PHILOSOPHIC WORDS

A Study of Style and Meaning
in the
Rambler and *Dictionary*
of
Samuel Johnson

BY

W. K. WIMSATT, JR.

ARCHON BOOKS
1968

Library of Congress Catalog Card Number: 68-16343
Printed in the United States of America

great wonders which they tell, of carrying in the air, transforming themfelves into other bodies, &c. are ftill reported to be wrought, not by incan-
tations or ceremonies, but by ointments, and anointing themfelves all over :
this may juftly move a man to think, that thefe fables are the effects of imagination : for it is certain, that ointments do all, (if they be laid on any thing
thick,) by ftopping of the pores, fhut in the vapours, and fend them to the
head extremely. And for the particular ingredients of thofe magical ointments, it is like they are opiate and foporiferous. For anointing of the fore-
head, neck, feet, back-bone, we know is ufed for procuring dead fleeps : and
if any man fay that this effect would be better done by inward potions ; an-
fwer may be made, that the medicines, which go to the ointments, are fo
ftrong, that if they were ufed inwards, they would kill thofe that ufe them :
and therefore they work potently, though outwards.

WE will divide the feveral kinds of the operations by tranfmiffion of
fpirits and imagination, which will give no fmall light to the experiments
that follow. All operations by tranfmiffion of fpirits and imagination have
this ; that they work at diftance, and not at touch ; and they are thefe being
diftinguifhed.

904. THE firft is the tranfmiffion or emiffion of the thinner (and more
airy) parts of bodies ; as in odours and infections ; and this is, of all the reft,
the moft corporeal. But you muft remember withal, that there be a number of thofe emiffions, both wholefome and unwholefome, that give no fmell
at all : for the plague, many times when it is taken, giveth no fcent at all :
and there be many good and healthful airs that do appear by habitation and
other proofs that differ not in fmell from other airs. And under this head
you may place all imbibitions of air, where the fubftance is material, odour-
like ; whereof fome neverthelefs are ftrange, and very fuddenly diffufed ; as
the alteration which the air receiveth in Ægypt, almoft immediately, upon
the rifing of the river of Nilus, whereof we have fpoken.

905. THE fecond is the tranfmiffion or emiffion of thofe things that we
call fpiritual fpecies ; as vifibles and founds : the one whereof we have handled, and the other we fhall handle in due place. Thefe move fwiftly, and at
great diftance ; but then they require a medium well difpofed, and their
tranfmiffion is eafily ftopped.

906. THE third is the emiffions, which caufe attraction of certain bodies
at diftance ; wherein though the loadftone be commonly placed in the firft
rank, yet we think good to except it, and refer it to another head : but
the drawing of amber and jet, and other clectrick bodies, and the attraction in gold of the fpirit of quickfilver at diftance ; and the attraction of
heat at diftance ; and that of fire to Naphtha ; and that of fome herbs to water, tho' at diftance ; and divers others ; we fhall handle, but yet not under
this prefent title, but under the title of attraction in general.

907. THE fourth is the emiffion of fpirits, and immateriate powers and
virtues, in thofe things which work by the univerfal configuration and fym-
pathy of the world ; not by forms, or celeftial influxes, (as is vainly taught
and received,) but by the primitive nature of matter, and the feeds of things.
Of this kind is (as we yet fuppofe) the working of the loadftone, which is
by confent with the globe of the earth : of this kind is the motion of gravity, which is by confent of denfe bodies with the globe of the earth : of this
kind is fome difpofition of bodies to rotation, and particularly from eaft to
weft : of which kind we conceive the main float and refloat of the fea is,
which is by confent of the univerfe, as part of the diurnal motion. Thefe

imma-

A page of volume iii of the *Works* of Francis Bacon,
London, 1740, marked by Johnson and his amanuenses
in compiling illustrations for his Dictionary. In the
Library of Yale University.

For

M. E.

NULLIUS IN VERBA

Motto of the Royal Society

NULLIUS ADDICTUS JURARE IN VERBA MAGISTRI,
QUO ME CUNQUE RAPIT TEMPESTAS DEFEROR HOSPES.

Horace, *Epistles,* I, i, 14–15

Motto of Samuel Johnson's Rambler

PREFACE

THE present study attempts three things which are not incompatible or inharmonious, which are even, I hope, advantageously interwoven, yet which can and should be distinguished. The three are (1) biography, the main subject of Chapter II and parts of Chapter IV; (2) linguistic history, the main subject of Chapter I and other parts of Chapter IV; (3) stylistic or rhetoric, the main subject of Chapters III and V. Of these the third may be said to depend logically upon the second, but not, I believe, upon the first, though the first and the third are often confused or made interdependent. In another place I have labored the view that the total complex of meaning or style which is a work of verbal art cannot be measured or even illuminated by inquiring what the author intended to write. What he does write, all that he implies, all the meaning he creates in words, whether consciously or unconsciously, is what he achieves. Or, to approach the matter another way, there are conceivably two kinds of evidence for what an author intended to say in a work—the internal and the external. The internal is what he succeeded in saying in the work, and the external, so far as it differs from or supplements the internal, is what he did not succeed in saying, and is not a part of the work. The stylistic study of Johnson's *Rambler* is then not an inquiry into the privacies of Johnson's mind, but, like linguistic study, an inquiry into public qualities of language. The matter is perplexed, however, in the case of Johnson by the fact that he is the author not only of prose essays but of a monumental English Dictionary and was even engaged upon the two simultaneously. No other English author presents either the same problem or the same opportunity for investigation. The Dictionary not only shows with a high degree of probability some of the private experience which must have entered into Johnson's prose composition, but is a record of the English language between about 1580 and 1750, and a public instrument of the highest authority for shaping the language after 1755. At different places in this study the Dictionary has been considered in different ways, now as record of personal experience, now as public monument. The result is, I believe, a close concord between the biographical and the linguistic and critical in this study, yet not a logical dependence of the two latter upon the former. The matter may be illustrated thus: It is a fact that "projection" is a term once

used seriously by chemists and alchemists, and that Johnson in the
Rambler applies it to cooking with a skillet in a country kitchen. It
is of course inconceivable that Johnson did not understand this joke
as well as we, who discover it by research; there was for him too a
smile behind the ponderosity, a ripple beneath the grave style. Yet
it is not his knowledge or intention which validates the joke, but
the public fact in the history of language—though both Johnson's
own knowledge and the public fact may be learned in his Dictionary from the definition of "projection" and the Baconian example.

Biography, one will perhaps observe at this point, is of many
shades; and the student whose interest in Johnson is determined
chiefly by the main tradition may scarcely wish to give the name
biography to Chapter II of this study or to Sections 1 and 2 of
Chapter IV. An apocryphal story about Johnson represents him as
saying: "Incident, Madam, incident is what the biographer wants.
Did he break his leg?" This bit of crudity rests on a misconception
which seems scarcely compatible with a reading of Johnson's *Lives
of the Poets*, but is not without relation to the figure of Johnson
himself as developed by his biographers. The lover of the anecdotal
Johnson will miss in the following study the roundness, or squareness, of his favorite character—the wig, the voice, the cats and tea
table, the conversations, the pistol butt. Even the alembics, retorts,
and furnaces observed in the garret over the Inner Temple chambers and at Streatham, though they might seem objects highly
relevant to this study, will receive no emphasis. The reason is two-
fold: First, these materials have not been found strictly relevant—
I have used them, judiciously I hope, when necessary to qualify, or
useful to support, conclusions on the whole of another quality.
And second, this study has been directed to a period of Johnson's
life before the anecdotal record begins. It is a part of my thesis that
long before the social manifestations, the hobnobbing at the laboratory of Beauclerk, the making of spirit in the garret over the Inner
Temple chambers, the bricks for the furnace at Streatham; before
the time of competence and comfort, during the obscure time of
hardship and Grubstreet struggle, we can find in the written and
printed record a rich account of Johnson's philosophic mind. The
impressive figure of Samuel Johnson is so largely the creation of one
genius in dramatic biography and of several smaller memorialists,
such is the value and prestige of these sources, that both the writing
and the reading of Johnson himself have very largely escaped the
kind of exploration which is usually directed toward intellectual
records of equal importance. We have literary editing of Johnson's
Lives of the Poets, and very recently a careful bibliographical and

textual editing of his poetry. Johnson's prose has received a certain number of useful annotations in books of selections for school use. Yet by and large the texture of Johnson's writing and the numerous clues to his reading remain almost unexamined. In a recent survey of Johnsonian scholarship during two centuries, Mr. R. W. Chapman has remarked that Boswell could not follow Johnson into the darker places of antiquity, that neither Boswell nor other biographers tell us much about Johnson's interest in the literature of the continental Renaissance. Another student [1] has complained that Boswell was so ignorant of the sciences that he failed completely to record an important side of Johnson's character. And especially the great bulk of the Dictionary has been avoided. No literary man ever left a more explicit and available record of his reading for a long period in a body of important literature. Yet the Dictionary has been an open challenge which students of Johnson's mind have failed to notice—or have noticed only too close. Not one tenth as much is to be known about the reading of Shakespeare, whose *Small Latin and Less Greek* has recently inspired the two heavy volumes of that title. It is of course not likely that the works of Johnson will ever be covered with a variorum panoply of annotation, or that his much Latin and considerable Greek will be minutely sifted. Johnson's was not the gorgeously ambiguous poetic gift out of which posterity spins admired multiplicities of meaning; the well of his memory and fusion of his images seem not so mysterious as to invite a laborious road to the Vanity of Human Wishes. Yet he read widely and vigorously, storing a part of his mind which does not appear upon the surface of the anecdotes, variegated and full of import as they are—a part submerged in the relative silence of the years before Boswell, recorded remotely inside the Dictionary, or transformed and obscurely shadowed in the abstract imagery of his prose. We know, for example, from an often quoted and dramatic anecdote in which Johnson kicked a stone, his attitude toward the phenomenalism of Berkeley. A close scrutiny of the Dictionary will show us certain works of Berkeley which Johnson had actually read. It will show us moreover certain epistemological doctrines of Locke which Johnson undoubtedly accepted in large part. A scrutiny of his prose will show the extent to which these doctrines affected his imagination, perhaps far beyond the conscious acceptance of intellect.[2]

1. Mr. John J. Brown. See *post* p. xii.
2. At the appropriate point I have taken advantage of the excellent approach to this matter in Professor Kenneth MacLean's *John Locke and English Literature of the Eighteenth Century* (New Haven, 1936). Cf. *post* p. 96.

So far as the present study is one of language and style, it is an attempt to refine upon a widely current and traditional idea of Johnson's Latinate, abstract, and sesquipedalian diction; to expound the "philosophical" implications of his diction; and hence to recall attention to a quality of his style which was noticed briefly by himself and by Boswell and Murphy but has passed without much notice in later Johnsonian criticism. It is a development of several pages of my earlier study *The Prose Style of Samuel Johnson* and diverges from the whole of that study in placing a greater emphasis upon origins. A corollary difference is that whereas the former analysis led me rather often into agreement with some of the strictures of Hazlitt and Walpole, concerning qualities of Johnson's prose which, being structural and logical, have enjoyed a high degree of stability from his own day to ours; I have here pursued paths which seem to go further in explaining why Boswell and others have praised the vividness of Johnson's imagination, a quality more dependent upon contexts, more associative and impermanent, and hence in need of being restored by the attentions of historical inquiry.

This study scarcely claims to present the only antecedents of Johnson's style or to explain all the qualities of his diction and imagery. The most frequent words in Johnson's *Rambler* are certainly the literal words of moral and psychological discourse. Johnson's theme is *magnanimity* and *pusillanimity*. As we read the *Rambler* we continually encounter *benevolence, beneficence, benefits, benefaction;* and their opposites, *malice* and *malignity,* the *malicious, malignant,* and *malevolent.* We hear of such virtues and pleasing traits as *alacrity, diligence, vigilance,* and *vivacity;* of such vices and weaknesses as *caprice, credulity, petulance, procrastination,* and *vanity;* of what is *flagitious, licentious,* and *sinistrous.* Johnson expresses such attitudes toward evil as *contempt, disgust, dejection,* and *despondency.* He and his characters are filled with *perturbation, vexation,* and *solicitude;* with *temerity* or *diffidence,* or they know moments of *tranquillity.* He treats of *felicity* and *infelicity,* especially of the latter. Nothing less than a concordance could do justice to the moral and psychological vocabulary of Johnson's *Rambler.* On the other hand, the words which are in a more special sense "philosophical" [3] and their contribution to our total concept of the style cannot be very well treated in a statistical way —though some such methods are in use among scholars for determination of disputed authorships.[4] The cold and abstracted sta-

3. Cf. Chap. I, p. 5.
4. Cf. G. Udny Yule, *The Statistical Study of Literary Vocabulary* (Cambridge, 1944).

tistics, let us say, three or four strikingly philosophic words, on the average, to a *Rambler,* when all *Ramblers,* even the least philosophic, are counted, will not do justice to the stylistic fact. In my earlier treatment of this matter I suggested that the philosophic quality of Johnson's prose lay in the peculiar effect of the most philosophic words wherever they do occur, and in a kind of extension or radiation of meaning through other classes of Johnson's words, which on the whole tend to be more abstract, more formal and learned than the words of daily speech. From the frequent words of moral and psychological discourse, as a kind of periphery and in places thinly metaphoric area of the philosophic, one may work, through several shades, toward a physico-philosophical core, which, if not the one pole or essential point of Johnson's thinking, is at least a very important one—and is the focus of this study. I have treated such extension of philosophic quality especially in Section 2 of Chapter V.

Within recent years the studies of Professor R. F. Jones have shown the effect of a scientific program and ideal of plain expression, as cultivated in the Royal Society, upon the prose of pulpit and essay. Other studies, notably those of Professor Marjorie Nicolson, have traced the themes of Galilean and Newtonian science in belletristic application. The aim of this study has been to show the effect not of theory or program upon style, nor of science upon themes, but of words upon style. Yet not in the simple sense that style is conceived as imitating style, so that one would test my thesis by asking whether Johnson's prose sounds like, or reminds one of, that of the Royal Society. It does not, and therein partly lies the interest. Aristotle observes in his *Physics* that doctoring begets not doctors but health. So a vigorous and original style is not begotten by literal imitation of other styles, but by a fusion of styles and ideas into the new idea and the new style. The most peculiar principles of Johnson's style are to be sought neither in earlier literary prose nor in philosophic prose as having a sufficiently interesting style of its own; nor are they to be sought in scientific principles considered seriously and accurately as such. It will not be contended in any part of this study that Johnson had more than a general—at times vague—and literary comprehension of science, sufficient for his purposes. Johnson's philosophic style proceeds from a system of ideas as expressed in a certain fashion of words, and the transformation which words and ideas undergo in his use, and to a less extent in that of other writers to be named, is at least as remarkable as the origin of these words and ideas. In the realm of literary study there is on the one hand *Forschung,* inquiry into facts and contexts which may by a further process be brought into literary criticism but which are in themselves opaque and not illuminated with literary significance. There is on the other hand the pure analysis of form, like and unlike, parallel and diverse, beginning, middle and end, the commonplace and abstracted sinews. The present study aims to strike between these extremes, at a point where the matter of literature, or in another terminology its context, undergoes a twist or transformation, becomes literary, and hence assumes the value of technique and of form.

There is a certain sense in which any study of Samuel Johnson is a far wider study—of an age and intellectual climate, of the English language and its literature. Such is the stature of the man and his deliberately formative effort in public intellectual history that general values attach to his biography more securely than to that of many a more sophisticated poet or essayist. Even so brief and special a study as the present, therefore, needs but to explain itself, not apologize, in professing to look beyond both Johnson the man and his writings. There is a reason why Johnson's Dictionary and *Rambler* appear in the title of this study; they are indeed the immediate objects of all but the first chapter. Yet the study is, I believe, appropriately entitled *Philosophic Words* and is concerned with the history of English language and style, or a phase of that history in which Johnson's Dictionary and his prose writings are the classic loci and climactic chapters.

In the course of this study I have had the advantage of consulting the unpublished findings of three other Johnsonian investigators. Mr. Lewis M. Freed's Cornell doctoral dissertation "The Sources of Johnson's Dictionary," 1939, was of signal assistance in the exploration of the otherwise almost uncharted hinterland of Johnson's Dictionary; certain of his statistical summaries are introduced in Chapter II. Mr. John J. Brown's Yale doctoral dissertation "Samuel Johnson and Eighteenth Century Science," 1943, is a comprehensive study in the biographical mode which I have found helpful in framing some parts of Chapters II and IV. Professor Curtis Bradford's Yale doctoral dissertation "Samuel Johnson's *Rambler*," 1937, afforded textual guidance which I have acknowledged more explicitly in Appendix A. The appearance in 1946 of *The English Dictionary from Cawdrey to Johnson*, by Professors DeWitt T. Starnes and Gertrude E. Noyes, was timely for my work upon Chapter II; I had previously been indebted to Professor Noyes for generous response to inquiries.

Professor Maynard Mack had the kindness to read the whole of this work in an intermediate draft and offered criticisms which were of the greatest assistance toward whatever degree of finish has been attained. Professor F. A. Pottle read the whole of the final draft. Among those who in other more personal ways have promoted the work—by advice, by information, by encouragement, by the reading of various parts—I take pleasure in naming especially my friends Professors Monroe C. Beardsley and Allen Hazen, Dr. George L. Lam, and Mr. Herman Liebert. To Mr. Liebert I owe special thanks for his cheerfulness in the long-term lending of books from his library of Johnsoniana and for his careful and expert reading of the work in page proof. For information about books which lay at a distance, I am especially indebted to Dr. R. W. Chapman, Professor Lane Cooper, Mr. Robert Haynes, Mr. P. Laithwaite, Dr. Archibald Malloch, Miss Elizabeth H. Wuks, and in general to the reference staffs of the libraries to be mentioned below. For various other kinds of assistance, I am grateful to my friends upon the scene at Yale, especially Drs. Charles H. Bennett, Grover Cronin, and John F. Fulton, Professor Gordon Haight, Dr. Warren H. Smith, Professors C. B. Tinker and Rulon S. Wells, Dr. Donald G. Wing, and Professor A. M. Witherspoon; and to others at a distance, especially Professors Curtis Bradford, J. L. Clifford, R. E. Moore, A. W. Read, and Miriam R. Small.

To Professor Philip B. Daghlian I owe a special debt for friendly and skilled assistance in bringing the word list of Appendix A toward its final shape. A study of so verbal or lexicographic a sort has involved the finding of many words in obscure places, the accumulation of minute files. I have received valuable help in this part of the labor from Yale undergraduates assigned at various times as my assistants by the Bursary Bureau: Messrs. John McClement, Augustus Schubert, Frank Hindley, and George Exon. Miss Margaret Sturgeon has worked expertly in the same cause.

Most of all, my wife has not only endured perusal of the drafts and revisions—the "future" note, the "abdicated" page—but has displayed a skill in searching that has come little short of the uncanny.

A book about words is in a special sense a fruit of the library. In the course of these studies I have borrowed books or received information from the Library of Congress and the Army Medical Library, the John Crerar Library, the libraries of Alma College, Chicago, Cornell, Harvard, Princeton, and Rutgers Universities, of Lichfield Cathedral, the Union Theological Seminary, and the New York Academy of Medicine. But most of all my debt is to the Library of Yale University—in a special way for permission to reproduce a page of Samuel Johnson's copy of the *Works* of Francis Bacon—but, far beyond that, for a courtesy and skilful assistance in opening the daily avenues of research such as, I believe, a scholar will travel widely without finding surpassed.

The work was completed while I held a Fellowship of the John Simon Guggenheim Memorial Foundation.

W. K. W., JR.

Silliman College, Yale University
   July, 1948

CUE TITLES

The Works of Samuel Johnson, Vols. i–xiii, 1787, are referred to throughout this study as *Works,* or, where a more specific title appears, simply by volume and page, e.g., *Debates* xii, 4. Or, where the reference is to one of Johnson's periodical essays, the number following the title is the number of the essay, and the next two numbers are, as usual, those of volume and page of the 1787 *Works,* e.g., *Rambler* 1, v, 4. Or again, if the title of a periodical essay is for any reason to be easily understood, the reference is more simply: 1, v, 4. For a few of Johnson's *Adventurers* not included in the collected works of 1787, *British Essayists,* ed. Alexander Chalmers, 1817, Vol. xxiii is referred to as *Chalmers* xxiii. Quotations from Johnson's Dictionary are taken throughout from the Second Edition, 1755–56, which differs from the First chiefly in some abbreviations of reference. The Johnsonian editions of G. B. Hill, *Letters of Samuel Johnson, Johnsonian Miscellanies,* Johnson's *Lives of the English Poets,* and Boswell's *Life of Samuel Johnson* (the first four volumes of the last in the revision of L. F. Powell) are referred to respectively as *Letters, Miscellanies, Lives,* and *Life. A Catalogue of the Valuable Library of Books of the Late Learned Samuel Johnson,* 1785, is referred to as *Catalogue of the Library of Samuel Johnson.* Editions of sources of Johnson's Dictionary, named in identifiable short titles throughout, may be found more completely described in Appendix B.

CONTENTS

CHAPTER I

Philosophic Words: Bacon to Johnson

THE tendency of the English is to express themselves pompously, said William of Malmesbury (*Angli pompatice dictare solent*).[1] And no doubt the tradition of big words in English has exhibited in its successive phases a generically constant stylistic value, of pomposity, grandiloquence, or impressiveness. It might be said, very broadly, that what were called "flourished" words in the criticism of the fourteenth century were called "aureate" in the fifteenth, "inkhorn" in the sixteenth, and "hard" by the dictionary makers of the seventeenth and eighteenth centuries, and that these were stylistically the same words that became "Johnsonese" and were given various epithets of disparagement by Macaulay and other Saxonists of the nineteenth century. These are the words which have in our day, by an eminent Teutonic historian of the language, been lamented as superfluous to the English vocabulary, stunting to the growth of native formations, undemocratic, and inharmonious with the native core of the language.[2] Yet a great deal of linguistic and literary history may be blurred over by such simplification. The gilded words of later fourteenth- and fifteenth-century poetry and prose, for example, would seem to have a stylistic character distinctly their own and in a special way to deserve the name "aureate" given them by Lydgate.

> Hale, sterne superne! Hale, in eterne,
>> In Godis sicht to schyne!
> Lucerne in derne, for to discerne
>> Be glory and grace devyne;
> Hodiern, modern, sempitern,
>> Angelicall regyne!
> Our tern infern for to dispern
>> Help, rialest Rosyne! [3]

In this rather mannered example from a later phase of the tradition, the stylistic effect is certainly of a far more special sort than what is conveyed by any term so general as "Latin," "precious,"

---

1. John C. Mendenhall, *Aureate Terms* (Lancaster, 1919), p. 31; cf. pp. 27, 34.
2. Otto Jespersen, *Growth and Structure of the English Language* (New York, 1923), pp. 152–153.
3. William Dunbar, *Ballad of Our Lady.*

or "elevated." The endings in *n* and *rn*, the short, echoing, concrete words, in semi-iconic support of a meaning of starriness and refulgence, make a style which is in a sense, whether good or bad, resplendent.[4] The flood of Latinate words let loose by the expansionists of the later sixteenth century, to take an opposite example, seem to have been a less discriminate gallimaufry of derivatives. There was less a vein of meaning or a prevailing cast of style than a search for heterogeneous riches, an ideal of elaborate and official impressiveness reminiscent of twelfth- and thirteenth-century letter writers of the School of Orleans. In such a parody at least as the well-known letter of Johannes Octo fabricated by Wilson for his *Arte of Rhetorique* the diction seems to deserve no better than the frequently bestowed epithet of "inkhorn."

You know my literature, you knowe the pastorall promotion, I obtestate your clemencie, to invigilate thus much for me, according to my confidence, and as you knowe my condigne merites for such a compendious living. But now I relinquish to fatigate your intelligence, with any more frivolous verbosities, and therfore he that rules the climates, be evermore your beautreux, your fortresse, and your bulwarke. Amen.

The stylistic value of inkhorn per se has been memorialized by Shakespeare himself in the conversation of the pedants Holofernes and Sir Nathaniel. "O! they have lived long on the alms-basket of words. I marvel thy master hath not eaten thee for a word; for thou art not so long by the head as *honorificabilitudinitatibus*." But even here there was a wealth of verbiage which the vital imagination of Shakespeare and other poets might inform with life in thousands of phrases—"multitudinous seas" and "knots intrinsecate."

The object of the present study is a vocabulary of "hard" words which began to be extensively cultivated shortly after the heyday of inkhorn, but which was yet quite different from either inkhorn or aureate or other earlier forms—the vocabulary of science or physical philosophy. Samuel Johnson was to say in the *Preface* to his Dictionary that the vocabulary of "natural knowledge" might be gathered from the works of Bacon alone; and we may assume at least that an important early monument of English scientific diction is the work of Francis Bacon, especially the ten centuries of his *Sylva Sylvarum: or a Natural History* (1626).

First, for separation; It is wrought by weight, as in the ordinary residence or settlement of liquors, by heat, by motion, by precipitation, or sub-

4. For aureate terms, see also Albert C. Baugh, *A History of the English Language* (New York, 1935), p. 229; J. W. H. Atkins, *English Literary Criticism: The Medieval Phase* (New York, 1943), pp. 168–171; Henry C. Wyld, *Some Aspects of the Diction of English Poetry* (Oxford, 1933), pp. 29–32.

limation; (that is, a calling of the several parts, either up or down, which is a kind of attraction:) by adhesion; as when a body more viscous is mingled and agitated with the liquor; which viscous body (afterwards severed) draweth with it the grosser parts of the liquor: and lastly, by percolation or passage.

If you provide against three causes of putrefaction, bodies will not corrupt: the first is, that the air be excluded, for that undermineth the body, and conspireth with the spirit of the body to dissolve it. The second is, that the body adjacent and ambient be not commaterial, but merely heterogeneal towards the body that is to be preserved.[5]

If we inquire into the history of the weightier words in these paragraphs, we shall find that a few of them (*sublimation, putrefaction, dissolve, adjacent*) had been used in approximately the same sense as early as the fourteenth century by Gower or Wyclif or in the sixteenth century by Elyot in his *Castel of Helth*. But others (*agitate, heterogeneal, percolation, precipitation, residence, separation*) seem to be used by Bacon in a sense either revived or but recently emphasized, and others still (*ambient, commaterial, adhesion, attraction, passage, settlement*) are recorded by the *Oxford English Dictionary*, in the technical usage of Bacon, from no writers earlier than Bacon himself. A writer upon the history of ideas in English words has pointed out the following staples of modern discourse the earliest examples of which in the *Oxford Dictionary* are from Bacon and other seventeenth-century scientists:

acid, astringency, cohesion, dissection, elasticity, equilibrium, fluid, hydraulic, intensity, polarity, pressure, spontaneous, static, suction, temperature (of heat and cold), tension (in physics), volatile (in a chemical sense and in a mechanical sense as an adjective).[6]

The history of this vocabulary—if the more relevant discussion of its meaning and stylistic value may wait briefly upon a bibliographic recital—is to be traced in the places where one would trace the history of experimental science and of mechanical or corpuscular philosophy in England, in the writers associated in the rise and flourishing of the Royal Society, those beginning with Bacon who prepared the way for its inquiries, those next who addressed their works to the Society or wrote under its "imprimatur," or in its *Philosophical Transactions*, and the philosophers who carried on a parallel campaign at the levels of metaphysics and theology. With-

5. *Natural History*, Nos. 302, 771.
6. Owen Barfield, *History in English Words* (New York, 1926), pp. 133, 148. Earliest examples in the *Oxford Dictionary* are of course not to be taken in an exclusive sense, yet the record of a group of words such as this is at least good evidence of a linguistic trend.

out attempting to retrace this history, one may say that words of the kind in question appear in various philosophic writings of an empirical cast, in the translated *Elements of Philosophy* of Hobbes, 1656, and his *Decameron Physiologicum: or, Ten Dialogues of Natural Philosophy*, 1678; in the Brownian and Cartesian defense of empirical method by Joseph Glanvill, *The Vanity of Dogmatizing* or *Scepsis Scientifica*, 1661 and 1665; [7] and in the *Essay Concerning Human Understanding* of Locke, 1690. They appear in the *Mathematical Magic* of Bishop John Wilkins, 1648; in the various scientific essays of Robert Boyle, for example, his *Experiments . . . Touching the Spring of the Air*, 1661, and his *Sceptical Chymist*, 1661; in the *Micrographia* of Robert Hooke, 1665; and in a classic of the new science written in English by Newton, the *Opticks* of 1704. An exotic and fantastic context for philosophic diction is to be found in the curious inquiries of Browne's *Pseudodoxia Epidemica*, 1646. The diction shades into technicalities in medical works like Gideon Harvey's *Morbus Anglicus*, 1666; Richard Wiseman's *Chirurgical Treatises*, 1676; or John Arbuthnot's *Essay Concerning the Nature of Aliments*, 1731, and *Essay Concerning Air*, 1735. In the eighteenth century it is systematized and preserved in such dictionaries as John Harris' *Lexicon Technicum*, 1704–10; John Quincy's *Lexicon Physico-Medicum*, 1719; and Ephraim Chambers' *Cyclopaedia*, 1728; or appears more popularized and diluted in the two volumes of J. T. Desaguliers' *Course of Experimental Philosophy*, 1734–44. Rather early it developed extensive theological affinities on the Platonic side, as in Henry More's *Divine Dialogues*, 1668; on the Biblical and chronological side, as in Sir Matthew Hale's *Primitive Origination of Mankind*,[8] 1675, and in a series of distinguished treatises of the physico-theological school: Thomas Burnet's baroque *Theory of the Earth*, 1684–90; the botanist John Ray's *Wisdom of God in the Creation*, 1691; the classicist Richard Bentley's *Folly and Unreasonableness of Atheism*—lecture sermons delivered on Mr. Boyle's foundation in 1792–93; the fossilist John Woodward's *Natural History of the Earth*, 1695; the Reverend Nehemiah Grew's *Cosmologia Sacra*, 1701; the Reverend William Derham's *Physico-Theology*—Boyle sermons published

---

7. For an account of the literature produced during this decade by Glanvill, Sprat and others in defense of empirical science and the Royal Society, see Richard F. Jones, *Ancients and Moderns* (St. Louis, 1936), chaps. viii and ix.

8. Barfield, *op. cit.*, p. 150, refers to a "queer jungle-growth of words . . . which sprang up about the middle of the seventeenth century," *contemporal, co-temporary, contemporize, isochronal, synchronal, synchronical, synchronism, synchronistic*, as well as *contemporary, contemporaneous, synchronize, synchronous*. Many of these appeared first in theological writings.

with copious notes in 1713; and the physician George Cheyne's *Philosophical Principles of Religion*, 1715.[9] These titles illustrate the boundaries of the scientific and literal area in which "philosophic" diction flourished. "Philosophic," it may be called, in the sense of Cheyne's *Philosophical Principles* or the Royal Society's *Philosophical Transactions*—the sense of *philosophical* 1b in the *Oxford English Dictionary:* "Pertaining to, or used in the study of, natural philosophy, or some branch of physical science; physical, scientific." The dignity of the term as applied to physical science is seen in the light of the *Oxford Dictionary* definition of *philosopher* 1: "A lover of wisdom . . . in a wide sense, including men learned in physical sciences (physicists, scientists, naturalists), as well as those versed in the metaphysical and moral sciences." A unity and systematization of wisdom, both physical and metaphysical, is indicated in this era by the term "philosophic" and is implicit in its frequent applications to physical sciences of all sorts. It was the era when chemistry, for example, which had been either alchemy or pharmacy, became in the eyes of Boyle a "distinct and noble branch of natural philosophy," and when at the same time even so physical a science as chemistry was not conceived as clearly distinct from metaphysical philosophy. Throughout the present study the terms "philosophic" and "scientific" will be used almost, but not quite, interchangeably—the latter in contexts where the emphasis is upon experimental and physical origins, the former for the most part where the emphasis is on the dignity connoted by a kind of diction.

2

ONE of the most obvious causes for the Latinity of seventeenth-century scientific diction is that many of the authors—Bacon, Newton, Ray, or Burnet, for example—wrote in Latin as well as in English, or at times rather than in English, and they often translated their own Latin into English or read or translated passages from Greek and Latin versions of Aristotle, Hippocrates, or Galen, from Celsus, Pliny, or Cicero, from Vesalius, Copernicus, Kepler, Gilbert, Galilei, Kircher, Gassendi, and a host of other Renaissance savants who wrote in Latin. Bishop Wilkins' *Mathematical Magic* affords the following clear illustration of the tendency:

9. Barfield, *op. cit.*, pp. 162–163, points out that such crucial words as *arrange, category, classify, method, organize, organization, regular, regulate, regularity, system, systematic*, in their modern meanings, appear in the language for the first time during this period.

The Species of local violent motion are by *Aristotle* reckoned to be these four.

Phys. 1.7   *Pulsio.*
c.3.   *Tractio.*
            Vectio.
            Vertigo.
Thrusting, Drawing, Carrying, Turning.[1]

The vocabulary of science, in short, was inherited from Latin and Greek writers. English dictionaries, notably that of Cockeram in 1623, and the *Glossographia* of Blount in 1656, gave their support by Englishing large squads of Latin words from Latin-English word lists.[2] Or, if we would inquire into final causes, we might be content to conclude, like one of the interlocutors in Boyle's *Sceptical Chymist,* speaking of Paracelsus and other chemical writers, that they affected "hard words and equivocal expressions . . . to make their art appear more venerable and mysterious." [3] It is difficult not to entertain such a suspicion when we find, for example, a medical writer of 1665 speaking of "immanous arthritick pains," "subitous and effroyable symptoms," "effroyable and supervulgar Convulsion Fits," or syrups and expectoratives which "auxiliate" a cough.[4] The suspicion may be illustrated in the next century from the *Logic* of Watts when he says that certain "names of sympathy, antipathy, substantial forms and qualities, . . . are but hard words, which only express a learned and pompous ignorance of the true cause of natural appearances"; [5] or from Quincy's *Lexicon,* where under the entry *heterogeneous,* he says: "This is a Term of a very lax Signification, and by the Chymists is come to serve almost for any thing they do not understand." *Homogeneous* and *heterogeneous,* he says, "are two hard Words that serve frequently for the Refuges of Ignorance; else the common Terms of Like and Unlike might serve for the same Purposes." [6]

1. *Mathematical Magic* (London, 1691), pp. 101–102. For a broader discussion of the debt of English medical terminology to classical and medieval Greek and Latin, see Edmund Andrews, *A History of Scientific English* (New York, 1947), chaps. iv, vii, viii, ix.
2. De Witt T. Starnes and Gertrude E. Noyes, *The English Dictionary from Cawdrey to Johnson* (Chapel Hill, 1946), pp. 31, 32, 42, 43.
3. *Works* (London, 1772), i, 521. "A Babylonish Dialect, which learned Pedants much affect" (*Hudibras* I, i, 93).
4. Gideon Harvey, *Morbus Anglicus: or the Anatomy of Consumptions* (London, 1672), pp. 37, 20, 39, 64.
5. Isaac Watts, *Logic* (London, 1745), pp. 75–76.
6. John Quincy, *Lexicon Physico-Medicum* (London, 1722), s.v. *heterogeneous.* Cf. the footnote definition of *heterogeneous* and *homogeneous* in Watts, *Logic,* ed. cit., p. 298.

These accounts, of genesis and of motive, while they do not go very far in saying what peculiar quality of meaning, if any, was attached to scientific diction, still suggest such an inquiry and may be found to foreshadow and complement its results. That scientific diction did have some special meaning and that the meaning may be difficult to define is indicated in one way by a kind of glossary style, which one may have noted in the example quoted above from Bishop Wilkins and which is frequently encountered in the English scientific writers of the era. The use of self-interpreting pairs of words had earlier been characteristic of inkhorn writers. "Devulgate or set forth," said Elyot, "explicating or unfolding," "difficile or hard," "education or bringing up of children." [7] So that Bacon had stylistic precedents for such phrases in his *Essays* as "the stroke or percussion of an envious eye," "a wound or solution of continuity." [8] In the *Natural History* the device often takes the form of instruction or directive:

Separation . . . is wrought . . . by precipitation, or sublimation; (that is, a calling of the several parts, either up or down).

All bodies ductile and tensile, (as metals that will be drawn into wires; wool and tow that will be drawn into yarn, or thread) have in them the appetite of not discontinuing strong.[9]

For induration, or mollification; it is to be enquired what will make metals harder and harder, and what will make them softer and softer.[10]

In the same vein one might cite Browne in his *Pseudodoxia*,[11] a technical writer like Gideon Harvey in his *Morbus Anglicus*,[12] Ray in his *Creation*,[13] Woodward in his *Natural History of the Earth*,[14]

7. Baugh, *A History of the English Language*, pp. 263, 265, 285. Cf. Jespersen, *Growth and Structure of the English Language* (New York, 1923), pp. 135–140, on synonymic relations between classical and other words in English.
8. *Essays* III and IX. Cf. *Natural History*, No. 944, "percussion of the envious eye . . . cast upon a person in glory."
9. *Natural History*, Nos. 302, 845.
10. *Physiological Remains, Works* (London, 1740), iii, 219.
11. *Pseudodoxia*, III, iv. The beaver is called *"animal ventricosum*, from his swaggy and prominent belly."
12. *Morbus Anglicus*, p. 110, "Restringents to stench and incrassatives to thicken the blood." Cf. esp. pp. 28, 46, 62.
13. *Wisdom of God in the Creation* (London, 1709), p. 158, "swiftness or pernicity." Cf. the unassimilated Latin words in this work: p. 258, *incessus;* p. 259, *situs;* p. 273, *decubitus;* p. 379, *inedia.*
14. *An Essay toward a Natural History of the Earth* (London, 1695), p. 180, "Corpuscles occurr or meet together," "Mineral Balls or Nodules."

or Arbuthnot in his *Essay on Air* [15] and *Essay on Aliments*.[16] By another method, that of marginal notes, Browne in his *Pseudodoxia* explains that *Antidotal* means "Against poison"; *diuretical*, "Provoking Urine"; *Antepileptical*, "Against the Falling Sickness"; and *Longimanous*, "Long-handed." [17] Cheyne in his medical treatises and his friend Arbuthnot, more lavishly, supply footnote glossaries. From Arbuthnot's *Essay Concerning Aliments* we learn, for example, the following synonyms:

mastication (chewing), saponaceous (soapy), attrition (rubbing, grinding), muriatick (briny), eructations (belchings), acrimony and tenacity (sharpness and glueness), propell (drive forwards), sanguification (making of blood), ramification (branching), homogeneous (of one kind), elasticity (spring), attenuated (made thin), evanescent (vanishing), elongation (lengthening), oleaginous (oily), anodyne (abating pain), eluted (washed away), farinaceous (mealy), depletion (emptying), viscid (tough, gluey), incide (cut, dissolve), aequilibrium (equal balance), influx (flowing in), rigidity (hardness, stiffness), lacerations (tearing, breaking), absorbent (that sucks in a liquid), vitrious (like glass), repletion (fulness).[18]

Browne in his address "To the Reader" had apologized for being carried into "expressions beyond mere English apprehensions." Arbuthnot's *Essay Concerning Aliments* is prefaced by a more precise "Explanation of some Chymical Terms" and by an apology for the "hard words" which he was "obliged to use." [19] Arbuthnot was writing, not for the gentlemen of his own profession, as he put it, but for anyone who might want to know how to eat correctly, and to him it seemed expedient, and what is of special note here, quite *possible*, to decode a professional language for popular understanding. Both Browne and Arbuthnot, it would seem, undertook to dispel an obscurity which they considered to lie rather in Latin roots than in abstruse ideas. The "hard words" were apparently harder than whatever they stood for.

The fact is that science, or at least qualitative science, in the seventeenth century, for all its specializing desires, had not moved very far away either from metaphysics, as we have observed, or

15. *An Essay Concerning the Effects of Air* (London, 1933), p. 25, "Repulsion or Flying off from one another."

16. *An Essay Concerning the Nature of Aliments* (London, 1735), p. 67, "much levigated or smooth." Cf. Ephraim Chambers, *Cyclopaedia* (London, 1728), s.v. *electricity:* "tersion or wiping, is almost universally necessary, as well as attrition or rubbing, to produce electricity."

17. *Pseudodoxia*, II, v; VII, xix.

18. *Essay Concerning the Nature of Aliments*, pp. 1, 2, 5, 8, 9, 16, 17, 27, 28, 30, 42, 43, 44, 52, 57, 121, 123, 125, 131, 141, 154, 156, 161, 167, 176, 190.

19. *Essay Concerning . . . Aliments*, Preface, p. A3ʳ.

from everyday life. "Science," laments a modern literary critic, "has withdrawn intellect from literature. It has divided truth from immediacy." [20] At the end of the eighteenth century Wordsworth thought of science as something so remote from daily life as to be no longer immediately available for poetry.[21] He might not have found it so in the year when Boyle published his *New Experiments Physico-Mechanical, Touching the Spring of the Air, and Its Effects; Made for the Most Part, in a New Pneumatical Engine.* Into a glass vessel, or "receiver," attached to a brass sucking-pump, Mr. Boyle and his associates introduced a *flaccid* lamb's bladder, exhausted the *ambient* air, and observed in the bladder a remarkable *intumescence;* they blew up the bladder before introducing it and had the pleasure of seeing it first swell and then break. They put in a lighted candle, observed that after two or three *exsuctions* of the air, the flame diminished, became blue, and went out. They observed the action of a magnet upon a needle hung in the receiver, the falling of quicksilver in a tube, the expansion of air under water, the motion of pendulums, the ticking of a watch, the death of a lark and a mouse.[22] There is a freshness of wonder, a manual and ocular immediacy, about these experimental adventures that links them to the exploits of Robinson Crusoe and shows that the philosophers as well as Crusoe are the ancestors of the balloon and submarine voyagers of Poe or Jules Verne. In this age even the abstruser formulae of Newton's *Opticks* are illuminated by vivid descriptions of how he let light through a small hole into a dark room and with a prism threw the spectrum of colors on the wall.[23] "Fortunate Newton," says Albert Einstein in his Foreword to the modern edition of the *Opticks,* "happy childhood of science!" And if we go back to Bacon, we are told to

Take an apple, and cut out a piece of the top, and cover it, to see whether that solution of continuity will not hasten a maturation:

for

we see that where a wasp, or a fly, or a worm hath bitten, in a grape, or any fruit, it will sweeten hastily.[24]

20. Max Eastman, *The Literary Mind* (New York, 1935), p. 241.
21. *Preface to Lyrical Ballads* (1800).
22. Experiments IV, V, X, XVI, XVII, XXI, XXVI, XXVII, XLI, in *Works* (London, 1772), i, 7–8, 18–19, 26, 32–34, 45–47, 61–62, 97–98. Boyle's experiments were repeated during social evenings by several generations of ingenious ladies and gentlemen. See the painting by Joseph Wright of Derby, "An Experiment with an Air Pump," mezzotint reproduced by Ruthven Todd, "Tracks in the Snow," *The Windmill,* ed. Reginald Moore and Edward Lane, i (1945), 32.
23. *Opticks* (New York, 1931), pp. 26, 45, 67, and *passim.*
24. *Natural History,* No. 325.

These were experiments which almost anybody might be expected to understand ("as much Anatomy as a Butcher knows, and moderate Skill in Mechanics," Arbuthnot asked in the reader of his *Essay* [25]), and they were experiments which many might be expected to emulate. The point need not be labored here that scientific virtuosos were many, and that among them might be found men of letters. As late as 1752, when the publication of Franklin's *Experiments and Observations on Electricity* had induced a wave of lightning-rod experiments, an astronomer writing in the *Gentleman's Magazine* invited all gentlemen who took "the laudable pains of keeping meteorological journals" to make their observations public; and a shopkeeper at Sir Isaac Newton's Head, Charing Cross, offered for sale suitable lightning rods with signal bells attached.[26] In the same era the maker of the English Dictionary, Samuel Johnson, was willing to undertake the revision of Chambers' *Universal Dictionary of Arts and Sciences* and was disappointed when the task was assigned to another.[27] Human activities had not yet been departmentalized.

The diction of such a science necessarily had an average generality and easiness of meaning—if once a possible ignorance of Latin roots were obviated by the use of self-translating doublets or marginal or footnote glossaries. There were indeed terms like *mechanical* as applied by Bacon to natural principles, or *gravity* and *gravitation* in the light of Newton's principles, or *focus* after its geometrical use by Kepler,[28] which took on a meaning not easily equated with that conveyed by approximate and plainer synonyms. There were highly specific and technical terms too, often in medicine or surgery, like those which abound in the treatises of Wiseman and Sharp: the *bubonceles, paraphymoses, empyemas, bronchotomies,* and *aneurisms.* A few other terms, the *tria prima,* for example, of the chemists, *salt, sulphur,* and *mercury,* had in technical language a meaning different from that in ordinary language. But the meaning of the far more frequent general terms—the *attrition, tenacity, absorbent, attenuated,* or *elongation* of Arbuthnot, the *separation residence, precipitation,* or *sublimation* of Bacon, words which might present a certain difficulty to understanding but could be adequately glossed with a synonym—must be looked for less in the realm of logic than in that of style and suggestion.

25. *Essay Concerning . . . Aliments,* Preface, p. A3^r.
26. *Gentleman's Magazine,* xxiii (August, 1752), 383; *Philosophical Transactions,* vol. xlvii, No. 96.
27. *Life* ii, 203, n. 3.
28. Barfield, *op. cit.,* pp. 144–145.

In defense of such words it may be said that they frequently took the place not of a single, plain English word but of a group of words (*homogeneous* = of one kind, *anodyne* = abating pain, *absorbent* = that sucks in a liquid), and hence they were more manageable. They could be modulated or manipulated in ways that would have forced the English phrases into makeshift postures. As the complexity of classifications in various branches of science increased, this synthetic and manipulable character of learned diction became even more stylistically convenient, and the diction itself both more difficult and more necessary.[29] In this respect the Latinate English of science approximated the systematic division and modulation of ideas which Bishop Wilkins aimed at in his algebraic *Real Character* written for the Royal Society—especially his "Connexive Particles" and his "Transcendental Particles."[30] Bishop Wilkins in his effort to supply a "distinct expression of all things and notions that fall under discourse"[31] produced a still-born language, a cryptic system of "integral" and "particle" shorthand symbols that far exceeded in degree of abstraction and generic orderliness all the living and dead languages which he rejected as models. But it is significant that in setting forth his system he found no analogy so convenient as the Latin language. His pages explaining the connexive Particles are marginally corroborated by columns of the Latin prepositions and case endings, and the Transcendental Particles are made clear by an eighteenfold enumeration of the Latin meanings conveyed in such suffixes as: *-esco, -osus, -lus, -aster, -tim,* or *-plex.*[32] The members of the Royal Society and their emulators in scientific writing would seem to have done what they could with the ideals of Bishop Wilkins' *Real Character,* as they did with the well-known prescription of Sprat,

29. Among the innumerable apologies for hard words that accompany scientific writing of the eighteenth century, the following from the Preface to John Hill's *History of Fossils* in 1748 is an excellent rationale: "As there is a Genus of Crystal distinguish'd from the rest by its being made up of a smaller number of planes than some other of the same Order, and compos'd of two pyramids join'd base to base without a column; in giving names to the several species of this Genus, the generical distinction to be first express'd must, in the common way of expression, take up many words, and must necessarily run thus, *Crystal compos'd of two pyramids, without an intermediate column, and compos'd of but few planes;* and to this the distinction of each species is to be added: Is it not better to save the tedious repetition of all these Words so often, by expressing the same sense in one; and making the name of the *Genus Pauraedrastylum.* . . . Words of this kind cannot but be of some length, but the meaning they convey pleads their pardon" (*A General Natural History,* Vol. i, *A History of Fossils,* Preface, p. a^v). Cf. Andrews, *op. cit.,* pp. 68, 161.

30. John Wilkins, *An Essay Towards a Real Character, and a Philosophical Language* (London, 1668), p. 318.

31. *Idem,* p. a^v.

32. *Idem,* Part III, chaps. i–vi, esp. pp. 298, 309–311, 318–320.

"so many things, almost in an equal number of words." They could scarcely use a language which, intending to embrace not merely mathematical ideas but the whole wealth of human experience, yet looked like algebra and was constructed on principles that attempted to be equally abstract. They used what was available within the heritage of learned English, a Latinate idiom which came nearest to having the same sort of expressive power.

This ductile expressive power of the Latin diction viewed in another light was a kind of irreducibility, a suggestion of radical meaning, and also of substantive dignity ("the deep latency of the substantial principles"),[33] which all the more recommended the diction to use in the scientific context. The plainer English words, we may generalize—*soapy, belchings, oily, gluey, stiffness,* to return to Arbuthnot's glossary—smell and feel too much of the impressionistic and undiscriminating talk of every day; in a scientific treatise they would have an irrelevant, too specific solidity of meaning. The Latin words both in their etymology and their ductility suggest something remote from the usual, some more precisely controlled and subtilized experience or more accurate observation —as the *sulphur, salt,* and *mercury* of the chemists referred not to the natural substances but to something sublimed in a retort. By their very removal from the ordinary, the Latin words suggest the principles of things—a reason or an explanation. Reasons could be made almost "as plentiful as blackberries." *Incrassatives* thicken the blood, and *induration* makes metals harder and harder, because such is the nature of *incrassatives* and of *induration.* In a less precise sense, the character of scientific words may be called simply that of specialization. One may accept, as a tentative frame for study, the statement of a recent writer on English language and poetry, that the vocabulary of science is paralleled by that of poetic diction in this period, the "phlogiston" of the chemists being on this view an analogue of the "finny tribe," or more precisely, one might suggest, of "the balmy spirit of the Western breeze." [34] The paradox of the vocabulary which we have been describing may be summarized in the statement that although the words did not refer to anything strictly other than what their plainer equivalents referred to, they were nevertheless very useful and were in fact the vocabulary of English experimental science and mechanical philosophy— or in the parallel statement, that the words were impressive and

33. Harvey, *Morbus Anglicus* (London, 1672), p. 13.
34. F. W. Bateson, *English Poetry and the English Language* (Oxford, 1934), p. 69. The phrase about the Western breeze appears in Johnson's Dictionary, s.v. *spirit,* the attribution being appropriately "Anonymous."

difficult, because Latin, and yet fairly easy when translated, because of the generic easiness of scientific ideas and the relative nearness of science in that era to life. This is a paradox which is full of implications for the history of philosophic diction in English literary style.

3

THE growth of metaphors from physical science is not, in general, to be traced by any simple chronology. The writer upon Aryan word history already quoted in this chapter says rather broadly that we drew out of our own bodies and from such human activities as cutting, stretching, and pulling the sensory concepts of force and pressure and the like; that we then externalized these concepts in tools and machines and turned them into abstract laws of mechanics; and that finally we proceeded to re-apply the laws to the familiar objects (our bodies) from which we had abstracted them, and to our minds, and so turned our previous notions inside out.[1] We may observe at least something like phases of such a history in some English words. In the word *pressure,* for example, which is used by Hobbes and Boyle in the seventeenth century in relation to air and other outside bodies, but which we find in Wyclif as a translation of the Vulgate *pressurae:*

> Whanne sche hath borun a sone, now sche thenkith not on the pressure, for joye, for a man is borun in to the world.

Or in the word *tension,* which the *Oxford Dictionary* tells us may have been taken into English directly from sixteenth-century medical Latin. *Tension* is used in 1533 by Elyot in his *Castel of Helth* in a physiological sense, by Boyle in 1685 to describe the condition of a bent bow, and much later by Shenstone of intellectual effort, and by Disraeli of the emotions or nerves. But it is a nice question whether the metaphors of Shenstone and Disraeli are based on the physiological or the physical use; and ultimately no doubt an insoluble question whether Latin *tendere* or its Aryan root referred to the mind or to an internal or an external action of the human body; and whether *premere* referred to a bodily pain or rather to the squeezing of grapes. The word *exacerbation* as defined in Edward Phillips' *New World of Words,* 1658, offers a curious illumination of the point. "A making sour," says Phillips. Of this rudimentary effort at definition it may be said at least that it is perhaps physical enough to include the recent seventeenth-century meaning of in-

1. Barfield, *History in English Words* (New York, 1926), pp. 149, 155, 177.

crease in severity of disease, but the word had its earlier psychological meaning of embitterment or irritation, a meaning reflected in Phillips' complementary remark: "in Rhetorick it is the same figure with Sarcasmus." The conclusion, in its most general form, would seem to be that in the history of words from the ancient languages into the modern, and within the modern, there are cycles or returns of meaning from physical to psychological and back, and at the same time parallel courses of meaning. The focus of the present study is upon a particular phase of meaning that occurred in the seventeenth and eighteenth centuries in English. We are content to say that the movement of experimental science resulted in a wide application of certain words to descriptions of the external world in a new context, and hence afforded in various degrees a basis for new psychological metaphors. Certain very ancient metaphors were rediscovered or at least revivified by the new literal statements of experimental science. Such words as *elasticity, equilibrium, intensity, polarity, static,* or *volatile* may be readily detected moving from the literal scientific realm to the metaphoric and psychological. In 1664 a physicist speaks of the elasticity of air, and in 1668 a moralist, of the elasticity of his "Appetitive Faculty"—"the spring" of his soul. Or in 1646 Browne in his *Pseudodoxia* speaks of the polarity of a magnet, and in 1767 Lord Chesterfield writes: "I find you are in motion and with a Polarity to Dresden."

Science in fact by its very emphasis on the isolation of phenomena, and often by the Cartesian duality of its analysis, tended to emphasize a distinction and yet a parallel between the inner and outer worlds and hence offered an invitation for a more complicated and subtilized description of the inner in terms suggestive of the outer. "Exhilaration," says Bacon, "hath some affinity with joy, though it be a much lighter motion." And "the running of the eyes with water . . . is an effect of dilatation of the spirits." [2] These are not metaphors, but they are not far from the kind of metaphor which the same mind would produce, in the *Advancement of Learning,* for instance, "grave solemn wits" in whom "it is nature to be somewhat viscous and inwrapped, and not easy to turn"; [3] or in the *Essays:* "Preoccupation of mind ever requireth preface of speech, like a fomentation to make the unguent enter"; [4] "The calling of a man's self to a strict account is a medicine, some-

2. *Natural History,* No. 721. Cf. No. 873.
3. II, xxiii, 33.
4. *Essay* xxv, *Of Dispatch.*

time too piercing and corrosive." [5] Another scientific writer of literary leanings, Joseph Glanvill, in his anti-Aristotelian and Cartesian *Scepsis Scientifica*, gives us the following account of sensory experience:

the different effects, which fire and water, have on us, which we call heat and cold, result from the so differing configuration and agitation of their Particles; . . . So that what we term heat and cold, and other qualities, are not properly according to Philosophical rigour in the bodies, their Efficients: but are rather Names expressing our passions; and therefore not strictly attributable to any thing without us, but by extrinsick denominations.

He gives us the following semi-metaphoric account of the relation between body and mind:

the boyling blood of youth, fiercely agitating the fluid Air, hinders that serenity and fixed stayedness, which is necessary to so severe an intentness: And the frigidity of decrepit age is as much its enemy, not only through penury of spirits, but by reason of its dulling moisture. And even in the temperate zone of our life, there are few bodies at such an aequipoiz of humours; but that the prevalency of some one indisposeth the spirit for a work so difficult and serious.

And the following full-fledged metaphor:

Interest is another thing, by the magnetisme of which our affections are almost irresistibly attracted. It is the Pole, to which we turn, and our sympathizing Judgments seldom decline from the direction of this Impregnant.[6]

It is in metaphors such as these perhaps that the distinctive capacities of scientific diction are most clearly realized. If we imagine *viscous* and *gluey*, or *equipoise* and *balance* to be points but a short distance apart when the words are applied to outside physical objects, then imagine lines drawn from a single point through the two words, it is somewhat further out on the resulting V that we find the words when they are applied to humoral or mental situations. It is one thing to say that a man has a *gluey* mind, but different, more restrained and perhaps less humorous, to say *viscous*— because *viscous* is more subtle and as applied to the mind may seem nearer the literal truth—as the "animal spirits" of Descartes would seem to have been considered more convenient than the solid body as a medium of contact with the soul. Through its lab-

5. *Essay* xxvii, *Of Friendship*. See Boyle's chemical and magnetic metaphors in his *Seraphic Love* (*Works*, 1772, i, 258, 261, 264, 269).
6. *Scepsis Scientifica* (London, 1665), pp. 65, 82, 98.

oratory and philosophic associations, *viscous* is a psychological word of more kindly implication.

4

OF SCIENTIFIC diction, both literal and in its metaphoric tendencies, as it occurred in scientific writers, one further thing may be said. As the themes of science, metaphysics, and morals blend, the tone of magniloquence which is latent in all scientific use, but soberly restrained in writers like Boyle, Locke, or Newton, swells somewhat and makes impressive alliances. In Derham's *Physico-Theology*, such terms as "terraqueous globe," "diurnal rotation," "fructiferous herbs," "lenticular humours," "teguments propagated," "evagation of sound," "repositories of generation," "ramifications," "inosculations," and "accommodations" are staples of discourse; and we may find it only a notable thickening of the scientific texture when he describes the loud echoes of a pistol shot in the mountains as "the magnifying of the sound by the polyphonisms or repercussions of the rocks, . . . and other phono-camptick objects." But in other passages he tells us of "unseemly contortions and incommodious vagations of the eye," or of "nervous commerce between the ear and mouth"; of animals he asks, "With what alacrity do they transact their parental ministry?" And mentioning the interior parts of the human ear—labyrinth, vestibulum, canals, and cochlea—he says: "But I shall not expatiate on these recluse parts." [1] A longer quotation from Woodward's *Natural History of the Earth*, with a certain metaphoric cast, shows how the man of science writes when he turns his thoughts to a moral subject. Woodward describes the state of man after the fall:

A strange imbecility immediately seized and laid hold of him: he became pusillanimous, and was easily ruffled with every little Passion within: supine, and as openly exposed to any Temptation or Assault from without. And *now* these exuberant Productions of the Earth became a continual Decoy and Snare unto him: they only excited and fomented his Lusts, and ministred plentiful Fewel to his Vices and Luxury; . . . he was laid open to all manner of Pravity, Corruption, and Enormity.

And on the next page he tells us that the cause of "corruption," the "fertility of the earth," was "universal," "diffusive," and "epidemical." [2]

1. *Physico-Theology* (London, 1714), pp. 133, 100, 129, 207, 129. The atmosphere is "this noble circumambient companion of our globe" (p. 13).
2. *An Essay Toward a Natural History of the Earth* (London, 1695), pp. 86–87.

If we conceive a graded series of styles, from that of the fossilist Woodward or the botanist Ray, when they write on moral and theological themes, through that of the classical clergyman Bentley, who uses metaphysics and physics in refutation of atheism, to the sermons and moral treatises of clergymen such as Robert South or Richard Allestree, the anonymous author of the *Decay of Piety* and *Government of the Tongue,* we move, by a kind of inverted proportion, from the scientific style with moral flourishes to the full-blown theological or moral style embellished by scientific arguments or scientific metaphors. A passage from Bentley's Fourth Sermon on the Boyle foundation will point the direction:

All matter is either fluid or solid, in a large acceptation of the words, that they may comprehend even all the middle degrees between extreme fixedness and coherency, and the most rapid intestine motion of the particles of bodies. . . . Now, because all the parts of an undisturbed fluid are either of equal gravity, or gradually placed and storied according to the differences of it, any concretion that can be supposed to be naturally and mechanically made in such a fluid, must have a like structure of its several parts; that is, either be all over of a similar gravity, or have the more ponderous parts nearer its basis.[3]

South in his *Sermons* would be less impressively philosophic about particles of matter, and at the same time metaphorical.

For as those who discourse of atoms, affirm, that there are atoms of all forms, some round, some triangular, some square, and the like; all which are continually in motion, and never settle till they fall into a fit circumscription or place of the same figure: so there are the like great diversities of minds and objects.[4]

Or he might sparingly employ the hard word. Speaking of discourse which like the sun had both light and agility:

It did not so properly apprehend, as irradiate the object. . . . It was vegete, quick, and lively.[5]

Or of the fault of being disposed to take pleasure in other men's sins:

It is . . . the very quintessence and sublimation of vice, by which, as in the spirit of liquors, the malignity of many actions is contracted into a little compass.[6]

3. Sermon IV, preached June 6, 1692, in *Works of Richard Bentley,* ed. Alexander Dyce (London, 1838), iii, 78–79.
4. *Sermons Preached upon Several Occasions* (Oxford, 1842), i, 5, Sermon I.
5. *Sermons,* i, 29, Sermon II.
6. *Sermons,* i, 376, Sermon XVII.

Meanwhile the poets had found philosophic diction assimilable to some of their purposes. Milton especially had been able to place it in contexts where it generated its maximum of volume and splendor:

> There lands the Fiend, a spot like which perhaps
> Astronomer in the sun's lucent orb
> Through his glazed optic tube yet never saw.
>
> What wonder then if fields and regions here
> Breathe forth elixir pure, and rivers run
> Potable gold, when with one virtuous touch
> The arch-chemic sun, so far from us remote,
> Produces, with terrestrial humour mixed,
> Here in the dark so many precious things.[7]

It was an effulgence which others might desire—Blackmore feebly in his pseudo-philosophic *Creation;* Philips in his *Cyder,* blending mellow Miltonic burlesque and affection for English soil and apples; Prior in the cosmological wisdom of his *Solomon;* Thomson in the meteors, the vicissitudes, the freezing air, the sun and sap of his *Seasons.*

Philosophic metaphors and words appeared almost everywhere in the realm of literate writing. During the literary career of the author who is to be the central object of this study, a philosophic allusion might grace an urbane epistolary style:

Monsieur Duclos observes, and I think very justly, *qu'il y a à présent en France une fermentation universelle de la raison qui tend à se développer.* Whereas, I am sorry to say, that here that fermentation seems to have been over some years ago, the spirit evaporated, and only the dregs left.[8]

Or the Burtonian wit of a facetious novelist:

To come at the exact weight of things in the scientific steelyard, the fulcrum, . . . should be almost invisible, to avoid all friction from popular tenets.[9]

Or more solidly the essays of the Rambler himself:

The notions of the old and young are like liquors of different gravity and texture which can never unite. The spirits of youth sublimed by health,

---

7. *Paradise Lost,* III, 589–591, 606–611. The Latinism of neo-classic English poetry was on the whole no doubt more Virgilian than philosophic. See Thomas Quayle, *Poetic Diction* (1924), chap. iv.

8. Chesterfield, *Letters,* to his son, April 22, 1751.

9. Sterne, *Tristram Shandy,* II, 19.

and volatilized by passion, soon leave behind them the phlegmatick sediment of weariness and deliberation.[10]

But Johnson's role in the history of philosophic words is a special one, determined partly by the fact that he devoted more than seven years to compiling *A Dictionary of the English Language.*

10. *Rambler* 69, v, 438.

CHAPTER II

Johnson's Dictionary

THE inkhorn controversy of the sixteenth century simmered down into the title pages and addresses to the reader of the seventeenth-century dictionaries, and English lexicography grew upon "hard words" and related curiosities: the terms of logic, law, physic, and astronomy specified in the physician Bullokar's *Expositor* of 1616; the encyclopedic Beasts, Birds, Boyes, Cities, Destinies, Divels, Dogges, Fayries, Fishes, Giants and the like which appear in the famous third part of Cockeram's *Dictionarie* of 1623; the polyglot neologisms prominent in Blount's *Glossographia* of 1656, as well as the terms of divinity, mathematics, heraldry, anatomy, war, music, and architecture advertised on his title page. Edward Phillips' *New World of Words* in 1658, with a title page that boasted forty-one arts and sciences, from theology and logic to hunting, fishing, and carving, included much curious and legendary material and many proper names, and is on the whole fairly representative of the exotic and esoteric vocabulary which accumulated in the English dictionaries of the seventeenth century.[1] In Phillips may be found: "*Aba*, a Tyrant of Hungaria, slain by his own Subjects near the River Tibiscus"; "*Cebratane*, . . . a Trunk to shoot at Birds with Clay Pellets"; "*Pen-guin*, a certain kind of Creature, of a mixt nature, between Beast, Bird and Fish; but chiefly Bird"; "*Weapon-Salve* (*Lat. Unguentum Armarium*) a sort of Sympathetical Ointment [which] cures a wound, by being applyed to the Weapon that made it." Phillips lists some authorities "Eminent in, or Contributory to"[2] the arts, sciences and "faculties" treated in his volume—Sir William Dugdale and Elias Ashmole, for example, in antiquities, the Honourable Robert Boyle in chemistry, John Evelyn in Agriculture and Architecture, Peter Lely in painting, Mr. Isaac Walton in fishing. But modern scholarship has concurred with Phillips' competitor Blount in questioning the good faith of the whole ambiguous claim, and the dictionary would in fact seem to reflect

---

1. Cf. Starnes and Noyes, *The English Dictionary from Cawdrey to Johnson* (Chapel Hill, 1946), esp. pp. 20, 21, 23, 27, 35, 37, 38, 49.
2. This "obscurely insinuating" phrase first appears in the edition of 1671 (Starnes and Noyes, *op. cit.*, pp. 52–54).

rather a random and secondhand virtuosity than a methodic interest in science. The learning is rather literary and miscellaneous than scientific. There is the flavor of *Quincunx* and *Pseudodoxia,* something of the "rhapsody of rags gathered from several dunghills."

During the nearly one hundred years that intervene between Phillips' *World of Words* and the epochal Dictionary of Samuel Johnson, English lexicography, especially in the works of John Kersey at the beginning of the eighteenth century, and those of Nathan Bailey later, made great progress not only toward linguistic inclusiveness but toward real technicality of scientific information. Kersey's *New English Dictionary* of 1702 was the first to introduce the bulk of common English words, and his revision of Phillips' *World of Words* in 1706 performed the same service for the new scientific vocabulary.[3] A striking feature of Bailey's revised folio *Dictionarium* of 1736, the most important predecessor of Johnson, and Johnson's check list in making his own Dictionary,[4] is its high degree of technicality. Bailey's folio explained "hard and technical Words, or terms of Art," in 62 "Arts, Sciences, and Mysteries" as follows:

Agriculture, Algebra, Anatomy, Architecture, Arithmetick, Astrology, Astronomy, Botanicks, Catoptricks, Chymistry, Chiromancy, Chirurgery, Confectionary, Cookery, Cosmography, Dialling, Dioptricks, Ethicks, Fishing, Fortification, Fowling, Gardening, Gauging, Geography, Geometry, Grammar, Gunnery, Handicrafts, Hawking, Heraldry, Horsemanship, Hunting, Husbandry, Hydraulicks, Hydrography, Hydrostaticks, Law, Logic, Maritime *and* Military Affairs, Mathematicks, Mechanicks, Merchandize, Metaphysicks, Meteorology, Navigation, Opticks, Otacousticks, Painting, Perspective, Pharmacy, Philosophy,

3. The author of the *New English Dictionary* of 1702 is known only as "J. K.," but his identity with Kersey would seem a safe assumption (Starnes and Noyes, *op. cit.,* pp. 70, 85).

4. Under the letters A, B, C in Johnson's Dictionary five entries are attributed to Bailey. Of these, *abatude, aptate, coomb* are found in either the 1730 or 1736 Bailey folio; *abased,* a term of heraldry, and *coom* are found only in 1736. Under the letter S some seventy words are attributed to Bailey, of which three, *sago, semi-spherical,* and *swine-Bread,* are found in 1736 but not in 1730, and seven others, *saick, sark, sarse, scatches, screak, sordet, stuke,* have some detail of etymology or definition which is lacking in 1730 but present in 1736. In short, Johnson did not use 1730 without 1736. There seems no reason to suppose that he did not rely altogether on the more complete 1736.

Other definitions from Bailey appear throughout the Dictionary with the attribution *Dict.* Cf. *Preface, Works* ix, 206. Mildred Struble, *A Johnson Handbook* (New York, 1933), p. 120, reports that of about 2,900 words under the letter A in Johnson's first edition 61 are defined as in Bailey's 1736 folio.

The accounts by Boswell, Percy, and Hawkins of Johnson's use of Bailey may be found in *Life* i, 218 and n. 1, and *Works* i, 175.

Physick, Physiognomy, Pyrotechny, Rhetorick, Sculpture, Staticks, Statuary, Surveying, Theology, *and* Trigonometry.

And Bailey lives up to his title page in a way that Phillips does not. With the help of the mathematician Gordon, the botanist Miller, the philologist Lediard, and others, Bailey was not so much the φιλόλογος of another part of his title page as a polymath of the widest smattering. The regular pattern of Bailey's Dictionary is that of a brief definition, followed by as many technical meanings as he has been able to find. After "Architecture . . . the Art of Building,"—we find *Civil* Architecture, *Military* Architecture, *Naval* Architecture, *Counterfeit* Architecture, Architecture in *Perspective,* and Architecture "represented in Painting and Sculpture as a Woman sitting upon a Piece of a Pillar, having all sorts of Tools and Instruments about her." The chemical signs (Aqua *Communis,* Aqua *Distillata,* Aqua *Fortis,* Aqua *Regalis,* Aqua *Vitae*) and the frequent heraldic, geometrical, astronomical, and mechanical diagrams are but graphic symptoms of a miscellaneous technicality and arcanism which crowds every page.

"The title which I prefix to my work," wrote Samuel Johnson in his *Plan of an English Dictionary,* "has long conveyed a very miscellaneous idea, and they that take a dictionary into their hands, have been accustomed to expect from it a solution of almost every difficulty." [5] It was left for Johnson, using the simplified title *A Dictionary of the English Language,* to write a dictionary which —with its approximately 40,000 words—was not the largest of his time [6] and was far from being the most technical, yet which, in its thoughtful definitions and illustrations on the historical principle, was both scientific and literary in the widest senses, the first general English dictionary—"for the use of such as aspire to exactness of criticism or elegance of style." [7] It is probably true, as Webster was to charge,[8] that Johnson's Dictionary multiplied the number

5. *Works* ix, 168.

6. Bailey's first folio Dictionarium of 1730 is estimated to contain about 48,000 words; Bailey's 1736 folio, about 60,000; the Scott-Bailey *New Universal Etymological English Dictionary* of 1755, about 65,000 (Starnes and Noyes, *op. cit.,* pp. 118, 122, 185). Angus Macdonald, "Johnson as Lexicographer," *University of Edinburgh Journal,* viii (Summer, 1936), 19, and a writer in *Lloyd's Evening Post* for February 8, 1777 (Vol. xl, p. 140), estimate for Johnson's Dictionary, respectively, about 41,000 and about 40,000 words, the latter figure being also the estimate of Professors Starnes and Noyes.

7. Johnson's Preface to the 1756 abstracted edition of the Dictionary. Cf. the review by Adam Smith, *Edinburgh Review,* No. I (January–July, 1755), p. 61. "Mr. Johnson has extended his views much farther. . . ."

8. Noah Webster, *A Letter to Dr. David Ramsay . . . Respecting the Errors in Johnson's Dictionary* (New Haven, 1807), pp. 5, 8–10. The comparison to the lan-

of outlandish and difficult words in written English, words no more truly English than so many Patagonian or Hottentot words; but that was not because there were more of these words in Johnson's Dictionary than in others, but because both dictionary and author were more interesting and had more authority.

2

THERE is a distinct degree of irony in Johnson's repeatedly humble and derogatory statements about his labors. "Beating the track of the alphabet with sluggish resolution," he says in his opening sentences to Lord Chesterfield in the *Plan*. "Not even the barren laurel" was believed to grow in the desolate province upon which he had entered "with the pleasing hope, that, as it was low, it likewise would be safe." [1] But it was in the same *Plan* that he announced his intention of selecting "such sentences, as, besides their immediate use, may give pleasure or instruction, by conveying some elegance of language, or some precept of prudence, or piety." [2] When the work had been accomplished, he looked back, in his *Preface*, with regret on the truncations which economy of space had forced upon him and on the limitations of his own learning and energy—yet with pride in the "innumerable passages" which he had "selected with propriety, and preserved with exactness; some shining with sparks of imagination, and some replete with treasures of wisdom." [3] He was one of those "whose fancy is active, and whose views are comprehensive" and who must therefore rest below their own aims. If he had been "doomed at last to wake a lexicographer," he had yet entertained the "dreams of a poet." [4] The *Preface* is the report of a man who has worked his way through a vast program of best-books reading and comes out charged with the importance of his experience.

I therefore extracted from philosophers principles of science; from historians remarkable facts; from chymists complete processes; from divines striking exhortations; and from poets beautiful descriptions.[5]

---

guage of the Hottentots is quoted from Horne Tooke, *Diversions of Purley*, i (Philadelphia, 1806), 182.

1. *Works* ix, 165–166. Cf. *Preface, Works* ix, 193, "Every author may aspire to praise; the lexicographer can only hope to escape reproach"; Dictionary, s.v. *lexicographer*, "a harmless drudge," and s.v. *Grubstreet; Rambler* and *Adventurer, post* p. 70; and Johnson's poem Γνῶθι σεαυτόν (*Post Lexicon Anglicanum auctum et emendatum*).

2. *Works* ix, 189.
3. *Works* ix, 220.
4. *Works* ix, 213, 218.
5. *Works* ix, 213.

If the language of theology were extracted from *Hooker* and the translation of the Bible; the terms of natural knowledge from *Bacon;* the phrases of policy, war, and navigation from *Raleigh;* the dialect of poetry and fiction from *Spenser* and *Sidney;* and the diction of common life from *Shakespeare,* few ideas would be lost to mankind, for want of English words, in which they might be expressed.[6]

The chief glory of every people arises from its authors; . . . I shall not think my employments useless or ignoble, . . . if my labours afford light to the repositories of science, and add celebrity to *Bacon,* to *Hooker,* to *Milton,* and to *Boyle.*[7]

The glow of such an enthusiasm is not altogether quenched even by the descending gloom and "frigid tranquillity" of Johnson's classic peroration.

Johnson's Dictionary, we are told, was read through twice by his contemporary, the historian Robertson;[8] in the nineteenth century it was read by Browning[9] and by Buckle.[10] At the simplest level of appreciation one notices that it contains not only very interesting quotations[11] but many which reflect the character and choice of the Johnson whom we know from other sources. One finds, for example, expressions of literary judgment, like the following from the *Spectator* under the word *idiomatick*[12]—an analogue of the *Rambler* on the diction of *Macbeth:*[13]

Since phrases used in conversation contract meanness by passing through the mouths of the vulgar, a poet should guard himself against the idiomatick ways of speaking.

And a passage of somewhat the same tenor from Broome's *Notes on the Odyssey* quoted twice, under words which might not seem promising, *cowkeeper* and *hogherd:*

6. *Works* ix, 215.
7. *Works* ix, 227. For Johnson's view of the pleasure and the difficulty of making a dictionary, see *Life* i, 189, n. 2.
8. *Miscellanies* ii, 352.
9. Mrs. Sutherland Orr, *Life and Letters of Robert Browning* (London, 1891), p. 53. He qualified himself for the profession of literature "by reading and digesting the whole of Johnson's Dictionary."
10. Alfred H. Huth, *The Life and Writings of Henry Thomas Buckle* (London, 1880), i, 40: "Began to read Johnson's English dictionary to enlarge my vocabulary," an entry in Buckle's diary.
11. One of Webster's objections to Johnson's Dictionary was that a large number of the illustrations "throw not the least light on his definitions" (*op. cit.,* p. 18). From a strictly lexicographic point of view, there is more than a grain of truth in Webster's charge.
12. Quotations are from Johnson's Dictionary (2d ed. 1755–56). For Johnson's freedom with the text of his sources, see his own *Preface, Works* ix, 213.
13. *Rambler* 168.

The terms cowkeeper and hogherd, are not to be used in our poetry; but there are no finer words in the Greek language.[14]

Johnson the moralist and student of human conduct appears in such miniature, self-contained fables from Sir Roger L'Estrange as the following under *lapidary:*

As a cock was turning up a dunghill, he espied a diamond: Well (says he) this sparkling foolery now to a lapidary would have been the making of him; but, as to any use of mine, a barley-corn had been worth forty on't.[15]

Or in aphoristic statements such as the following from Bacon's *Apophthegms* under *naked:*

A philosopher being asked in what a wise man differed from a fool? answered, send them both naked to those who know them not, and you shall perceive.[16]

His well-known regard for the homely details of biography, expressed in *Rambler* 60 and *Idler* 84, appears often through the Dictionary in a kind of thumbnail biography or biographical incident from Bacon, from Swift's *Thoughts on Various Subjects,* from Knolles or Camden.[17]

Cromartie after fourscore went to his country-house to live *thriftily,* and save up money to spend at London.

Swift.

An old lord of Leicestershire amused himself with mending *pitchforks* and spades for his tenants gratis.

Swift.

They misliked nothing more in King Edward the Confessor than that he was *Frenchified;* and accounted the desire of foreign language then to be a foretoken of bringing in foreign powers, which indeed happened.

Camden's Remains.

14. Cf. *nineteen, obsolete* (Swift and Dryden on hard words); *track* v.a. (Dryden on Jonson: "He was not only a professed imitator of Horace, but a learned plagiary in all the others; you track him everywhere in their snow"). Cf. *nonage, opera, solemn, sum, summerhouse, till, triplet, tolerate, unconfined, unconstraint, youth.*
15. Cf. *plump, smoothness, tatterdemalion, throat, waggish.*
16. Cf. Bacon under *baggage, bottle, breakfast, brusher, gallipot, gamester, gentry, juvenile, smother, twilight;* Locke under *sore;* Swift under *vain;* Jonson under *parapet* and *petulancy.*
17. Cf. *canonist, carpingly, freespoken, laundress, nimblewitted, pew, poem, shave, spender, stoop, step, stuff* v.a., *thumb.* Johnson's marked copy of Bacon (see Appendix B) shows that he originally selected from the *Apophthegms* and *Ornamenta Rationalia* many more aphorisms and pointed anecdotes than actually appear after the retrenchments of which he complains in his *Preface.*

And one may sometimes trace a Johnsonian prejudice or whim in the Dictionary, as when one turns from the example last quoted to the word *gallicism:*

A mode of speech peculiar to the French language: such as, he *figured* in controversy; he *held* this conduct; he *held* the same language that another had *held* before: with many other expressions to be found in the pages of *Bolingbroke.*

Or (since Johnson objected to Bolingbroke for more than one reason), when one comes to the word *irony:*

A mode of speech in which the meaning is contrary to the words: as, *Bolingbroke was a holy man.*

Or to the word *sophistically,* where he quotes Swift to good effect:

Bolingbroke argues most *sophistically.*[18]

Johnsonians have often noted that the Dictionary contains not a few special tokens of the author's character—certain Tory whimsies, anti-Scot jests, and occasional mellow loyalties to Grubstreet and to Lichfield.[19] "Johnson's Dictionary," says a recent writer, "embodies a personality."

We can trace his progress so closely at times that we almost surprise him among a jumble of books, turning with an outflung arm to his assistants, or handing over with a contemptuous shrug his copy of the 1736 edition of Skelton, after marking in black lead pencil the passage he has chosen.[20]

"Had Johnson left us nothing but his Dictionary," says Carlyle in a more seriously panegyric vein, "one might have traced there a great intellect, a genuine man." [21] Two of the most serious strains of meaning which run through the Dictionary, and two which we can connect most clearly with the Johnson whom we know in other ways, are the scientific and the religious, the second related to the first by the physico-theological tie which is the motif of so much English writing of the period from which Johnson drew his sources. It was perhaps no surprise to Johnson's first readers to find a sermon from South or a text from *Proverbs* under the word *sensualist* or the word *slothfulness.*

18. Cf. my more complete account, "Johnson's Treatment of Bolingbroke in the Dictionary," *MLR*, xliii (January, 1948), 78–80.

19. William P. Courtney, *A Bibliography of Samuel Johnson* (Oxford, 1915), pp. 46–48. Cf. my short note "Johnson and Scots," *TLS*, xlv (March, 1946), 115.

20. Walter B. C. Watkins, *Johnson and English Poetry before 1660* (Princeton, 1936), p. 1.

21. *On Heroes, Hero-Worship, and the Heroic in History*, Lecture v, "The Hero as Man of Letters."

Let atheists and sensualists satisfy themselves as they are able; the former of which will find, that, as long as reason keeps her ground, religion neither can nor will lose hers.

Slothfulness casteth into a deep sleep, and an idle soul shall suffer hunger.

But even to a clerical reader of the year 1755 the religious cast of the Dictionary may have seemed more pervasive and special when he found under *split* v.a. 3 a homiletic image from the *Decay of Piety:*

God's desertion, as a full and violent wind, drives him in an instant, not to the harbour, but on the rock where he will be irrecoverably split.

Or under *shuffle* two arguments from South: [22]

In most things good and evil lie shuffled, and thrust up together in a confused heap; and it is study which must draw them forth and range them.

When lots are shuffled together in a lap or pitcher, what reason can a man have to presume, that he shall draw a white stone rather than a black?

Six mighty works of the physico-theological school, Ray's *Wonders of God in the Creation,* Grew's *Cosmologia Sacra,* Derham's *Physico-Theology,*[23] Burnet's *History of the Earth,* Bentley's *Sermons* on the Boyle foundation, Cheyne's *Philosophical Principles,* and works of a similar tenor like More's *Antidote against Atheism* and Hale's *Primitive Origination of Mankind,* provided Johnson with miniature versions of the teleological argument for insertion under the most widely varied, concrete, and commonplace words. Under *fusee* one finds the analogy of the watch from Hale:

The reason of the motion of the balance is by the motion of the next wheel, and that by the motion of the next, and that by the motion of the fusee, and that by the motion of the spring: the whole frame of the watch carries a reasonableness in it, the passive impression of the intellectual idea that was in the artist.

Under *liniment* an example of animal economy from Ray:

22. See some religious quotations of various shades under: *science, sect, senselessly, sensuality, seriously, settle, shallowbrained, shrewdly, shrink, slip, sottishly, spirtle, struggle, sum, surmise, syllogism.*
23. See Johnson's recommendation of Ray and Derham in his Preface to Dodsley's *Preceptor,* 1748 (*Works* ix, 416). The philosophic schoolmaster, says Johnson, "will every day find a thousand opportunities of turning the attention of his scholars to the contemplation of the objects that surround them, of laying open the wonderful art with which every part of the universe is formed, and the providence which governs the vegetable and animal creation." Derham was Sunday reading for Johnson at Inchkenneth in the Hebrides (*Life* v, 323).

The wise author of nature hath provided on the rump two glandules, which the bird catches hold upon with her bill, and squeezes out an oily pap or liniment, fit for the inunction of the feathers.

As John Ray had seen the Wonders of God everywhere in the Creation, Johnson's readers found the same wonders everywhere in the variegated realm of discourse of which his Dictionary was the alphabetized mirror.

3

To DESCRIBE the element of science in a dictionary is perhaps not a dramatic undertaking and in the present instance will not advance the logic of our argument through many or complicated stages. Yet some rehearsal at least of the most conspicuous scientific materials in Johnson's Dictionary and of the main numerical facts is necessary to underpaint, as it were, the argument that is to follow. Johnson's Dictionary is one which presents to the eye of the most casual inspector large typographical blocks of scientific materials. "I resolved to show . . . my attention to things," he says in his *Preface,*

to pierce deep into every science, to enquire the nature of every substance of which I inserted the name, to . . . exhibit every production of art or nature in an accurate description, that my book might be in place of all other dictionaries whether appellative or technical.[1]

We have then such families of scientific articles as the more than 350 descriptions of plants taken from Philip Miller's *Gardeners Dictionary,* ranging in length from an inch or so of type—for example, under *apricot, bishopsweed, chocolate, dogbane, earthnut, figwort, ivy*—to a substantial part of a column, as under *elm, flower, pear, plum, tree, tulip, vine,* and *wheat.*[2]

Bishopsweed. . . . The name of a plant. This is an umbelliferous weed, with small striated seeds; the petals of the flowers are unequal, and shaped like a heart. The seeds of the greater bishopsweed are used in medicine, and should be sown in an open situation, early in the spring.

[1] 1. *Works* ix, 218.

2. Cf. Lane Cooper, "Dr. Johnson on Oats," *PMLA,* lii (September, 1937), 788–796. Names of plants are in all about 650, with other definitions and definitive illustrations from Chambers, Hill, Quincy, and Mortimer's *Art of Husbandry.* James Harrison, editor of the 7th edition of the Dictionary, 1786, points out that about a hundred of the descriptions from Miller (e.g., under *ahouai, Alexanders, apricot, archangel, arse-smart, asarabaca*) were omitted or severely truncated in the revised 4th edition of 1773 (*Harrison's Edition,* The Editor's Preface).

Under the word *plant* an article a column in length gives twenty-seven species of plants according to the botanist Ray.[3] A more casual interest in the natural history of animals, fishes, and birds [4] does not exclude under the word *animal* a lengthy classification attributed to Ray [5] and a few other substantial articles, from Dom Augustin Calmet's *Dictionary of the Holy Bible* and other encyclopedias.[6] A widely inclusive and perhaps haphazard selection of some 350 substances—e.g., *alum, ammoniac, antimony, coal, copper, crystal, emerald, emery, iron, isinglass, lime, metal, nitre, nutmeg, opium, potash, salt, stone*—are described in the first pages of the Dictionary (up to the word *citrine*) chiefly from Ephraim Chambers' *Cyclopaedia*, but after that chiefly from two works of John Hill, his *Materia Medica* and *History of Fossils*.[7]

Quicksilver, called mercury by the chymists, is a naturally fluid mineral, and the heaviest of all known bodies next to gold, and is the more heavy and fluid, as it is more pure; it is wholly volatile in the fire, and may be driven up in vapour by a degree of heat very little greater than that of boiling water; it is the least tenacious of all bodies, and every smaller drop may be again divided by the lightest touch into a multitude of others. The specifick gravity of pure mercury is to water as 14020 to 1000, and as it is the heaviest of all fluids, it is also the coldest, and when heated the hottest: the ancients all esteemed quicksilver a poison. . . .

Hill.

Mercury is very improperly called a metal, for though it has weight and similarity of parts, it is neither dissolvable by fire, malleable, nor fixed: it seems to constitute a particular class of fossils, and is rather the mother

3. I am unable to say from which of several botanical works by Ray this is derived. Cf. Chambers, *Cyclopaedia* (1741), s.v. *plant;* James, *Medicinal Dictionary,* s.v. *botany.*

4. An early critic of Johnson's Dictionary enumerates seventy birds which are omitted (*A Letter from a Friend in England to Mr. [John] Maxwell . . . with a Character of Mr. Johnson's English Dictionary* [Dublin, 1755], cited by Stanley Rypins, "Johnson's Dictionary Reviewed by His Contemporaries," *PQ,* iv [July, 1935], 282).

5. Johnson's tables of animals according to Mr. Ray agree verbatim with those in Chambers' *Cyclopaedia* (1741), s.v. *animal*—a translation with some omissions and some elaborations from the two Latin tables in John Ray's *Synopsis Methodica Animalium Quadrupedum et Serpentini Generis* (London, 1693), pp. 53, 60 (John Crerar Library).

6. e.g., under *armadillo, chameleon, dromedary, eagle, elephant, ossifrage, ostrich, porcupine, seacow, stork, swan,* and *woodlouse.*

7. *Nitre* has nearly a whole column from Hill's *History of Fossils.* Hill's *Materia Medica* was published in May of 1751. More than 100 of the names of substances have articles from Chambers or Hill or from both. Many shorter illustrations are from Bacon, Boyle, Quincy, and Woodward's *Natural History of Fossils*—from the latter especially, the illustrations for precious stones.

or basis of all metals, than a metal itself: mercury is of considerable use in gilding, making looking-glasses, in refining gold, and various other mechanical operations besides medicine.

Chambers.

In the area of medicine, surgery, and anatomy, a few longer articles, e.g., under *bone, breast, finger, kidney, midriff, pulse, skull, tonsil, tooth, vein,* are quoted from the *Lexicon Physico-Medicum* of John Quincy, and more than 400 [8] shorter illustrations from Quincy's *Lexicon,* Wiseman's *Chirurgical Treatises,* Sharp's *Surgery,* Harvey's treatise on *Consumptions,* Floyer on *Humours,* Arbuthnot's treatises on *Aliments* and on *Diet,* Bacon's *Natural History* and Browne's *Pseudodoxia.*

The putrid vapours, though exciting a fever, do colliquate the *phlegmatick* humours of the body.

Harvey.

The bones of the toes, and part only of the *metatarsal* bones, may be carious; in which case cut off only so much of the foot as is disordered.

Sharp's Surgery.

The areas of mathematical, astronomical, and optical science are represented by about 60 definitions from the *Lexicon Technicum* of John Harris and the *Cyclopaedia* of Chambers; and by perhaps an equal number [9] of very technical illustrations from Cheyne's *Philosophical Principles,* Derham's *Physico-Theology,* Newton's *Opticks,* Wilkins' *Mathematical Magic,* and various essays of Boyle.

Sir Isaac Newton has made it probable, that the comet, which appeared in 1680, by approaching to the sun in its *perihelium,* acquired such a degree of heat, as to be 5000 years a cooling.

Cheyne's Philosophical Principles.[10]

In a small group of words relating to meteorological and electrical phenomena, the word *comet* is noteworthy for its long article taken from the encyclopedias of Trévoux and Chambers; the word *barometer* for perhaps the longest article in the Dictionary, one of a column and a half, from the *Lexicon Technicum* of Harris. The words *accurate, bolis, meteor, lightning, regular, thunder, will with a wisp,* and *wind* form a family illustrated from the Lucasian Professor John Colson's translation of Musschenbroek's *Elementa Physicae.* Under the word *electricity* Johnson himself contributed

8. Technical terms of medicine and related sciences number in all about 900.
9. Technical terms of this class number in all about 300.
10. Cf. *quadrible,* where Derham refers to Sir Isaac Newton; *mesologarithms,* where Harris refers to Kepler.

a brief original essay. After quoting the inadequate definition from Quincy's *Lexicon:*

A property in some bodies, whereby, when rubbed so as to grow warm, they draw little bits of paper, or such like substances, to them,

he continued the history of electricity to the date of his Dictionary, with allusions to the pioneer work of Stephen Gray and to the lightning-rod experiments that had followed recently in the wake of Franklin's *Experiments and Observations:*

Such was the account given a few years ago of electricity; but the industry of the present age, first excited by the experiments of *Gray,* has discovered in electricity a multitude of philosophical wonders. Bodies electrified by a sphere of glass, turned nimbly round, not only emit flame, but may be filled with such a quantity of electrical vapour, as, if discharged at once upon a human body, would endanger life. The force of this vapour has hitherto appeared instantaneous, persons at both ends of a long chain seeming to be struck at once. The philosophers are now endeavouring to intercept the strokes of lightning.[11]

The names of the chemical substances in Johnson's Dictionary are a medley of the learned and the humble, *ammoniac* and *antimony, nutmeg* and *salt;* the names of the plants from Miller's *Gardeners Dictionary* are of the English soil—*arse-smart, bladder-nut, cabbage, daffodowndilly, figmarigold, rupture wort*—the flowers "that come before the swallow dares," the "rathe primrose" and "tufted crowtoe," "myrtles brown" and "ivy never sere." It was only in the articles about these words that the lexicographer encountered the substances *factitious, friable, porous, volatile, tenacious, viscous,* and *indurated,* the exotic florilegium of specimens *umbelliferous, papilionaceous, vulnerary, labiated, membranaceous, squamose, verticillate.*[12]

In certain other sciences, a much more considerable number of words defined in the Dictionary are themselves learned and technical: in medicine and anatomy such words as

anastromatick, anastomasis, aneurism, anorexy, antalgick, antaphroditick, antapoplectick, antarthritick, anthypchondriack,

in mathematicks, astronomy, and mechanicks the terms massed under such prefixes as *bi-, epi-, equi-, hex-, para-, pent-, plani-, poly-, quad-, quin-,* and *sesqui-,* and, more dispersedly, families

11. Corrected text from the edition of 1773. See my short article, "Johnson on Electricity," *RES,* xxiii (July, 1947), 257–260.
12. See *alum, mummy, quicksilver; balm, basil, bear's breech, bean, betony, birdsfoot, bishopsweed, bladder-sena, bladder-nut, bottle-flower, broom.*

of words like *astrolabe, azimuth, asymptote, hydrostatical, hydrometry, selenography, sideration, thermometer, thermoscope.*

But again, to make a further distinction and to emphasize it even more, our discussion of philosophic words in Chapter I must have prepared us for the fact that by far the greater number of philosophic words in Johnson's Dictionary, and the more significant for our study, are those of more general and extensible meaning, the terms of the broader science of things in general. Not the miscellaneous big or "hard" words which have appeared so plentifully in the lists extracted from Johnson's Dictionary by Noah Webster [13] and subsequent critics—but a special class of learned words —many indeed rather hard, some less so. In the realm of medical generality, such words as *alexipharmick, anodyne, cathartical, emollient, phlegmatick, salutiferous;* in the inorganic physical realm, the words of heat and cold, *assation, cremation, calefaction, frigifaction*—of light and darkness, *candent, interlucent, scintillation, umbrosity*—of the secondary qualities impressed upon the senses of sight, hearing, taste, and smell, *colorifick, pellucid, prismatick, sonorifick, acerbity, saporifick, odoriferous.* And in far greater numbers still the words of even more abstract categories of meaning. The following lists must be understood as even more rigorous selections than the foregoing, presented only to suggest the pervasive occurrence of the vocabulary of abstract scientific categories throughout the Dictionary.[14]

Of motion:

aberrance, accelerate, gradient, graduation, gyration, ingression, locomotion, oscillation, progression, quiescence, sequacious, trepidation, velocity

Of mechanical action:

abduce, abscind, coaction, collision, concussion, conquassate, impact, impellent, impinge, impulse, obduce, obtund, percussion, refract, transilience, transmission, trusion

13. *Op. cit.*, pp. 8, 10. There are perhaps about 700 nonphilosophic big words in the Dictionary, such—to name a few not chosen by Webster—as *agonothetic, belomancy, cynegiticks, gynecocracy* ("petticoat government"), *ingannation* ("A word neither used nor necessary"), *myropolist, naumachy, reboation, screable, vitilitigate.* Sir Thomas Browne is the source of some of these words; Bailey's *Dictionarium,* of others. Many are given without authority.

14. Johnson occasionally specifies the scientific character of a word. See *fixidity,* "A word of Boyle"; *frigorifick,* "A word used in science"; *frustum,* "A term of science"; *strata,* "A philosophical term"; *stratify,* "A chymical term"; *stratum,* "A term of philosophy"; *striae,* "In natural history . . ."; *venal* 2, "A technical word."

Of shape and structure:

anfractuous, configuration, conflexure, elliptical, gibbosity, globosity, involution, nodosity, protuberance, recurvation, tortuosity

abarticulation, catenation, interstitial, intertexture, ramification, reticulated, superficies

Of qualities of matter:

crassitude, density, elasticity, flaccid, flexibility, malleability, porosity, rigidity, tenacity, tenuity

Of fluids in particular:

colliquation, dilution, distillation, ebullition, effervescence, fluctuation, immerge, interfluent, liquefaction, percolate, solution, tincture, viscosity

Of mixture and joining:

adhesion, amalgamate, coalescence, cohesion, immiscibility

Of increase and decrease and equality:

aggregate, accretion, comminuible, congestion, conglobate, conglomerate, diminution, increment, plenitude, superaddition, superfluitance

equability, equilibrium, equipoise, equipollence, equiponderance [15]

Of purity and homogeneity and their opposites:

adulteration, defecate, purgation, sophisticate

adjectitious, adscititious, adventitious, congruity, consentaneous, discriminate, extrinsical, heterogeneal, homogeneal.

With these may be mentioned a few more metaphysical and "scholastic" [16] terms:

consubstantiate, immanent, incorporeal, materiation, supersubstantial.

The illustrations of these general philosophic terms are taken from a wide range of philosophic authors: from Bacon, Boyle, Newton, and Arbuthnot; Glanvill, Locke, Bentley, Watts, and Cheyne; Browne, Hale, Grew, Ray, and Derham; and the technical dictionaries of Quincy, Harris, and Chambers—in ways which will be the further object of our study in this and in parts of succeeding chapters.

15. Cf. *imponderous, librate, overpoise, perpension, ponderal, preponderance, superponderate.*
16. See the definitions of *quiddity* and *ubiety.*

The survey of philosophic material which we have just made
may be summarized statistically in the following statements: In
the first volume of the Dictionary, or under the letters A to K, there
are at least 10,000 quotations of various shades from philosophic
writings—the largest numbers from Locke, Browne, Arbuthnot,
Bacon's *Natural History*, and Boyle—a total which constitutes
about one fifth of all the illustrations in the first volume.[17] Of the
words defined in the whole Dictionary, it is my conservative estimate that there are more than 3,000 of general philosophic import,
and about 2,000 technical hard words and homely names of plants
and substances technically described—the total of more than 5,000
including about one word in every eight of the Dictionary. These
proportions are perhaps not an unusual bulk of science for an English dictionary. But it seems safe to say that they do represent a
familiarity with the literature and vocabulary of science which
was unusual for a man of letters, even in Johnson's day, when
science and letters were still closely compatible.

It is true that the making of the Dictionary is not the only
avenue by which Johnson may have arrived at philosophic ideas
and words.[18] The biographer of Johnson will note the 4,000-odd
philosophic books, including works of Bacon, Browne, Wilkins,
Boyle, Glanvill, Newton, Woodward, Locke, Arbuthnot, and
Cheyne, some of which Johnson may have sampled while making
the Catalogue of the Harleian Library for the bookseller Osborne
in 1743 and 1744,[19] or what is more certain but less specific, the

17. See the statistical tabulation in Mr. Lewis M. Freed's Cornell doctoral dissertation, "The Sources of Johnson's Dictionary" (1930), p. 45. Taking the totals
of all authors who appear fifty times or more in the first volume, I arrive at the following summary: quotations from poets about 24,000 (including Shakespeare 8,694,
Dryden 5,627, Milton 2,733, Pope 2,108, Spenser 1,546); from literary prose
writers, 10,000 (including Bacon in his literary and historical works 1,563, Addison
2,439, Swift 1,761); from religious writers, 5,000 (including Hooker 1,216, South
1,092); from the Bible, 2,270; from the law dictionaries of Ayliffe and Cowell, the
Farrier's Dictionary and Mortimer's *Art of Husbandry*, a total of about 1,533. For the
10,000 philosophic quotations the authors who appear most frequently are: Locke
1,674, Browne 1,070, Arbuthnot 1,029, Bacon in his *Natural History* and *Physiological Remains* 920, Boyle 592, Watts 509, Woodward 460, Hale 337, Ray 336,
Glanvill 321, Wiseman 309. Most of the 334 quotations from Bentley are from his
highly philosophic *Sermons* on the Boyle foundation.
     For some variations from Mr. Freed's count, see the tabulation of prose sources of
the first volume of the Dictionary in Eula G. Stark, "Samuel Johnson's Reading for
the Dictionary," Chicago master's dissertation (1928).
18. For Johnson's reading, mainly classical, in his father's bookshop at Lichfield
and as a student at Oxford, see Aleyn Lyell Reade, *Johnsonian Gleanings*, Part III
(London, 1922), pp. 166–167; Part v (London, 1928), pp. 27–30, 213–229.
19. *Catalogus Bibliothecae Harleianae*, ii (London, 1743), 761–908, 923–933,
941–943, 955–958; iii (London, 1744), 138–148, 228–232; iv (London, 1744), 410–

conversational sources of information to which Johnson had ready access in his early London years. About 1749, for example, Samuel Dyer, who "was going through a course of chemistry under Dr. Pemberton, of Gresham College," retailed "descriptions of processes" at the Ivy Lane Club. To these Johnson "would listen . . . attentively." [20] In medicine, the science in which Johnson, through hypochondriac inclination and the ready laboratory of his own disordered constitution, had by the end of his life gained the greatest proficiency, his early lessons would seem to have been learned as he translated the lives of Actuarius, Aegineta, Aretaeus, Boerhaave, Ruysch, and other famous physicians for the *Medicinal Dictionary* of Dr. James.[21] "My knowledge of physick," he told Boswell, "I learnt from Dr. James." [22] Later in life he recommended to Boswell the *English Malady* and *Essay of Health and Long Life* by the "learned, philosophick and pious" Dr. Cheyne,[23] books which unlike Cheyne's *Philosophical Principles of Religion* were not chosen as Dictionary sources but which had appeared as early as 1733 and 1724. Johnson had come to London in an age when natural philosophy was a general study, the serious pursuit of virtuosos and cranks, the fad of the sophisticated. He could scarcely have had literary aspirations, much less have been a leading workman for the booksellers, without being exposed to the ideas of philosophy on every hand—in the *Transactions* and the *Abridged Transactions* [24] of the Royal Society, in the popularized systems and

440, 706–739. In estimating the number of books which Johnson handled it is necessary to take into account, however, the fact that Vols. iii and iv, for the second Harleian sale, repeat a number of titles which appear in Vol. ii, for the first sale. See, e.g., ii, 762 (No. 12540) and iii, 140 (No. 1707), Roger Bacon's *Opus Majus*, ed. Jebb, 1733. Practically all, if not all, the philosophic sources of the Dictionary are present. We have the anecdote of Johnson's felling Osborne with a folio, and it has been connected with Johnson's browsing in the Harleian books (*Works* i, 150; *Miscellanies* ii, 347), yet I believe too much could easily be made of Johnson's opportunity and of his inclination. Johnson and Oldys catalogued 36,941 titles in the four volumes of the Harleian Catalogue proper. Of the Latin, French and English annotations sprinkled through the volumes, only a very few (e.g., the short Latin notes on Roger Bacon and Francis Bacon, ii, 761–762) are attached to philosophic titles.

20. *Works* i, 414; *Life* i, 190–191.

21. Allen T. Hazen, *Samuel Johnson's Prefaces and Dedications* (New Haven, 1937), pp. 68–72; "Samuel Johnson and Dr. Robert James," *Bulletin of the Institute of the History of Medicine*, iv (June, 1936), 455–465; "Johnson's Life of Frederic Ruysch," *Bulletin of the History of Medicine*, vii (March, 1939), 324–334.

22. *Life* iii, 22.

23. *Life* i, 65; iii, 26–27, 87, 473.

24. Cf. *Considerations on the Case of Dr. Trapp's Sermons Abridged by Mr. Cave*, a piece written by Johnson in 1739, though first published in the *Gentleman's Magazine*, lvii (July, 1787), 555–557. "How few will read or purchase forty-four large volumes of the Transactions of the Royal Society, which, in abridgement, are

dictionaries of a J. T. Desaguliers, a Benjamin Martin or a John
Hill, in the monthly essays and communications which appeared
in the *Gentleman's Magazine.* In 1755, the year when the Dictionary was published, Johnson wrote for the aged inventor Zachariah
Williams *An Account of an Attempt to Ascertain the Longitude at
Sea,* and the following year for the *Literary Magazine* he reviewed
the *Philosophical Transactions,* Birch's *History of the Royal Society,* Newton's *Arguments in Proof of a Deity* addressed to Bentley, and four other books on scientific subjects. Perhaps as early
as 1754 [25] Johnson had entered upon what may by courtesy be
called his own experimental activities. At any rate he described
himself as "Sober the amateur chemist" in an *Idler* of November 18,
1758; he visited the laboratory of Beauclerk at Windsor in 1759,[26]
and during the next few years was busy with the alembic, retorts
and receivers reported by Hawkins and Boswell in the garret over
the chambers in the Inner Temple.[27] Later still we find the outdoor
laboratory at Streatham.[28] Last of all, in Johnson's library when he
died, nearly thirty years after the publication of the Dictionary,
were several hundred books on various sciences: the classic Latin
and Greek medical works of Hippocrates, Aretaeus, Galen, and
Celsus; [29] the works of medieval and Renaissance chemists and
physicists, Roger Bacon, Paracelsus, William Gilbert, Helmont,
and Boerhaave; [30] the anatomists Vesalius and Fallopius; the naturalist Conrad Gesner.[31] There were also certain medical and
physical works in English published before the date of Johnson's
Dictionary.[32] It is possible that some of the books in Johnson's

---

generally read, to the great improvement of philosophy." Johnson quotes the *Philosophical Transactions* in the Dictionary, s.v. *lough,* "Lough *Ness* never freezes." Cf.
Philosophical Transactions . . . Abridged by John Lowthorp (London, 1731), ii,
321–322. The Dictionary article and attribution *Phil.,* s.v. *dipping needle,* appear to
be derived from Harris' *Lexicon Technicum.*

25. If we accept as accurate Mrs. Piozzi's account, repeated by Murphy, of
Murphy's discovery of Johnson "making aether" (*Miscellanies* i, 306, 407–408; cf.
Life i, 356). Cf. John J. Brown, "Samuel Johnson's 'making aether,'" *MLN,* lix
(April, 1944), 286. An early date for Johnson's experiments is further suggested by
the presence in Johnson's library at his death of handbooks dated in this period, one
of which he ordered from Millar about 1752 (see note 32).

26. *Life* i, 248–250.

27. *Works* i, 392, 414; *Life* i, 436; cf. *Life* ii, 155; iii, 398; iv, 237.

28. *Miscellanies* i, 307; *Letters* i, 179, 183.

29. *Catalogue of the Library of Samuel Johnson,* Nos. 59, 237, 225, 470, 259. Cf.
No. 86, Haller methodus studii medici; No. 259, Mead praecepta medica. Cf. S. C.
Roberts, "Johnson's Books," *The London Mercury,* xvi (October, 1927), 615–624.

30. *Idem,* Nos. 317, 111, 80, 412, 398. Cf. No. 418, Beccheri physica subter-
ranea; No. 309, Conspectus Chemiae, Stahlii; No. 558, Gassendi opera.

31. *Idem,* Nos. 475, 111, 233, 337.

32. e.g., No. 125, Cheselden's anatomy (cf. Dictionary, s.v. *brain*); No. 44,
Hales' statics (cf. *Life* v, 247); No. 614, Macquer's Chymistry, 2 v. 1754 [?]; No.
615, Lewis's Chymistry, 1746; Helsham's lectures, 1739 (cf. *Letters* i, 31; ii, 303).

library at his death had survived the perambulations of his years of poverty, his removal from the house in Gough Square to the lodgings in Staple Inn and Gray's Inn in 1759 and to the Inner Temple in 1760. The scientific volumes in the last library, at Bolt-court, like the scientific reviews of 1756 and the chemical experiments, have at any rate the relation of consequential evidence to the philosophic experience of Johnson's earlier years.

Johnson's work upon the Dictionary itself, however, his reading of some two score philosophic authors and of the three or four best scientific encyclopedias of his day, and the extraction of examples from these, remains the most important chapter, if not of his medical education (where his earlier work for Dr. James's Dictionary has a superior claim) at least of his education in almost every other branch of natural philosophy. From a strictly biographical point of view, the Dictionary furnishes the most reliable evidence of what Johnson read—and of what passages had especially caught his attention. For purposes of linguistic history and stylistic analysis, in that it illustrates the meaning of select English words from eminent writers—Bacon, Boyle, Newton, and Arbuthnot, no less than from Shakespeare, Swift, and Pope—the Dictionary is by far the most important Johnsonian document relating to science. For the period up to 1755 it is scarcely to be challenged. The Dictionary is furthermore not simply a source or a guide to the sources of Johnson's words and ideas, but is in itself an important incident in the history of philosophic words and in that of the interaction between natural philosophy and the rest of life and literature.

4

THE evidence which we have surveyed may perhaps already have invited the reflection that the science of Johnson's Dictionary is that of a generation or of a century before the Dictionary appeared —both in the range of authorities chosen and in Johnson's emphasis as it falls among these authorities. There are many more quotations from Browne or from Bacon than from Chambers or from Watts. This is what one would expect from Johnson's linguistic views, his announced program of illustrating the language from the period of its maturity and splendor. But, what is of more significance for assessing the science in Johnson's Dictionary, this comparative archaism is also what one would expect from the history of eighteenth-century science, and especially of science in England. Johnson's Dictionary appears at the end of a half-century during which theoretical science had paused—in the shadow of

Newton. There had been no thinking comparable to that of Boyle and Newton, no English classics of science like the *New Experiments Physico-Mechanical Touching the Spring of the Air* or the *Opticks*. Franklin's *Experiments and Observations on Electricity made at Philadelphia in America* appears just in time to be reflected in Johnson's specially composed paragraph which we have quoted a few pages back. Johnson's Dictionary appears in the era of technology, the activities of the practical English industrial bent, the roller-spinning machine of Lewis Paul—with which Johnson himself seems to have been in some degree acquainted.[1] In the Royal Society and its *Transactions* it is the era of mathematics and, especially in the biological sciences, of Baconian observation and description, the amiable William Arderon's fish in a jar of water, the collecting of shells and flowers.[2] *Hypotheses*, Newton had said, *non fingo*. In Johnson's Dictionary, then, one finds a natural philosophy which had endured for several generations and was still currently authoritative, and which in its closeness to life and simplicity was, as we have argued in our first chapter, capable of certain easy yet interesting relations to life and literature.

A juncture of the scientific and the ordinary might be illustrated from Johnson's Dictionary by an indefinite variety of plain words which on consultation disclose not only a scientific source but an equivalent or related hard philosophic word or set of words. Thus:

stut. Divers stut: the cause is the refrigeration of the tongue, whereby it is less apt to move; and therefore naturals stut.

Bacon.

stench. Restringents to stench and incrassatives to thicken the blood.

Harvey on Consumptions.

swaggy. The beaver is called animal ventricosum, from his swaggy and prominent belly.

Brown.

twirl. The twirl on this is different from that of the others; this being an heterostropha, twirls turning from the right hand to the left.

Woodward on Fossils.

unlocks. A lixivium of quick lime unlocks the salts that are entangled in the viscid juices of some scorbutick persons.

Arbuthnot.[3]

1. John J. Brown, "Samuel Johnson and the First Roller-Spinning Machine," *MLR*, xli (January, 1946), 16–23.

2. See John Hill's *Review of the Works of the Royal Society* (London, 1751), and George R. Potter, "The Significance . . . of Hill's Review," *University of California Publications in English*, xiv (1943), esp. 165, 174–180.

3. Cf. *slit, soil* v.a. 1, *squeeze* v.n., *stroke, stump, unboiled, unburnt, unfrozen, unglue, unsalted, unscreened, unsoured, unsown, unsteeped.*

In formulating his own definitions Johnson often creates the same juxtaposition. The well-known *cough*, "a convulsion of the lungs, vellicated by some sharp serosity," and *network*, "any thing reticulated or decussated, at equal distances, with interstices between the intersections," are only extreme examples of the lexicographer's effort to find for what is concrete and familiar a more analytic and philosophic equivalent.

saw. A dentated instrument, by the attrition of which wood or metal is cut.

shot 2. The missive weapon emitted from any instrument.

sneeze. To emit wind audibly by the nose.

spar. To fight with prelusive strokes.

speaking trumpet. A stentorophonick instrument; a trumpet by which the voice may be propagated to a great distance.

stone 1. Stones are bodies insipid, hard, not ductile or malleable, nor soluble in water.[4]

"Sometimes," explains Johnson in his *Preface*, "easier words are changed into harder, as *burial* into *sepulture* or *interment, drier* into *desiccative, dryness* into *siccity* or *aridity, fit* into *paroxysm;* for the easiest word, whatever it be, can never be translated into one more easy." [5]

"I could not," he says at another point in his *Preface*, "visit caverns to learn the miner's language, nor take a voyage to perfect my skill in the dialect of navigation, nor visit the warehouses of merchants, and shops of artificers, to gain the names of wares, tools and operations, of which no mention is found in books." [6] But the scientists had been to these places before Johnson, and—in a pattern different from but complementary to that of the definitions which we have just considered—their pages supplied him with illustrations for many homely words. "The Language of Artizans, Countrymen, and Merchants, before that of Wits, or Scholars," Sprat had said in his famous description of a scientific style.[7] And Boyle had testified:

I learn'd more of . . . the Nature of Stones by conversing with two or three Masons, and Stone-cutters, than ever I did from *Pliny* or *Aristotle.*[8]

4. Cf. *periwig* ("Adscititious hair"), *peppermint, peruke* v.a., *scallop, scissors, smoke, snowball, suds* 1, *swoon, weekly, whereness, wipe, yawn.* George Colman's "Letter from Lexiphanes, containing Proposals for a *Glossary* or *Vocabulary* of the Vulgar Tongue" burlesques this feature of Johnson's Dictionary: "*See-Saw,—*Alternate Preponderation. . . . *Helter-skelter,—Quasi Hilariter & Celeriter,* signifying Motion of equal Jocundity and Velocity" (*Prose on Several Occasions* [London, 1787], ii, 94–95).

5. *Works* ix, 212.

6. *Works* ix, 220.

7. *The History of the Royal Society* (London, 1722), Part I, sec. xx, p. 113.

8. *Some Considerations Touching the Usefulnesse of Experimental Naturall Phi-*

Under *digger* in Johnson's Dictionary we find Boyle in the mines.

When we visited mines, we have been told by diggers, that even when the sky seemed clear, there would suddenly arise a steam so thick, that it would put out their candles.

Under *druggist* we find Boyle in a shop buying "common nitre"; under *drugster* he buys oil of turpentine; under *distiller* he sends for spirit of salt. Under *featherdriver,* "One who cleanses feathers by whisking them about," and under *stonecutter,* the illustration is from Derham's *Physico-Theology;* under *tallow-chandler,* from Harvey on the *Plague.*[9] The humbler, concrete, and makeshift expressions for degrees of sensory experience are very likely in Johnson's Dictionary to lead to scientific writers—the names of colors, for example, to Woodward, Boyle, or Newton. Thus, under *brownish, bluishness, greenish:* [10]

A brownish grey iron-stone, lying in this strata, is poor, but runs freely.

I could make, with crude copper, a solution without the bluishness that is wont to accompany its vulgar solutions.

Of this order the green of all vegetables seems to be, partly by reason of the intenseness of their colours, and partly because, when they wither, some of them turn to a greenish yellow.

In much the same way, under *watery, weigh, wheyish, whet,* and *wisp* we find Bacon's descriptions of experiments in his *Natural History.* Under *taffeta* and *thread* we find, with Shakespeare and others, Boyle again, talking of changeable colors.

A similar interpenetration of materials may be discerned when the word *lentil* is defined from Miller's *Gardeners Dictionary* and is illustrated by the "ground full of lentils" in II *Samuel;* when the word *thigh* is anatomically defined from Quincy's *Lexicon* and illustrated by Jacob's thigh out of joint in *Genesis;* or, to choose a more elaborately rounded treatment, when under the word

------

losophy, The Second Tome (Oxford, 1671), Essay III, p. 5. Cf. Jones, *Ancients and Moderns,* p. 277.

9. Cf. *glassgrinder, goldbeater, pewterer, pumper, varnisher, wiredrawer.*

10. Cf. *blueness, fleshcolour, foliomort, feuillemorte, green, hazel, hazelly, high-coloured, oilcolour, purplish, seagreen, silvery, sky-colour, ultramarine, umber, verdi-grise, verditure, vermilion, watercolours, white, whitish, whitishness, willowish, yellow, yellowish, yellowness.*

Cf. *sweeten, sweetish, tastable, tasteless.*

Cf. the quotations from Boyle, Browne, Locke, Glanvill, and others under such epistemological terms as *scientifically, secretist, sententiosity, signality, signation, solvible, speculate, supposal, sureness, syllogistick, unaccurateness, watchfully.*

ATTRA'CTICAL. *adj.* [from *attract*.] Having the power to draw to it.

Some ſtones are endued with an electrical or *attractical* virtue.   *Ray on the Creation.*

ATTRA'CTION. *n. ſ.* [from *attract*.]

1. The power of drawing any thing.

The drawing of amber and jet, and other electrick bodies, and the *attraction* in gold of the ſpirit of quickſilver at diſtance ; and the attraction of heat at diſtance ; and that of fire to naphtha ; and that of ſome herbs to water, though at diſtance ; and divers others, we ſhall handle. *Bacon's Nat. Hiſt.*

Loadſtones and touched needles, laid long in quickſilver, have not admitted their *attraction.*   *Brown's Vulgar Errours.*

Attraction may be performed by impulſe, or ſome other means ; I uſe that word, to ſignify any force by which bodies tend towards one another.   *Newton's Opticks.*

2. The power of alluring or enticing.

Setting the *attraction* of my good parts aſide, I have no other charms.   *Shakeſp. Merry Wives of Windſor.*

ATTRA'CTIVE: *adj.* [from *attract*.]

1. Having the power to draw any thing.

What if the ſun
Be centre to the world ; and other ſtars,
By his *attractive* virtue, and their own,
Incited, dance about him various rounds.   *Paradiſe Loſt.*

Some the round earth's coheſion to ſecure,
For that hard taſk employ magnetick power ;
Remark, ſay they, the globe, with wonder own
Its nature, like the fam'd *attractive* ſtone.   *Blackmore.*

Bodies act by the attractions of gravity, magnetiſm, and electricity ; and theſe inſtances make it not improbable but there may be more *attractive* powers than theſe.   *Newt. Opt.*

2. Inviting ; alluring ; enticing.

Happy is Hermia, whereſoe'er ſhe lies ;
For ſhe hath bleſſed and *attractive* eyes.
                          Shakeſp. Midſum. Night's Dream.

I pleas'd, and with *attractive* graces won,
The moſt averſe, thee chiefly.   *Paradiſe Loſt, b.* ii.

ATTRA'CTIVE. *n. ſ.* [from *attract*.] That which draws or incites allurement ; except that *attractive* is of a good or indifferent ſenſe, and *allurement* generally bad.

The condition of a ſervant ſtaves him off to a diſtance ; but the goſpel ſpeaks nothing but *attractives* and invitation.
                                                                         South.

ATTRA'CTIVELY. *adv.* [from *attractive*.] With the power of attracting or drawing.

ATTRA'CTIVENESS. *n. ſ.* [from *attractive*.] The quality of being attractive.

ATTRA'CTOR. *n. ſ.* [from *attract*.] The agent that attracts ; a drawer.

If the ſtraws be in oil, amber draweth them not ; oil makes the ſtraws to adhere ſo, that they cannot riſe unto the *attractor.*   *Brown's Vulgar Errours, b.* ii.

A'TTRAHENT. *n. ſ.* [*attrahens*, Lat.] That which draws.

Our eyes will inform us of the motion of the ſteel to its *attrahent.*   *Glanville's Scepſis.*

Part of a page of Johnson's Dictionary, First Edition, folio, 1755. The Baconian quotation is from *Natural History* No. 906. See frontispiece.

swan [11] a lengthy natural and historical account from Dom Augustin Calmet's *Historical, Critical, Geographical, and Etymological Dictionary of the Holy Bible* is followed by three quotations from Shakespeare:

> And I will make thee think thy swan a crow,

a comment from Peacham on the drawing of the swan, a quotation from Dryden, and a concluding description from Locke of "the idea which an Englishman signifies by the name swan."

The swan mentioned in *Romeo and Juliet,* we may remember, was Romeo's first love, who was to seem a crow beside the ladies Benvolio would show him. An approximation to metaphor in such loosely associative Dictionary treatments may be perhaps more clearly seen if one will return and set beside the quotation from Newton under *greenish* the companion quotation from Spenser's *Prothalamion:*

> With goodly greenish locks all loose, unty'd,
> As each had been a bride.

Or with the quotation from Boyle under *drugster,* that from Atterbury:

Common oil of turpentine I bought at the drugster's.

They set the clergy below their apothecaries, the physicians of the soul below the drugsters of the body.

Atterbury's antithesis between *drugsters* of the body and physicians of the soul is an antithesis between literal and metaphoric which makes a certain metaphoric advance upon literal *drugster.* The case is curiously near to that of a similar word, *varnisher,* again illustrated from Boyle:

An oil obtained of common oil may probably be of good use to surgeons and varnishers.

But in a secondary meaning—"A disguiser; an adorner"—illustrated thus from Pope:

> Modest dulness lurks in thought's disguise;
> Thou varnisher of fools, and cheat of all the wise.

The same parallel is found more compactly in Johnson's Dictionary in a number of burlesque passages which the physician Arbuthnot and his friend Pope had written in *The Memoirs of*

11. Cf. *aspalathus, calamus, mushroom, pike, petard, stork, sugar, wheat.* For Calmet's *Dictionary* see Appendix B.

Martinus Scriblerus. Under *marble* and again under *percussion* we find the following passage:

Marbles taught him percussion and the laws of motion; nutcrackers the use of the lever, and tops the centrifugal motion.

Under *abductor* we find:

He supposed the constrictors of the eye-lids must be strengthened in the supercilious; the abductors in drunkards, and contemplative men, who have the same steady and grave motion of the eye.

And under *pineal,* after an explanation of Descartes' use of the term to name the "gland which he imagined the seat of the soul":

Courtiers and spaniels exactly resemble one another in the pineal gland.[12]

In his *Plan of an English Dictionary* Johnson names seven kinds of meaning which a lexicographer ought to take into account—the natural or primitive, the consequential, the metaphorical, the poetical, the familiar, the burlesque, and that which is peculiar to any great author [13]—a gradation of meanings, in which the natural, the metaphorical, and the burlesque may be considered major divisions. In the facetious and burlesque applications of Pope and Arbuthnot just quoted the approach to simile and metaphor is clear. A boy with marbles is like a physicist studying percussion. It is noteworthy that in the *Plan* Johnson illustrates the metaphoric grade of meaning in three philosophic examples: "the *zenith* of advancement, the *meridian* of life, the *cynosure* of neighboring eyes." [14] In the *Preface,* reviewing the program which he had actually carried out in the Dictionary, he says again:

As by the cultivation of various sciences, a language is amplified, it will be more furnished with words deflected from their original sense; the geometrician will talk of a courtier's zenith, or the eccentrick virtue of a wild hero, and the physician of sanguine expectations and phlegmatick delays.[15]

The materials of science, in fact, and the history of scientific words in English for the past century and a half provided Johnson with perhaps his main opportunity for illustrating the metaphoric growth of meaning. There was, as we have seen, a strain in the empirical writers whose books Johnson read, a character of the very tradi-

12. Cf. *bobcherry, embolus, hydraulical, straddle, tennis.*
13. *Works* ix, 183–184; cf. *Preface, Works* ix, 210, 216.
14. *Works* ix, 196.
15. *Works* ix, 224.

tion, which promoted the metaphor between matter and spirit [16] and hence the metaphoric use of scientific terms. Such a metaphor was, in fact, one of the great metaphors of the English language during the period when most of the sources of the Dictionary were written. And Johnson's Dictionary was the first English dictionary to give an adequate reflection of this fact.

In the *Dictionarium* of Johnson's foremost predecessor Nathan Bailey we find, for example:

Accelerate. to hasten, to quicken, or put on.
Acrimony. Sharpness, Eagerness, Tartness.
Adhesion. a cleaving or sticking unto.

Adhesion. ⎱
Adherence.⎰ [in *Natural Philosophy*] signifies the State of two Bodies, which are joined or fastened to each other, either by the mutual Interposition of their own parts, or the Compression of external Bodies.

While Johnson was in the course of preparing his Dictionary, in 1749, another competitor, the Newtonian popularizer Benjamin Martin, inspired perhaps by Johnson's program of definitions announced in the *Plan*, published his *Lingua Britannica Reformata*, a dictionary which included in the improvements proclaimed on its title page a "diacritical" system of

Enumerating the Various Significations of Words in a Proper Order, viz. Etymological, Common, Figurative, Poetical, Humorous, Technical &c in a Manner not before attempted.

It is significant, however, that Martin, as he explains in Section V of his Preface, collected the various meanings of words from earlier dictionaries, especially from the English-French part of Boyer's *Dictionnaire Royal* and the Latin-English part of Ainsworth's *Thesaurus*. The result was that Martin's meanings were for the most part already established and defined meanings—long petrified metaphors—and where he drew from Boyer, were meanings of common and unphilosophic English or French words (*keen*, 1 sharp, that cuts well. 2 sharp, or subtle; *kickshaw*, 1 a French ragoo. 2 a slight business), or where he drew from Ainsworth, were of common Latin words (to *lament*, 1 to bewail, weep, or mourn for. 2 to take on sadly).[17] But if we turn to such philosophic words as *accelerate, acrimony, adhesion,* we find that his treatment is no

16. Cf. the passages from Bacon's *Natural History* quoted *ante* p. 14, and Johnson's Dictionary, s.v. *dilatation, exhilaration, propulsion.*

17. Starnes and Noyes, *The English Dictionary*, pp. 150–156. Martin is cited in Johnson's Dictionary under *camera obscura* and *cessionary.*

less rudimentary than that of Bailey. In the most ambitious of these three examples the resemblance is in fact verbatim.

Accelerate. to hasten or make speed.
Acrimony. sharpness, or sourness in bodies, by which they corrode or dissolve others.
Adhesion. 1 a cleaving or sticking to. 2 (in Philosophy) it is the state of two bodies, which are joined or fastened to each other, either by the mutual interposition of their own parts, or the compression of external bodies.

But Johnson, meanwhile, was relying on earlier dictionaries—Bailey, Phillips, or Ainsworth—for occasional hard words or other words which he had missed in the reading of his sources. For the graded meanings of the main vocabulary of the English language —"words fitted to live" [18]—he was relying on the authors from Shakespeare and Bacon to Swift and Arbuthnot, and on his own endurance and capacity in a great program of recognizing, distinguishing, and defining. The difference between Johnson and his forerunners Bailey and Martin is fairly illustrated in his treatment of the three words already quoted. *Accelerate* has for Johnson a primary sense with five illustrations, from Bacon, Glanvill, Newton, Arbuthnot, and Thomson:

1. To make quick, to hasten, to quicken motion; to give a continual impulse to motion, so as perpetually to increase.

Take new beer, and put in some quantity of stale beer into it; and see whether it will not accelerate the clarification, by opening the body of beer, whereby the grosser parts may fall down into lees.

Bacon's Natural History, No. 307.

> Lo! from the dread immensity of space
> Returning with accelerated course,
> The rushing comet to the sun descends.
> *Thoms[on's] Sum[mer].* 1. 1690.

It has also a secondary sense, pointedly distinguished from the physical and scientific first sense, and illustrated from Bacon and Watts.

2. It is generally applied to matter, and used chiefly in philosophical language; but it is sometimes used on other occasions.

In which council the king himself, whose continual vigilancy did suck in sometimes causeless suspicions, which few else knew, inclined to the accelerating a battle.

Bacon's Henry VII.

18. Percy W. Long, quoted in Starnes and Noyes, *op. cit.*, p. 185.

Acrimony in Johnson's Dictionary is:

1. Sharpness, corrosiveness.

There be plants that have a milk in them when they are cut; as, figs, old lettuce, sow-thistles, spurge. The cause may be an inception of putre-faction: for those milks have all an acrimony, though one would think they should be lenitive.

Bacon's Natural History.

The chymists define salt, from some of its properties, to be a body fusible in the fire, congealable again by cold into brittle glebes or crystals, sol-uble in water, so as to disappear, not malleable, and having something in it which affects the organs of taste with a sensation of acrimony or sharp-ness.

Arbuthnot.

2. Sharpness of temper, severity, bitterness of thought or language.

John the Baptist set himself, with much acrimony and indignation, to baffle this senseless arrogant conceit of theirs, which made them huff at the doctrine of repentance, as a thing below them, and not at all belong-ing to them.

South.

The definition of sense 1 of the word *adhesion* embodies a special distinction:

1. The act or state of sticking to something. *Adhesion* is generally used in the natural, and *adherence* in the metaphorical sense: as, *the adhesion of iron to the magnet;* and *adherence of a client to his patron.*

An illustration from Boyle and one from Locke refer to the adhe-sion of particles of matter; one from Prior is more widely applied:

  —Prove that all things, on occasion,
  Love union, and desire adhesion.

An example which brings us to the verge of the meaning next defined:

2. It is sometimes taken, like *adherence,* figuratively, for firmness in an opinion, or steadiness in a practice.

The same want of sincerity, the same adhesion to vice, and aversion from goodness, will be equally a reason for the rejecting any proof whatso-ever.

Atterbury.

 A further important difference between Johnson and his most philosophic predecessor Bailey, though it does not appear in the examples just quoted, is that Bailey, in accord with his technical bent, and in a way that sometimes emphasizes the more recent

chronology of word histories,[19] makes the philosophic meaning,
when he gives it, a special instance of a more general meaning,
whereas Johnson, as Latinist and etymologist, conceiving a more
remote history of words and an over-all drift of metaphor from
physical to spiritual, makes the philosophic or physical meaning the
primitive or natural, the psychological meaning secondary. Thus
ardent for Bailey is "hot as it were burning, very hot; also vehement, eager, zealous," to which he adds "Ardent *Spirits* [with
Chymists] such Spirits as being distilled from fermented Vegetables, &c. will take Fire and burn as Brandy, &c." But *ardent* for
Johnson is "1. Hot; burning; fiery," with an example from Newton's
Optics; "2. Fierce; vehement; having the appearance or quality of
desire," with an example from Dryden; "3. Passionate; affectionate:
used generally of desire," with an example from Prior. *Asperity*
for Bailey is "the Inequality or Roughness of the Surface of any
Body; whereby some Parts of it stick out beyond the Body, so as
to hinder the Hand from passing over easily and freely," with an
almost completely redundant definition added under the heading:
[with *Philosophers*]. *Asperity* for Johnson is "1. Unevenness; roughness of surface," with an example from Boyle; "2. Roughness of
sound; harshness of pronunciation," a meaning which he does not
illustrate; "3. Roughness or ruggedness of temper; moroseness;
sourness; crabbedness," with illustrations from the religious writers
Allestree and Rogers. Or *attraction* is for Bailey "drawing to, the
drawing of one Thing to another," with a special application [in
Mechanicks] and a second, Newtonian, application [in *natural
Philosophy*], "that universal Tendency that all bodies have towards
one another. . . ." For Johnson *attraction* is more simply "1. The
power of drawing anything," with examples from Bacon, Browne,
and Newton; "2. The power of alluring or enticing," with an example from Shakespeare.

It is true that Johnson was more meticulous and explicit about
metaphoric meanings under the letter A [20] than under the letters
from B to Z—but then there is no other part of the Dictionary
where Johnson is so meticulous in every way as under the letter
A.[21] The definitions and illustrations just adduced are the formal
examples of a method in the arrangement of material which ap-

---

19. 1. Cf. *ante* p. 14.

20. Cf. *abscind*, "To cut off, either in a natural or figurative sense"; *absorpt*, "Used as well, in a figurative sense, of persons, as in the primitive, of things"; *absterse*, "Less analogical than absterge"; *aggravate*, "Used only in a metaphorical sense."

21. Cf. Philip B. Gove, "Notes on Serialization and Competitive Publishing (John-son's and Bailey's Dictionaries, 1755)," *Oxford Bibliographical Proceedings and Papers*, v (1936–39), 312. As examples of Johnson's irregularity of effort see the isolated clusters of citations from Phillips' *World of Words* under *bugle, bull-finch,*

pears repeatedly, though often more elliptically, throughout the Dictionary. Most often the distinction into primary and secondary meanings, as in the examples above, is retained, though without reference to "natural," "philosophical," and "metaphorical" meanings.[22] In other cases, several examples under a single definition show metaphoric relationship,[23] or a single illustration under a single definition is a metaphor.

obumbrate. The rays of royal majesty, reverberated so strongly upon Villerio, dispelled all those clouds which did hang over and obumbrate him.

Howel.

occecation. Those places speak of obduration and occecation, so as if the blindness that is in the minds, and hardness that is in the hearts of wicked men, were from God.

Sanderson.

opiate n. They chose atheism as an opiate, to still those frightning apprehensions of hell, by inducing a dulness and lethargy of mind, rather than to make use of that native and salutary medicine, a hearty repentance.

Bentley.

percolate. The evidences of fact are percolated through a vast period of ages.

Hale's Origin of Mankind.

We may conclude our discussion of metaphor in the Dictionary by referring to some of Johnson's quotations from his own works.

bull-bee, bull-head, or under *cat's-tail, cavagion, caudlebeak, cauf;* or his use of Sir Thomas Hanmer's glossary of Shakespearean words only after the word *cosier* (Allen Walker Read, "The Contemporary Quotations in Johnson's Dictionary," *ELH,* ii (November, 1935), 250. An abbreviation of references all through the second edition of the Dictionary is due not to Johnson but, as Gove points out, to a compositor's program of saving time and type.

22. See, for example, *aridity, cholerick, circulation, coarctation, cohesion, coincident, compunction, conspicuousness, defecate* v.a., *depression, derivation, deviation, devolve, diffuse* v.a., *digestion, dissolve* v.n., *divarication, ductile, eccentrick, epidemical, exulcerate, fervent, fixation, flatulent, flexibility, fluctuation, fluent, flux, foment, frigidity, gravity, humour, imbibe, immerse, implication, impulse, inclination, incoherence, incorporate* v.a., *indissoluble, induration, inflammation, inflexible, influx, insinuate* v.a., *inspiration, instil, intermixture, irradiate, languid, lax, lubricity, lucid, luculent, luminary, mortification, obliquity, penetration, pestilential, phlegmatick, polite, preponderate, pressure, progression, pungency, purgation, purification, result, sanguine, solidity, solution, sublimation, subtile, superficial, supine* adj., *suspend, temper, titillation, trepidation, tumid, tumorous, turgid, vacant, vacuity, vapour* n., *ventilate, volatile, volubility.*

23. See *cathartical, combustible, compense, condense* v.a., *concoct, constituent, contiguous* 2, *derive* v.a. 1, *disseminate* v.a., *evaporate, ferment, fulgour, imbue, incitation, incorporate* v.n., *index, infection, ingredient, fuliginous, intension, irruption* 1, *laboratory, lassitude, lethargick, magnetism, medicament, munite, noxious* 1, *petrify, predispose, predominate, preponderance, preservative, progressive, scarify, stupify, tincture* v.a., *tinge, transfusion, unsophisticated, vapour* v.a., *vitiate.* The adjacent treatment of cognate words often clarifies the metaphoric relation.

Johnson acknowledges his own authorship of 33 quotations in the
Dictionary, and of these 11 illustrate words which fall within the
range of our inquiry: *dissipate, expiration, instillation, lacerate,
medicate, relax, stagnant, transmute, virility, vacant.*[24] The pattern
of definition and quotation for several of these words is significant.

dissipate v.a.
> 1. To scatter every way; to disperse.
> > The heat at length grows so great, that it again dissipates
> > and bears off those corpuscles which it brought.
> > > *Woodward.*
>
> > It is covered with skin and hair, to quench and dissipate
> > the force of any stroke, and retard the edge of any weapon.
> > > *Ray.*
>
> > The circling mountains eddy in,
> > From the bare wild, the dissipated storm.
> > > *Thomson.*
>
> 2. To scatter the attention.
> > This slavery to his passions produced a life irregular and
> > dissipated.
> > > *Savage's Life.*
>
> 3. To spend a fortune.
> > The wherry that contains
> > Of dissipated wealth the poor remains.
> > > *London.*

stagnant. Motionless; still; not agitated; not flowing; not running.
> What does the flood from putrefaction keep?
> Should it be stagnant in its ample seat,
> The sun would through it spread destructive heat.
> > *Blackmore.*
>
> 'Twas owing to this hurry and action of the water, that the
> sand now was cast into layers, and not to a regular settlement,
> from a water quiet and stagnant.
> > *Woodward.*
>
> Immur'd and buried in perpetual sloth,
> That gloomy slumber of the stagnant soul.
> > *Irene.*

24. The other words are *elegant, dog* v.a., *just, faint, ground* v.a., *disjoint, follow, from* 3, *idler, important, intimidate, imposture, lord, march* v.n., *obscurely,
penitence, polish* v.a., *proverbial, spare* v.a., *stormy, sultaness, unconquered.* See
W. K. Wimsatt, Jr. and Margaret H. Wimsatt, "Self-Quotations and Anonymous
Quotations in Johnson's Dictionary," *ELH*, xv (March, 1948), 60–68.

transmute v.[a.] To change from one nature or substance to another.

> Suidas thinks, that by the golden fleece was meant a golden book of parchment, which is of sheep's-skin, and therefore called golden, because it was taught therein how other metals might be transmuted.
>
> *Raleigh.*

> That metals may be transmuted one into another, I am not satisfied of the fact.
>
> *Ray on the Creation.*

> Patience, sov'reign o'er transmuted ill.
>
> *Vanity of Human Wishes.*

Here Johnson remembers his own work to complete a metaphoric pattern with an example which his original excursions into English literature had by chance failed to provide.[25]

Or there may have been times when Johnson could not remember the example from his own writing or had not yet written it.

fugacity. 1. Volatility; quality of flying away.

> Spirits and salts, which, by their fugacity, colour, smell, taste, and divers experiments that I purposely made to examine them, were like the salt and spirit of urine and soot.
>
> *Boyle.*

2. Uncertainty; instability.

suavity. 1. Sweetness to the senses.

> She desired them for rarity, pulchritude, and suavity.
>
> *Brown.*

2. Sweetness to the mind.

volatility. 1. The quality of flying away by evaporation; not fixity.

> Upon the compound body, chiefly observe the colour, fragility, or pliantness, the volatility or fixation, compared with simple bodies.
>
> *Bacon.*[26]

2. Mutability of mind; airiness; liveliness.

These patterns are incomplete as they stand in the Dictionary. We may complete them by turning to Johnson's *Rambler*, where poets lament "the fugacity of pleasure," good humour is defined as "a constant and perennial . . . suavity of disposition," and the author speculates "whether a secret has not some subtle volatility." [27]

25. Cf. *instillation, lacerate.*
26. Other examples from Bacon, Hale, Newton, Arbuthnot.
27. *Ramblers* 143, vii, 16; 72, vi, 7; 13, v, 82.

CHAPTER III

The Rambler

IN a debate in the House of Commons, March 10, 1741, over the wages of seamen:

Sir ROBERT WALPOLE . . . rose and spoke as follows:—Sir, every law which extends its influence to great numbers in various relations and circumstances, must produce some consequences that were never foreseen or intended, and is to be censured or applauded as the general advantages or inconveniences are found to preponderate. Of this kind is the law before us, a law enforced by the necessity of our affairs, and drawn up with no other intention than to secure the publick happiness, and produce that success which every man's interest must prompt him to desire.[1]

Johnson's *Debates in Parliament,* the reports which he wrote for the *Gentleman's Magazine* during the years 1740 to 1743, tend toward a rhetorical emptiness which may reflect what was actually said in Parliament (Johnson was praised for the fidelity of his dramatization) or may only corroborate what is known from external sources, that he invented upon very scant evidence. Yet the speeches of Johnson's parliamentarians are not without marks of peculiar interest for the student of his mind and style. In one vein, there are such examples of his early Swiftian, ironic manner as the retort of Pitt to the elder Horace Walpole, on the "atrocious crime of being a young man,"[2] the passages about raw commanders called "from the frolicks of a school, or forced from the bosoms of their mothers,"[3] the portrait of the fugitive Pretender.[4] In another vein, there are certain figurative uses such as the following, attributed to Lord Hervey, in a debate over the high cost of an army:

The rise of our stocks, my Lords, is such a proof of riches, as dropsical tumours are of health; it shews not the circulation, but the stagnation of our money.[5]

1. *Works* xii, 299.
2. *Works* xii, 306.
3. *Works* xii, 54, 100.
4. *Works* xii, 46.
5. *Works* xiii, 309; cf. xii, 19, 75, 114, 303; xiii, 176, 389, 447, 461–462.

Or, in the long and acrimonious debate over the duty on spirituous liquors, the following medico-moral passage, again attributed to Lord Hervey:

. . . these liquors, my Lords, liquors of which the strength is heightened by distillation, have a natural tendency to inflame the blood, to consume the vital juices, destroy the force of the vessels, contract the nerves, and weaken the sinews, . . . they not only disorder the mind for a time, but by a frequent use precipitate old age, exasperate diseases, and multiply and increase all the infirmities to which the body of man is liable. . . .[6]

An anti-administration speaker in the House of Commons employs a metaphor from a different branch of philosophy.

Our Sovereign is always sure of knowing the true sense of his people, because he may see it through the proper, the constitutional medium: but then this medium must be pure, it must transmit every object in its real form and its natural colours.[7]

And a peer defending the administration, from yet another:

. . . it is always to be remembered, my Lords, that in public transactions, as in private life, interest acts with less force as it is at greater distance, and that the immediate motive will generally prevail.[8]

Johnson wrote the *Debates in Parliament* during two or three years, 1740 to 1743,[9] when so far as is known neither his education, at Lichfield and at Oxford, nor his literary employments in London had offered any important introduction to the literature of science—unless we may count as such the life of Boerhaave written for the *Gentleman's Magazine* in 1739, and the lives of Barretier, Morin, and Sydenham written or translated during the years when the *Debates* were written. It was perhaps soon after he wrote the last of his *Debates,* the one for February 22, 1743, that he entered, with Oldys, upon the task of examining or browsing through the 37,000-odd volumes of the Harleian Library, for the *Catalogue,* which appeared in 1743 and 1744. Some 5,000 of those volumes, as we have seen, dealt with various branches of philosophy. At about the same time, apparently, he began to work with Dr. James upon the three-volume *Medicinal Dictionary* of 1743 and 1745, to which he contributed an expanded version of his earlier life of Boerhaave and lives of other eminent physicians and botanists. It is also probable that at some time during these years the idea of an English Dic-

6. *Works* xiii, 391. In the same debate, see "state empirics" and "empirical politicians," xiii, 425, 507.
7. *Works* xiii, 92.
8. *Works* xiii, 37.
9. *Life* i, 505, 509.

tionary, the scheme in which Addison, Philips, and Pope had been interested,[10] began to form in Johnson's mind, though it is impossible to say when the proposal was broached to him by Robert Dodsley or when his first readings began. The first sketch of the *Plan* was dated April 30, 1746,[11] and the contract, June 18 of the same year.[12] The clarity of philological detail in the *Plan*, its "enlarged, clear, and accurate views," suggest that by 1746 he had already made a good start in gathering materials. The Dictionary "had grown up in his mind insensibly," he told Boswell.[13] The beginning of the year 1744 would not be too early a date to observe the effects of Johnson's reading for the Harleian *Catalogue*, for Dr. James's Dictionary, or even for his own Dictionary, upon his writing. In Johnson's *Proposals for the Harleian Miscellany*, a composition of seven paragraphs issued in January, 1744, he remarked that "Volumes, considerable only for their Size, are handed down from one Age to another, when compendious Treatises, of far greater Importance, are suffered to perish." As indeed:

the compactest Bodies sink into the Water, while those, of which the Extension bears a greater Proportion to the Weight, float upon the Surface.

He observed further that the best method of preventing these losses was "to unite these scattered Pieces into Volumes." Or:

to consolidate these Atoms of Learning into Systems, to collect these disunited Rays, that their Light and their Fire may become perceptible.[14]

The same vein appears a little more than two years later in the *Plan of an English Dictionary* when Johnson argues: "it is not enough that a dictionary delights the critic, unless, at the same time, it instructs the learner." As:

it is to little purpose that an engine amuses the philosopher by the subtlety of its mechanism, if it requires so much knowledge in its application as to be of no advantage to the common workman.

And again when he promises: "Thus, my Lord, will our language be laid down, distinct in its minutest subdivisions, and resolved into its elemental principles."

10. Mary Segar, "Dictionary Making in the Early Eighteenth Century," *RES*, vii (April, 1931), 210–213; Joseph Spence, *Anecdotes*, ed. Samuel W. Singer (London, 1820), pp. 310–311.

11. *The R. B. Adam Library* (Oxford, 1929), Vol. ii, "A Short Scheme for Compiling a New Dictionary of the English Language," p. (19).

12. *Works* i, 344, n.†.

13. *Life* i, 182.

14. Hazen, *Samuel Johnson's Prefaces and Dedications* (New Haven, 1937), p. 51.

And who upon this survey can forbear to wish, that these fundamental atoms of speech might obtain the firmness and immutability of the primogenial and constituent particles of matter, that they might retain their substance while they alter their appearance, and be varied and compounded, yet not destroyed.[15]

In these analogies, though the point need not be labored, it may be that one perceives a deeper concentration of color, a greater deliberacy and initiation into the ideas of philosophy, than in the images which Johnson had earlier put into the speeches of his parliamentarians.

In the opening pages of the *Plan*—a passage which, together with its analogue in the *Preface* to the Dictionary, we have quoted in our second chapter—Johnson narrates the rejection of terms of science by the academicians of France, but observes the actual admission and naturalization of such terms in current language through metaphoric use and the assimilation of habit.[16] "It was at this time," according to one of Johnson's minor biographers—the time when he "inscribed" his *Plan* to Chesterfield—that Johnson, by his own later confession, "aimed at elegance of writing, and set for his emulation" a part of one of the philosophic sources of the Dictionary, the Preface of Chambers to his *Cyclopaedia*. Chambers' Preface, to be sure, displays no unusual efforts at imagery, and neither the Preface nor the Proposal, which according to Boswell was the model named by Johnson, is likely to be accepted as an adequate antecedent for the prose style of Johnson. Yet in dignity of diction and in a formal squareness of phrasing the Preface actually bears a resemblance, greater I believe than has been noticed, to the style of Johnson, especially to that of his lexicographical essays. The allusion to such lexicographical topics as, in the opening paragraph, the Vocabulary of the Academy *della Crusca* and the Dictionary of the French Academy, the gravity of Chambers' account of the difficulties that lay in his way—some natural and "appendant to the very design," others "superadded" by accident, the "latitudinarian practice" of language authorized by custom, the licenses which "relax the bands of grammar, and annul the difference between words"—Chambers' praise of nature for going out of her way to "annex a sort of pleasure . . . to the knowledge even of things not immediately useful," or his apology for passages from other languages "not sufficiently naturalized" and "sentiments . . . not sufficiently di-

15. *Works* ix, 168, 179–180.
16. *Works* ix, 169.

gested"—these and other details will perhaps remind one of Johnson's *Plan* of a Dictionary and *Preface*.[17]

The most important prose composition which Johnson produced between the *Plan* and the completion of the Dictionary was the *Rambler*. Except for the *Debates in Parliament*, the *Rambler* is the largest bulk of Johnson's prose united under a single title, only the *Lives of the Poets* approximating it. The *Debates in Parliament* and the *Rambler* stand massively and antithetically at either end of the ten-year period during which Johnson undertook his most formative labors for the booksellers. Johnson once said, "My other works are wine and water; but my *Rambler* is pure wine."[18] And though it may be doubted that the finest passages of Johnson's prose are to be found in the *Rambler*, yet the *Rambler* is, in the elaboration and complexity of its structures and in the weight of its vocabulary, the most concentrated, and in its length the most sustained, example of the peculiarities which distinguish the prose of Johnson's maturity. To the end of his life Johnson remained the Rambler.[19]

2

ONE of the most persistent themes in the *Rambler*, and one that seems a natural emanation of the Johnson we know, is the lament for pedantic or fanatic science, the ridicule of mathematician, mechanist, inventor, empiric, and virtuoso. The satirical efforts of Johnson's forerunners, in the *Tatler*, the *Spectator*, and the *Guardian*, had been directed against the more simply observational activities of the new science (Natural History as distinguishable from Natural Philosophy), the collection and description of insect, pebble, moss, and shell; the method for catching eels; the report on the porcupine swallowed by a snake.[1] Johnson himself, on the evidence of such *Ramblers* as 82 and 83 about the virtuoso Quisquilius (who incidentally gives us the fine Johnsonian word *papilionaceous*),[2] has been considered an opponent of Baconian nat-

17. See Thomas Tyers, A Biographical Sketch of Dr. Johnson, Miscellanies ii, 347–348; Life i, 218–219; Chambers' Cyclopaedia (London, 1741), Vol. i, pp. ii, xx, xxi, xxiii, xxv. Chambers' Latin epitaph, written by himself, in the North cloister of Westminster Abbey (Life i, 219, n. 1) is an example of lapidary style which Johnson could not have despised.

18. Life i, 210, n. 1.

19. Cf. Miscellanies i, 347, n. 3, 348.

1. Tatler, Nos. 119, 216, 221, 236; Spectator, Nos. 21, 54, 121, 242, 262; Guardian, Nos. 24, 95, 107, 112, 156. See Carson S. Duncan, The New Science and English Literature in the Classical Period (Menasha, 1913), pp. 165–170; George R. Potter, loc. cit. ante p. 38, n. 2.

2. 82, vi, 67.

uralism.[3] "To hew stone, would have been unworthy of *Palladio;* and to have rambled in search of shells and flowers, had but ill suited with the capacity of *Newton.*" [4] But the melancholy misgivings of the Rambler about science can embrace the whole range, from the activities of Quisquilius and the gifted dabbler Polyphilus [5] to those of the heavy pedant Gelasimus, who devoted himself to studying the "resistance of fluids" and was "the first who fully explained all the properties of the catenarian curve." Upon achieving eminence and mingling with society, Gelasimus was humiliated to find that "algebraic axioms" had no weight with ladies, and that they were little interested in "his theories of the tides, or his approximation to the quadrature of the circle." [6] Gelidus—a portrait, it has been said,[7] of John Colson, Lucasian Professor of Mathematics at Cambridge and translator of one of the scientific sources of Johnson's Dictionary, the *Elementa Physicae* of Musschenbroek [8]—Gelidus, upon hearing that his brother had been shipwrecked, thought immediately of "meteorological observations." He was the sort of philosopher who would neglect "the endearments of his wife, and the caresses of his children, to . . . calculate the eclipses of the moons of Jupiter." [9] The scholarly Amazon Misothea "scarcely condescended to make tea, but for the linguist, the geometrician, the astronomer, or the poet." [10] Even the most legitimate pursuit of knowledge has the sad result of isolating the savant from his fellow men. "With what satisfaction" can the politician talk to the chemist (who never thinks of anything but salt and sulphur), or the astronomer to the grammarian (who thinks an etymology more important than Jupiter and all his satellites)? [11] The naturalist has no interest in the philologer, nor the botanist in the astrologer, nor the lawyer in the physician; and war

---

3. C. H. Conley, *The Reader's Johnson* (New York, 1940), p. 12. Johnson's later experiments, recorded in a diary, included such Baconian simplicities as plucking and shaving his own hairs to see how long they would take to grow back, or laying out vine leaves to see how much weight they lost in drying (*Life* iii, 398, n. 3).

4. 83, vi, 76. Cf. 5, v, 31.

5. 19, v, 125, 129.

6. 179, vii, 228–229.

7. By Mrs. Piozzi, *Miscellanies* i, 179. Johnson came to London with a recommendation to Colson from Gilbert Walmsley (*Life* i, 101).

8. Cf. *ante* p. 30.

9. 24, v, 159.

10. 113, vi, 268. Even the realms of allegory, the Garden of Hope, the place of Justice, are peopled by an alchemist who awaits the hour of "projection," by the inventors of a diving bell, of a submarine, of an optical instrument, of a universal medicine (67, v, 425–428; 105, vi, 218–219). Cf. *Adventurer* 45, ix, 14; 99, ix, 89; 119, ix, 126–127.

11. 99, vi, 181.

and peace mean nothing to him "that is growing great and happy electrifying a bottle." [12]

Gelasimus, who is named from the fact that he tried to be merry in an awkward way, and Gelidus are orientalized as Gelaleddin in *Idler* 75. Johnson told Mrs. Piozzi that "he had his own outset into life in his eye" when he wrote the story of Gelaleddin, and likewise that Sober the chemical trifler in *Idler* 31 was "intended as his own portrait." [13] It is irrelevant to the present argument to urge this kind of evidence against Boswell's estimate of the early Johnson, a young man "distinguished for his complaisance" among the ladies of Lichfield and Ashbourne. [14] But it is difficult not to see strong grounds of sympathy between Johnson himself and the gallery of unfortunate pedants in the *Rambler*. [15] In the letter to Chesterfield, Johnson was to call himself "a retired and uncourtly scholar."

At any rate, he who touches pitch shall be defiled therewith. If Johnson's expressed view of science is on the whole melancholy, these literal uses of science at the same time attest an underlying affection, and what attests it even more is the wide assortment of scientific ideas that are assimilated in various metaphoric ways to moral and psychological themes throughout the *Rambler*. "That the country, and only the country, displays the inexhaustible varieties of nature, and supplies the philosophical mind with matter for admiration and enquiry, never was denied," says the Rambler, "but my curiosity is very little attracted by the colour of a flower, the anatomy of an insect, or the structure of a nest." And he adds, "I am generally employed upon human manners, and therefore fill up the months of rural leisure with remarks on those who live within the circle of my notice." [16] Yet the Rambler is able on other occasions to bridge this chasm between the country and the city, and to see nature in the larger sense—a nature found in books, almost certainly, rather than in rambles—[17] as an analogue of the specific human nature on which his attention is focused.

As the industry of observation has divided the most miscellaneous and confused assemblages into proper classes, and ranged the insects of the

12. 118, vi, 304.
13. *Miscellanies* i, 178.
14. *Life* i, 82; cf. i, 94–95.
15. Cf. 14, v, 93, the man of letters who spends his early years in the privacies of study and when he has gained knowledge enough to be respected, enters life either diffident and bashful or too hot and dogmatical, "disabled by his own violence, and confused by his haste to triumph." Cf. 173, vii, 197; 157, vii, 104; and 117, vi, 292.
16. 138, vi, 423.
17. "Should I wish to become a botanist, I must first turn myself into a reptile" (*Life* i, 377, n. 2).

summer, that torment us with their drones or stings, by their several tribes;

so, he observes,

the persecutors of merit, notwithstanding their numbers, may be likewise commodiously distinguished into Roarers, Whisperers, and Moderators.[18]

Again, he employs a more precise observation:

Natural historians assert, that whatever is formed for long duration arrives slowly to its maturity. Thus the firmest timber is of tardy growth, and animals generally exceed each other in longevity, in proportion to the time between their conception and their birth.

The same observation may be extended to the offspring of the mind. Hasty compositions, however they please at first by flowery luxuriance . . . can seldom endure the change of seasons.[19]

Or again:

Of the birds of passage, some follow the summer; and some the winter, because they live upon sustenance which only summer or winter can supply;

but of the annual flight of human rovers it is much harder to assign the reason, because they do not appear to find or seek any thing which is not equally afforded by the town and country.[20]

An even more important and characteristic group of *Rambler* images are those drawn from medicine and anatomy. The themes of health, illness, and medicine in fact run so deep in Johnson's mind that here it is not easy to distinguish the literal from the figurative. Medicine is connected with morals in at least two main ways that seem sometimes separate and sometimes blended, in the analogy between physical and moral ills and in the fact that physical suffering is both the partial cause of sin and the badge and punishment of our fallen state. Throughout Johnson's writing the reference to medicines and diseases is pervaded with the same sorrowful air of profound moral meaning. Nouradin the wealthy merchant of Samarcand was seized with a "slow malady" and called for help upon the "sages of physick," who "filled his apartments with alexipharmicks, restoratives, and essential virtues";

18. 144, vii, 24.
19. 169, vii, 169. Cf. 146, vii, 36, "Reputation, which is never to be lost, must be gradually obtained, as animals of longest life are observed not soon to attain their full stature and strength."
20. 135, vi, 407. See 48, v, 310; 2, v, 11; 72, v, 8; 64, v, 411; 5, v, 30; 193, vii, 308, brief similes from botany and animate nature.

he was "invigorated with cordials, or soothed with anodynes"; but a "frigorifick torpor" encroached upon his veins, he "fell in convulsions, became delirious, and expired." [21] The lugubrious tone of this oriental example is little different from that of the following passage in a reflection on the mischiefs of idleness and the salubrious effects of activity.

Whatever hope the dreams of speculation may suggest of observing the proportion between nutriment and labour, and keeping the body in a healthy state of supplies exactly equal to its waste, we know that, in effect, the vital powers unexcited by motion, grow gradually languid; that as their vigour fails, obstructions are generated; and that from obstructions proceed most of those pains which wear us away slowly with periodical tortures.[22]

In one of the favorite opening patterns of a *Rambler* essay—a philosopher's version, as it were, of epic simile—a formal statement of some melancholy physiological principle, some amplification of the theme of man's corruptibility and moribundity, serves the purpose of analogue in an elaborate social or moral application and diffuses a sad color of decay through larger structures of ideas.

It is observed by those who have written on the constitution of the human body, and the original of those diseases by which it is afflicted, that every man comes into the world morbid, that there is no temperature so exactly regulated but that some humour is fatally predominant, and that we are generally impregnated, in our first entrance upon life, with the seeds of that malady, which, in time, shall bring us to the grave.[23]

"This remark," continues the Rambler, "has been extended by others to the intellectual faculties. . . ." Again:

Anatomists have often remarked, that though our diseases are sufficiently numerous and severe, yet when we enquire into the structure of the body, the tenderness of some parts, the minuteness of others, and the immense multiplicity of animal functions that must concur to the healthful and vigorous exertion of all our powers, there appears reason to wonder rather that we are preserved so long, than that we perish so soon, and that our frame subsists for a single day, or hour, without disorder, rather than that it should be broken or obstructed by violence of accidents, or length of time.[24]

21. 120, vi, 313–315. During the pretended sickness of Captator he was "lethargick or delirious" and the "table was filled with vials and gallipots" (198, vii, 336). Cf. 167, vii, 160; 140, vi, 437.
22. 85, vi, 85–86.
23. 43, v, 276.
24. 45, v, 292.

THE

RAMBLER.

No. 156. Price 2d.

To be continued on TUESDAYS *and* SATURDAYS.

SATURDAY, *September* 14, 1751.

Nunquam aliud natura, aliud sapientia dicit.

JUV.

VERY Government, fay the Politicians, is perpetually degenerating towards Corruption, from which it muft be refcued at certain Periods by the Refufcitation of its firft Principles, and the Reeftablifhment of its original Conftitution. Every animal Body, according to the methodick Phyficians, is by the Predominance of fome exuberant Quality continually declining towards Difeafe and Death, which muft be obviated by a feafonable Reduction of the peccant Humour to the juft Equipoife which Health requires.

IN the fame Manner the Studies of Mankind, all, at leaft, which, not being fubject to rigorous Demonftration, admit the Influence of Fancy and Caprice, are perpetually

A page of the *Rambler,* First Edition, folio. See pp. 58–59.

"The same reflection," says the Rambler, "arises to my mind, upon observation of the manner in which marriage is frequently contracted. . . ." [25] In briefer and more dispersed, though no less metaphoric expressions, the motif of disease and its remedy or prevention is one of the most persistent in the *Rambler*. We hear of a *"frigid* and *narcotick infection"* which must be checked "at the first discovery by proper *counteraction";* of *preservatives, medicines,* and *physick* of the mind; of *catharticks* of vice and of the soul, *lenitives* of passion, *symptoms* of the writer's malady, the *contagion* of examples, and argumental *delirium.* We hear of "the *antidotes* with which philosophy has *medicated* the cup of life," or learn that the *antidote* against sorrow is employment, that austerity is the proper *antidote* to indulgence. In No. 207, as the Rambler approaches the end of his task, he feels the *instillations* of the *frigid opiate* of weariness.[26]

This pattern of medical imagery is one which harmonizes obviously with certain lugubrious shades of Johnson's moral temper as we know it through his biography. Another strain of imagery—that of the controlled and dispassionate sciences which deal with inorganic matter—may at first seem less redolently Johnsonian. Yet it is, I believe, equally characteristic and is more abstractly and pervasively related to details of Johnson's psychological meaning. In chemical analysis, for example—the separating of substances into elemental particles, homogeneous and heterogeneous—lay an abstract principle of likeness, difference, and isolation, which was capable of entering into a wide variety of somber or at least sober human contexts. In the *Plan* of a Dictionary, we remember, Johnson had already drawn an analogy between the "fundamental atoms of speech" and the "primogeneal and constituent particles of matter." [27] In the *Rambler*:

as the chemists tell us, that all bodies are resolvable into the same elements, and that the boundless variety of things arises from the different proportions of very few ingredients:

so a few pains and a few pleasures are all the materials of human life, and of these the proportions are partly allotted by providence and partly left to the arrangement of reason and of choice.[28]

25. Cf. especially 156, vii, 95, the triple parallel of body politic, animal body, and the principles of truth; 112, vi, 258–259, the doctrine of Celsus about laxity of medical regimen applied to mental health; and 151, vii, 63, the effects of time upon the human body compared to "the climatericks of the mind." For shorter medical similes, see 6, v, 35; 80, vi, 55; 96, vi, 107; 107, vi, 227; 150, vii, 57.
26. See *post* Appendix A, the italicized words.
27. *Works* ix, 179–180.
28. 68, v, 430. Cf. 184, vii, 254; and *Adventurer* 95, ix, 82, the extended analogy

Again:

to him whose genius is not adapted to the study which he prosecutes, all labour shall be vain and fruitless, vain as an endeavour to mingle oil and water, or in the language of chemistry, to amalgamate bodies of heterogeneous principles.[29]

Or again:

the notions of old and young are like liquors of different gravity and texture which can never unite. The spirits of youth sublimed by health, and volatilized by passion, soon leave behind them the phlegmatick sediment of weariness and deliberation.[30]

A frequent boiling, evaporation, and chemical effervescence appears as the symbol of subtlety, ephemerality, excitement, or emotion.

It may with some reason be doubted . . . whether a secret has not some subtle volatility, by which it escapes imperceptibly at the smallest vent, or some power of fermentation, by which it expands itself so as to burst the heart that will not give it way.[31]

Thus, in a short time, I had heated my imagination to such a state of activity and ebullition, that upon every occasion it fumed away in bursts of wit, and evaporations of gayety.[32]

Certain infusions, instillations, and impregnations find their way into the current of thought.

Our thoughts, like rivulets issuing from distant springs, are each impregnated in its course with various mixtures, and tinged by infusions unknown to the other, yet at last easily unite into one stream, and purify themselves by the gentle effervescence of contrary qualities.[33]

Those petty qualities, which . . . are every moment exerting their influence upon us, and make the draught of life sweet or bitter by imperceptible instillations. . . . operate unseen and unregarded, as change of air makes us sick or healthy, though we breathe it without attention, and only know the particles that impregnate it by their salutary or malignant effects.[34]

---

between human passions and the "primogeneal colours" discovered by Sir Isaac Newton.

29. 25, v, 166. (Johnson's opinion about genius and effort is of course the opposite of this statement.) Cf. 14, v, 94, polite discourse gliding over men of letters "as heterogeneous bodies, without admitting their conceptions to mix in the circulation." Cf. 111, vi, 354; 139, vi, 430; 174, vii, 200.

30. 69, v, 438.

31. 13, v, 82.

32. 101, vi, 195. Cf. Appendix A, *ebullition, effervescence, evaporation, fermentation, flatulence, volatile.*

33. 167, vii, 162; cf. 101, vi, 195; 141, vii, 2.

34. 72, vi, 7.

Certain related ideas of concentration and diffusion are realized in images drawn from broader physico-chemical and corpuscular sciences. Thus, in one striking analogy, set in a cosmological frame of reference:

It is said by modern philosophers, that not only the great globes of matter are thinly scattered through the universe, but the hardest bodies are so porous, that, if all matter were compressed to perfect solidity, it might be contained in a cube of a few feet.

In like manner, if all the employment of life were crowded into the time which it really occupied, perhaps a few weeks, days, or hours, would be sufficient for its accomplishment, so far as the mind was engaged in the performance.[35]

More often the idea of mental or moral radiation is found in images of light rays.

That merit which gives greatness and renown, diffuses its influence to a wide compass, but acts weakly on every single breast; it is placed at a distance from common spectators, and shines like one of the remote stars, of which the light reaches us, but not the heat.[36]

Certain "powerful minds" are said to "carry light and heat through the regions of knowledge." [37] And he who seeks to follow every-body's advice will

harass his mind, in vain, with the hopeless labour of uniting heterogene-ous ideas, digesting independent hints, and collecting into one point the several rays of borrowed light, emitted often in contrary directions.[38]

On the same principle:

An object, however small in itself, if placed near to the eye, will engross all the rays of light; and a transaction, however trivial, swells into im-portance when it presses immediately on our attention.[39]

The expansion of the universe by the telescope had for nearly a hundred and fifty years enlarged the poetic imagination [40] in a way which one might typify in the shield of Milton's Satan, hang-ing upon his shoulders

like the moon, whose orb
Through optic glass the Tuscan artist views.

35. 8, v, 46–47.
36. 78, v, 46.
37. 23, v, 151.
38. 23, v, 151.
39. 106, vi, 224. Cf. Appendix A, *irradiation, radiation, scintillation.*
40. Cf. Marjorie Nicolson, "The 'New Astronomy' and English Literary Imagina-tion," *Studies in Philology,* xxxii (July, 1935), 442 ff.

The Rambler, drawing less upon the cosmological aspects of astronomy than upon principles of optics involved in the lens, has brought these stimuli of the imagination closer to common human character and the social scene. The telescope itself appears in homely similes:

As a glass which magnifies objects by the approach of one end to the eye, lessens them by the application to the other,

so vices are extenuated by the inversion of that fallacy, by which virtues are augmented.[41]

Ruricola, a man placed in a "remote country" and eager for news, complains:

I am perplexed with a perpetual deception in my prospects,

like a man pointing his telescope at a remote star, which before the light reaches his eye has forsaken the place from which it was emitted.[42]

And the microscope, an instrument which had created the "infinity of worlds" within an atom into which Pascal had gazed, and the unlovely complexions of the ladies of Brobdingnag,[43] was available to the Rambler for somewhat less profound and for certainly less fantastic purposes.

It is well known, that, exposed to a microscope, the smoothest polish of the most solid bodies discovers cavities and prominences; and that the softest bloom of roseate virginity repels the eye with excrescences and discolorations.

In like manner:

we may, by diligent cultivation of the powers of dislike, raise in time an artificial fastidiousness, which shall fill the imagination with phantoms of turpitude, shew us the naked skeleton of every delight. . . .[44]

Almost the same figure occurs in a shorter metaphor: "Rules are the instruments of mental vision," and, "Some seem always to read with the microscope of criticism," while "others are furnished by criticism with a telescope." [45] Finally, Johnson's interest in the lens is illustrated in the following rich if literal passage about glass:

41. 28, v, 183.
42. 61, v, 388. "Who but Donne would have thought that a good man is a telescope?" (*Life of Cowley*, Par. 78, *Lives* i, 26).
43. Cf. Marjorie Nicolson, *The Microscope and English Imagination* (Northampton, 1935), pp. 51, 68.
44. 111, vi, 260. For Johnson's later interview with the king in which he showed his ignorance of the compound microscope, see *Life* ii, 39.
45. 176, vii. 214. "The critic Eye, that microscope of Wit" (*Dunciad*, ix, 233).

Who, when he saw the first sand or ashes, by a casual intenseness of heat melted into a metalline form, rugged with excrescences, and clouded with impurities, would have imagined, that in this shapeless lump lay concealed so many conveniencies of life, as would in time constitute a great part of the happiness of the world? Yet by some such fortuitous liquefaction was mankind taught to procure a body at once in a high degree solid and transparent, which might admit the light of the sun, and exclude the violence of the wind; which might extend the sight of the philosopher to new ranges of existence, and charm him at one time with the unbounded extent of the material creation, and at another with the endless subordination of animal life; and, what is yet of more importance, might supply the decays of nature, and succour old age with subsidiary sight. Thus was the first artificer in glass employed.[46]

The lens was the characteristic instrument of astronomy and optics. Another simpler and more ancient instrument, the balance, was characteristic of a wider range of mechanical and mathematical sciences, or was in a peculiar way the symbol of these sciences and of their application to the even wider realms of political and moral force. In the *Debates in Parliament*, especially in those over policies of the Seven Years' War, phrases like "balance of power" and "balance of Europe" had been used by Johnson with a frequency and brevity which indicate that the status of cliché was enjoyed by the image.[47] In occasional tendencies to realize the image ("the balance of Europe . . . in our hands," "folly and ambition . . . changing the weights," "law . . . inactive, like a balance loaded equally on each side"),[48] and in such embellishments as the words *equipoise, equilibrium*, or *preponderate*,[49] we may, however, see something typical of Johnson the stylist even at that date. In the *Rambler*, the image is more consistently turned inward, to psychological uses, and is manipulated with far greater emphasis and philosophic affection. In the very first *Rambler* Johnson weighs the reasons for and against his project.

Having accurately weighed the reasons for arrogance and submission, I find them so nearly equiponderant, that my impatience to try the event

46. 9, v, 56–57.
47. The *Oxford English Dictionary* quotes "balance of Europe" from 1677. Cf. *Debates in Parliament, passim*, e.g., *Works* xiii, 226, 230, 257, 266, 267, 271, 273. For an elaborate image of the balance of power, see Bolingbroke's *Letters on History*, Letter vii, *Works* (Philadelphia, 1841), ii, 258. Cf. the quotation from Swift in Johnson's Dictionary, s.v. *balance*.
48. *Works* xii, 142; xiii, 316, 142.
49. *Equipoise, Works* xii, 364, 371, 378; xiii, 54, 96, 227, 326, 361, 373, 468; *equilibrium*, xii, 221, 236; xiii, 150, 236; *preponderate*, xii, 299; xiii, 199, 291, 513. *Equiponderant* was reserved for the *Rambler*.

of my first performance will not suffer me to attend any longer the trepidations of the balance.[50]

A little later we find:

the equipoise of an empty mind, which, having no tendency to one
motion more than another but as it is compelled by some external power,
must always have recourse to foreign objects.[51]

And again:

It appears, upon a philosophical estimate, that, supposing the mind, at
any certain time, in an equipoise between the pleasures of this life, and
the hopes of futurity, present objects falling more frequently into the
scale would in time preponderate, and that our regard for an invisible
state would grow every moment weaker.[52]

The image is one of the most frequently repeated throughout the
Rambler.[53]

In the second of the two examples just produced, it may be noted
that the "equipoise of an empty mind" gives way to a less explicit
image of "motion"; the mind is "compelled by some external
power." In general, the balance is but one of the Rambler's more
concrete symbols of a human mind conceived as a recipient and
recorder of conflicting external impulses, pushes and retardations,
motives, temptations, fears and desires. It can be said most clearly
in the Rambler's own words:

The advance of the human mind towards any object of laudable pursuit,
may be compared to the progress of a body driven by a blow. It moves
for a time with great velocity and vigour, but the force of the first impulse is perpetually decreasing, and though it should encounter no
obstacle capable of quelling it by a sudden stop, the resistance of the
medium through which it passes, and the latent inequalities of the
smoothest surface, will in a short time by continued retardation wholly
overpower it.[54]

To act is far easier than to suffer; yet we every day see the progress of
life retarded by the *vis inertiae,* the mere repugnance to motion, and find
multitudes repining at the want of that which nothing but idleness
hinders them from enjoying.[55]

Or, the figure may be not of push, resistance, or inertia, but of the
more mysterious gravitational power of attraction.

50. 1, v, 5.
51. 5, v, 30.
52. 7, v, 44.
53. Cf. Appendix A, s.v. *balance, oscillation, preponderation.*
54. 127, vi, 358.
55. 134, vi, 402.

To loose the attention equally to the advantages and inconveniences of every employment is not without danger; new motives are every moment operating on every side; and mechanicks have long ago discovered, that contrariety of equal attractions is equivalent to rest.[56]

All attraction is increased by the approach of the attracting body. We never find ourself so desirous to finish, as in the latter part of our work, or so impatient of delay, as when we know that delay cannot be long.[57]

There are many natures which can never approach within a certain distance, and which, when any irregular motive impels them towards contact, seem to start back from each other by some invincible repulsion. There are others which immediately cohere whenever they come into the reach of mutual attraction, and with very little formality of preparation mingle intimately as soon as they meet.[58]

Or the source of imagery may be the more anciently known magnet.

Wealth is the general center of inclination, the point to which all minds preserve an invariable tendency, and from which they afterwards diverge in numberless directions.[59]

Mr. Frolick the Londoner came into the country with a great reputation and a boastful style of talking, but Ruricola on failing to find in him "any uncommon enlargement" of faculties, concluded ironically that he was perhaps "benumbed by rural stupidity, as the magnetic needle loses its animation in the polar climes." [60] Again, persons of average charm are advised "to enter into the crowd, and try whom chance will offer to their notice, till they fix on some temper congenial to their own,"

as the magnet rolled in the dust collects fragments of its kindred metal from a thousand particles of other substances.[61]

The facetious subject of *Rambler* 199 is an artificial magnet for the detection of infidelity in wives.

It is characteristic of all the types of philosophical image in the *Rambler* that they occur not only in explicit and firmly drawn similes and analogies but more dispersedly and pervasively, in at-

56. 153, vii, 76.
57. 207, vii, 389.
58. Cf. *Adventurer* 45, ix, 17, the elaborate analogy between socio-individual contrariety of impulse and the celestial balance of centrifugal and centripetal forces; Johnson's Adversaria for *Adventurer* 45 quoted by Boswell in *Life* i, 207; and *Adventurer* 34, ix, 7, the analogy between the acceleration of gravity and that of falling into poverty.
59. 131, vi, 383.
60. 61, v, 393.
61. 160, vii, 121.

tenuated and shorter metaphors or in phrases which have only a coloring of philosophy.[62] Johnson's assimilation of scientific images to the prevailing abstraction of his style is so thorough, or to put it an opposite way, his realization of the imagery latent in even the most abstract philosophic word is so keen, that a very accurate degree of metaphoric interaction between abstract and ordinarily almost imageless words often occurs in his writing. A cursory twentieth-century reader may scarcely feel the remotely suggested image of astral light in the following:

The honour paid to their memory is commonly proportionate to the reputation which they enjoyed in their lives, though still growing fainter, as it is at a greater distance from the first emission.[63]

Or the allusion to corpuscularian mechanical action in the following:

The first transports of new felicity have subsided, and his thoughts are only kept in motion by a slow succession of soft impulses. Good-humour is a state between gaiety and unconcern; the act or emanation of a mind, at leisure to regard the gratification of another.[64]

I have in this view of life considered men as actuated only by natural desires, and yielding to their own inclinations, without regard to superior principles by which the force of external agents may be counteracted.[65]

Or in the following the allusion to the same kind of action under the aspect of a Lockean epistemology of physically impressed ideas.

The works and operations of nature are too great in their extent, or too much diffused in their relations . . . to be reduced to any determinate idea. It is impossible to impress upon our minds an adequate and just representation of an object.[66]

No man can at pleasure obtund or invigorate his senses, prolong the agency of any impulse, or continue the presence of any image traced upon the eye, or any sound infused into the ear.[67]

The epistemological aspect of philosophic diction and certain abstract extensions of the philosophic throughout Johnson's prose are subjects which will be considered at more length in a later part of this study.[68]

---

62. See, for example, *post* Appendix A, *corrosion, ductility, fluctuation, frigorifick, resiliency.*
63. 146, vii, 38.
64. 72, vi, 7–8.
65. 151, vii, 68.
66. 125, vi, 344.
67. 78, vi, 42. Cf. 138, vi, 425, quoted *post* p. 97.
68. *Post* pp. 94–113; Secs. 1 and 2 of Chap. V.

3

It was a way of writing which the Rambler had established as his own—a momentum which carried through the years when he had folded his legs and enjoyed "the bread and tea of life," to the end. Neither the Rambler nor his parodists would forget it. In the Lucianic dialogue of the Scotch purser, "horrible" Campbell, written about 1764, the English Lexiphanes is made to speak of "agglomerated asperities," "a subaqueous voyage," or "an ambulatory circumrotation in the Park," or in one of the many passages which Campbell quotes almost verbatim from the *Rambler*, of "imagination . . . heated to such a state of activity and ebullition, that on every occasion it fumes away in evaporations of gaiety." [1] Almost twenty years later, a second Scotchman, Callander, in his *Deformities of Dr. Samuel Johnson*, supplying his own italics, observes that "an *emanation* of royal munificence has, of late, relaxed the Doctor's *frigorifick* virtue," and, objecting to an opinion in Johnson's *Life of Dryden:*

Some *narcotic* seems to have *refrigerated* the red liquor which circulates in the Doctor's veins, and to have *hebetated* and *obtunded* his powers of *excogitation.* . . . Perhaps his admirers may answer, that my remark is but the *ramification* of envy, the *intumescence* of ill nature, the *exacerbation* of "gloomy malignity." [2]

Without attempting a detailed account of Johnson's practice through the whole of his career, one may observe in passing that during the fourth and fifth years after the Dictionary—when the Rambler had become the Idler—some of his most noteworthy efforts are a satirical portrait of himself as "Sober" with his chemical furnace, distillations, and essences,[3] a ridicule of experimental dabblers which culminates in a savage account of vivisection,[4] an extended eulogy of English mechanical philosophy and the Royal Society,[5] certain astronomical and teleological reflections in an

1. Archibald Campbell, *Lexiphanes* (2d ed. London, 1767), pp. 6, 25, 13, 11. See the phrases quoted from *Lexiphanes* in the *OED*, s.v. *abscission, agglomerated* 2, *circumrotation* 3, *pneumatology* 3, *tortuosity* 2.

2. J. Thomson Callander, *Deformities of Dr. Samuel Johnson* (2d ed. London, 1782), pp. 14, 20.

3. 31, viii, 124. Cf. 64, viii, 257–258, the sketch of Ranger among the virtuosos; 55, viii, 220–224, the complaint of the author who undertook to write the natural history of his county. The twenty-nine essays which Johnson contributed to the *Adventurer* (L. F. Powell, "Johnson's Part in the *Adventurer*," *RES*, iii [October, 1927], 420–429) are examples of Johnson's creative prose toward the end of the Dictionary work (March 3, 1753 to March 2, 1754) which I have found it convenient to cite at various other points. See *post* Index, Johnson, Samuel, *Adventurer*.

4. 17, viii, 65–66.

5. 91, viii, 364–368. Cf. 88, viii, 354–356, the criticism of vain expectations raised by the program of the same Society.

essay on the Flight of Time,[6] and an invocation of the shades of
Locke and Malebranche in an essay on the nature of thought.[7]
And while the *Idler* on the whole is sparing of philosophic metaphor, one of the best-known essays is wholly devoted to a light-
hearted exaggeration of philosophic analogy. Punch, says a "profound investigator," a "philosopher" of the Idler's acquaintance,

is a liquor compounded of spirit and acid juices, sugar and water. The
spirit, volatile and fiery, is the proper emblem of vivacity and wit; the
acidity of the lemon will very aptly figure pungency and raillery, and
acrimony of censure.[8]

During the months in which Johnson wrote the last *Idlers,* he wrote
also the chapters of *Rasselas* on the art of flying and the history of a
learned astronomer,[9] allegorical versions of the essays on scientific
vanity in *Rambler* and *Idler.* One finds in *Rasselas* a pervasive,
quietly accurate, and elegant use of philosophic images, "the
swifter migration of wings," and the "pendent spectator," [10] the
"emersion of a satellite of Jupiter," [11]

manners pliant and minds susceptible of new impressions, which might
wear away their dissimilitudes by long cohabitation, as soft bodies by
continual attrition conform their surfaces to each other.[12]

In later works the full-blown simile is less frequent, but the short
metaphors, the turns of philosophic phrase, remain among the most
characteristic traits of Johnson's writing—in the *Preface to Shakespeare* a "mind . . . refrigerated by interruption"; [13] in the political tracts a "fever of epidemick patriotism," [14] a crowd "condensed
and heated" which "begins to ferment with the leaven of sedi-
tion," [15] a "nation combustible," "a meteor formed by the vapours
of putrefying democracy"; [16] in the *Western Islands* an "epidemical

6. 43, viii, 171–174.
7. 24, viii, 93.
8. 34, viii, 135. Cf. 1, viii, 4, "The diligence of an *Idler* is rapid and impetuous, as
ponderous bodies forced into velocity move with violence proportionate to their
weight."
9. Chaps. vi, xli–xliv. Callander (*op. cit.,* p. 20) points out that "The Newtonian
system had reached the happy valley; for its inhabitants talk of the earth's *attraction*
and the body's *gravity.*"
10. *Works* xi, 16, 18 (chap. vi).
11. *Works* xi, 116 (chap. xlii).
12. *Works* xi, 83 (chap. xxx). Cf. xi, 50 (chap. xvi), "volatility of fancy"; xi, 37
(chap. xii), "soft reciprocation of protection and reverence." Cf. chap. xlix, Imlac's
discourse on the nature of the soul.
13. *Works* ix, 300.
14. *The False Alarm, Works* x, 24.
15. *Idem,* x, 26. Cf. pp. 3, 12, 15, 28, 32, 33.
16. *Falkland's Islands, Works* x, 68. Cf. pp. 42, 54, 59, 60–61, 63.

enthusiasm" for religious change, the "magnetism" of Lord Mon-
boddo's conversation; [17] in the *Lives of the Poets*, certainly the least
philosophic of all Johnson's writing, "ebullitions of imagination," [18]
the "emission . . . of the Proposals for the *Iliad*," the "coalition of
congenial notions." [19]

In 1763 Johnson wrote to his new friend Boswell:

The dissipation of thought, of which you complain, is nothing more than
the vacillation of a mind suspended between different motives, and
changing its direction as any motive gains or loses strength.[20]

In 1766 he wrote to Boswell:

Do not accustom yourself to enchain your volatility by vows.[21]

And in June of 1784, in the last conversation between Johnson and
Boswell:

Sir, it is in the intellectual world as in the physical world; we are told by
natural philosophers that a body is at rest in the place that is fit for it;
they who are content to live in the country, are *fit* for the country.[22]

It would be inept in such a context to speak of anything like a
Ruling Passion. Yet Johnson's bent for philosophic imagery and
diction was among the most permanent attachments of his mind—
like the habit of bullying and bouncing which he himself observed
to prevail even during his attack of paralysis and aphasia of 1783.
It stuck to his "last sand."

17. *Works* x, 318, 326. Cf. the philosophical discussion of Lough Ness, pp. 348–
349.
18. *Life of Young, Lives* iii, 397.
19. *Life of Pope*, Pars. 106, 243; *Lives* iii, 129, 190.
20. *Life* i, 471.
21. *Life* ii, 21.
22. *Life* iv, 338.

CHAPTER IV

The Relation Between Rambler *and* Dictionary

JOHNSON'S 203 *Ramblers,* published from March 20, 1750 to March 14, 1752, were written, we must suppose, in the closest conjunction with the labor upon his Dictionary, while Johnson was completing his collection of examples and was beginning the actual composition of copy under the first letters of the alphabet. His ironic attitude toward the task of dictionary-making is expressed in *Rambler* 106:

Others spend their lives in remarks on language, or explanations of antiquuities, and only afford materials for lexicographers and commentators, who are themselves overwhelmed by subsequent collectors.[1]

His weariness in *Rambler* 141:

The task of every other slave [except the wit] has an end. The rower in time reaches the port; the lexicographer at last finds the conclusion of his alphabet.[2]

And the conscience of the lexicographer appears in the apologia of the last *Rambler:*

I have labored to refine our language to grammatical purity, and to clear it from colloquial barbarisms, licentious idioms, and irregular combinations. Something, perhaps, I have added to the elegance of its construction, and something to the harmony of its cadence. When common words were less pleasing to the ear, or less distinct in their signification, I have familiarized the terms of philosophy, by applying them to popular ideas, but have rarely admitted any word not authorized by former writers; for I believe that whoever knows the *English* tongue in its present extent, will be able to express his thoughts without further help from other nations.[3]

We may picture Johnson, I believe, as writing his bi-weekly *Ramblers* during hours diverted from the labor of reading the

1. 106, vi, 226. Cf. *Adventurer* 39, *Chalmers* xxiii, 252, "Men who daily spend fifteen or sixteen hours in study . . . employed their minds . . . in the low drudgery of collating copies, comparing authorities, digesting dictionaries. . . ." Cf. *ante* p. 23.
2. 141, vii, 5.
3. 208, vii, 395. Cf. *Idler* 91, viii, 366.

sources of the Dictionary or of composing the copy which about November 1, 1751, he promised to supply to Strahan at the rate of a sheet a day.[4] Or when daytime hours had been devoted to the Dictionary, we may suppose that he spent the night in forced marches to meet the printing deadline of the *Rambler*—"the stated calls of the press twice a week." The copy, we are told, was seldom sent to the press till late in the night before the day of publication.[5] The printer's boy would often come to the house where Johnson was entertained and "wait while he wrote off a paper for the press in a room full of company." [6] In the small duodecimo notebook which later came into the possession of Boswell, Johnson seems to have collected the materials for 30 *Ramblers* before he began. The rest had to come, as Boswell puts it, "from the stores of his mind," his "great fund of miscellaneous knowledge." [5] It would be strange if this miscellaneous knowledge, or at least some of the most immediately available and active parts of it, were not at this period the by-product of Dictionary labors. In the first volume of the Dictionary Johnson used about 480 quotations from Clarendon's *History of the Rebellion,* more than 200 from Ralegh's *History of the World,* and about 240 from Knolles' *History of the Turks.*[7] "The phrases of policy, war, and navigation," he said in the *Preface,* might be taken from Ralegh alone.[8] In *Rambler* 122 we have Johnson's dissertation upon the English historical genius, with his criticism of the styles of Ralegh, Clarendon, and Knolles. Another Dictionary author who seems to have made a marked impression upon Johnson was Watts. In Watts' *Improvement of the Mind,* a book which Johnson quoted more than 150 times in the first volume of the Dictionary, and for which he repeatedly expressed his esteem in later years,[9] he read of the "Man who dwells all his Days among Books . . . a mere Scholar . . . a contemptible sort of Character in the World."

4. *Letters* i, 25, 27. On April 3, 1753, Johnson wrote in his diary the entry quoted by Boswell: "I began the second vol. of my Dictionary, room being left in the first for Preface, Grammar, and History, none of them yet begun" (*Life* i, 255). The completed Dictionary was published on April 15, 1755.

5. *Life* i, 203–204; cf. iii, 42.

6. *Miscellanies* ii, 414.

7. Lewis M. Freed, "The Sources of Johnson's Dictionary," Cornell doctoral dissertation (1939), pp. 45 ff. Cf. *ante* p. 34, n. 17. The importance of the Dictionary to Johnson's acquaintance with Knolles is of course qualified by his earlier use of Knolles in writing *Irene.*

Idler 69, on English translations, is another essay which seems to rely heavily on Dictionary reading.

8. *Works* ix, 215.

9. *Life* iv, 311; *Works* xi, 198, *Apophthegms; Lives* iii, 308–309, *Life of Watts.*

A Hermit who has been shut up in his Cell in a College, has contracted a sort of Mould and Rust upon his Soul, and all his Airs of Behaviour have a certain aukwardness in them; but these aukward Airs are worn away by degrees in Company: The Rust and the Mould are filed and brusht off by polite Conversation.[10]

This was at least a very congenial view to the creator of the lugubrious gallery of *Rambler* pedants and scholars noticed in our last chapter. In a different though related application, in a *Rambler* on sorrow, the image of rust upon the soul was closely echoed.

Sorrow is a kind of rust of the soul, which every new idea contributes in its passage to scour away.[11]

A large and miscellaneous family of Latin, Greek, and Italian label portraits in Watts' *Improvement*—Arithmo, Vanillus, Scitorio, Polycles, Scintillo, Sobrino, Audens, Furio, Jocander, to name but a few [12]—were among the most recent in the classic genealogy of the *Rambler's* own inventions: his Athanatus, Bucolus, Captator, Nugaculus, Papilius, Philomedes, Prospero, Quisquilius, and Vagario.[13] From various other authors Johnson as Rambler happily recalled, here and there, the very quotations which he used in the Dictionary. What illustrates a word in the Dictionary embellishes an idea in the essays. We may note a Dictionary quotation from Dryden and one from Milton juxtaposed in a paragraph of No. 86, or in other *Ramblers* a quotation from King Henry's rebuke of Prince Hal, another from Hal's battlefield tribute to Falstaff, an example of Spenser's "studied barbarity" in the eclogue, a speech from Addison's *Cato*, and a passage from Hooker about destitution, all of which appear in the Dictionary under words where a suspicious person might search for them.[14] An italicized phrase, *cathartics of the soul*, in *Rambler* 87 will be found, if we consult

10. *Improvement of the Mind* (London, 1741), p. 44.
11. 47, vi, 307. Cf. *Spectator*, No. 316.
12. *Improvement*, pp. 9–23.
13. *Ramblers* 54, 138, 197, 103, 141, 72, 200, 82, 59, 27. The *Rambler* contains more than a hundred such names. They probably owe something also to the sparingly drawn label portraits of William Law's *Serious Call*, 1728, an occasional Dictionary source (e.g., under *mortification* and *town*) and the book to which Johnson owed his religious conversion (*Life* i, 68). Cf. *Life* iv, 4, n. 3.
14. Cf. 86, vi, 93 and *Dictionary*, s.v. *fate* 3 and *joyless;* 145, vii, 31 and *hackney* (the same misquotation); 72, vi, 10 and *spare* v.a. 3; 37, v, 241 and *missay* 2; 9, v, 55 and *aghast;* 28, v, 187 and *destitution.*
For the appearance in the *Rambler* of such more occasional and archaic Dictionary sources as Caxton, the ballad of the *Children in the Wood*, Sir Thomas More, and Aleyn's poetical *History of Henry VII*, see Walter B. C. Watkins, *Johnson and English Poetry before 1660* (Princeton, 1936), pp. 44, 48, 50, 76. See Caxton quoted in the Dictionary, s.v. *puissance.*

cathartick in the Dictionary, to be a quotation of a quotation from Plato in Addison's *Spectator*, No. 507.

2

ONE might not unreasonably expect certain philosophic elements in the *Rambler* to show the same relation to the Dictionary. Having in mind Johnson's statement that he had never read Bacon until he was compiling the Dictionary,[1] one might point to a *Rambler* quotation from Bacon's *Ornamenta Rationalia* [2] paralleled in the Dictionary under *behaviour,* to a quotation from the Epistle Dedicatory of Bacon's *Essays* [3] paralleled in the Dictionary under *last,* to paraphrases from the *Essay of Studies* [4] and *Essay of Youth,*[5] and allusions to the *History of Winds* [6] and the *New Atlantis.*[7] Boyle too is an author known to Johnson perhaps entirely through the Dictionary. And the knowledge is reflected in the *Rambler* by an allusion to a remark of Boyle's about reciprocal communication of mechanical knowledge [8] and by another to his *Essay on the Spring of the Air.*[9] Or, to turn to some other conspicuously scientific ideas appearing in the *Rambler:* an allusion to "tearing down bulwarks with a silk-worm's thread" in *Rambler* 117 may very well derive from picture and text about the power of pulleys in Bishop Wilkins' *Mathematical Magic.*

By the help of these arts it is possible (as I shall demonstrate) for any man to lift up the greatest Oak by the roots with a straw, to pull it up with a hair, or to blow it up with his breath.[10]

The facetiously philosophic *Rambler* 199, upon an artificial magnet for detecting infidelity in wives, finds a likely inspiration in the second of Browne's chapters on the magnet in the *Pseudodoxia:* "Dioscorides puts a shrewd quality upon it . . . who therewith discovers the incontinency of a wife, by placing the Loadstone under her pillow." [11] The allusion in *Rambler* 169 to the gestation and longevity of animals might easily be accounted for by a pas-

1. *Life* iii, 194; cf. iii, 220–221.
2. 38, v, 246. Cf. *Ornamenta Rationalia,* No. 63, *Works* (London, 1740), iii, 297.
3. 106, vi, 226.
4. 137, vi, 420.
5. 140, vi, 436.
6. 14, v, 92.
7. 117, vi, 298. Cf. 7, v, 366; *Adventurer* 85, ix, 61; 131, ix, 142.
8. 201, vii, 352. "It is observed in some of the writings of Boyle. . . ." (Folio text.)
9. 106, vi, 225. Cf. *Adventurer* 99, ix, 88.
10. *Mathematical Magic* (London, 1691), p. 96. I owe this example to Mr. John J. Brown's Yale doctoral dissertation, "Samuel Johnson and Eighteenth-Century Science" (1943), p. 166.
11. Bk. II, chap. iii, near the end. The *Rambler* reference to the discovery of the

sage about the gestation of animals in Bacon's *Natural History:*
"Those that are longer in coming to their maturity or growth, are
longer in the womb." [12] Or by another in Browne's *Pseudodoxia:*

Of Animals viviparous such as live long, go long with young, and attain
but slowly to their Maturity and stature . . . so the Elephant that liveth
an hundred, beareth its young above a year, and arriveth unto perfection
at twenty.[13]

In *Rambler* 135 the "birds of passage" of which "some follow the
summer, and some the winter, because they live upon sustenance
which only summer or winter can supply" might have been suggested by a passage in Ray's *Wisdom of God in the Creation,*[14] or
even more likely by a chapter "Of the Migration of Birds" in Derham's *Physico-Theology:*

It is . . . very odd . . . that some certain place is not to be found in all
the terraqueous globe affording them convenient food and habitation
all the year, either in the colder climes, for such as delight in the colder
regions, or the hotter for such *birds of passage* as fly to us in summer.[15]

Rambler 41 argues the limited capacity of brutes from their failure
to show progress in arts: "The sparrow that was hatched last spring
makes her nest the ensuing season, of the same materials, and with
the same art, as in any following year." [16] In Ray's *Wisdom of God,*
on the page before that about the migration of birds, Johnson had
read:

Birds of the same kind make their Nests of the same Materials, laid in the
same Order, and exactly of the same Figure . . . neither were any of
the same kind ever observ'd to make a different Nest, either for Matter
or Fashion.[17]

---

longitude (67, v, 426) must be taken in connection with a current agitation which
culminated for Johnson in 1755 when he wrote for the inventor Zachariah Williams
An Account of an Attempt to Ascertain the Longitude at Sea. Cf. R. W. Chapman,
"Johnson and the Longitude," *RES*, i (October, 1925), 458–460.
    12. No. 759.
    13. Bk. III, chap. ix; cf. Bk. VI, chap. v, "The Elephant (As Aristotle affirmeth)
carrieth the young two yeares. . . ." Bk. IV, chap. x of Derham's *Physico-Theology*
is devoted to the duration of life in animals.
    14. *Wisdom of God in the Creation* (London, 1709), p. 149.
    15. *Physico-Theology* (London, 1714), p. 358, Bk. VII, chap. iii. Cf. Eleazar
Albin, *A Natural History of Birds* (London, 1738), i, 8, "The Cuckow."
    16. 41, v, 264. Johnson returned to the same argument in a conversation with
Boswell and Goldsmith, 7 May, 1773 (*Life* ii, 249).
    17. *Wisdom of God,* p. 148. Cf. *The Ornithology of Francis Willughby,* trans.
John Ray (London, 1678), p. 16. Cf. *Wisdom of God,* p. 150, quail lighting on ships
at sea, with *Life* ii, 55, 248, on the migration of woodcocks. Cf. John J. Brown, *op.
cit.,* p. 183.

Yet Johnson deals, after all, in the commonplaces of science: the *catenarian curve,*[18] the *quadrature* of the circle,[19] the resistance of fluids,[20] the satellites which the telescope of Galilei had discovered moving about the planet Jupiter—celebrated satellites which of course were to be found in half a dozen of the Dictionary sources,[21] but which, it is no less relevant to note, had been a few months earlier the subject of a book published at London by the astronomer James Hodgson: *The Theory of Jupiter's Satellites with the Construction and Use of the Tables for Computing Their Eclipses.*[22] Johnson deals in traditions about animal life which went back to antiquity and had been repeated by Renaissance naturalists and by Sir Thomas Browne, in teleological observations such as were among the most frequent topics of scientific and popular discourse during the seventeenth and eighteenth centuries. The idea that the longevity of animals is proportionate to their periods of gestation appears in Pliny's *Natural History.* The striking example of the elephant is cited by both Pliny and Browne from Aristotle.[23] Parallels between the *Rambler* and the Dictionary sources such as we have just seen might doubtless be multiplied, but it must be said at this point that the effect of Johnson's Dictionary reading upon his prose is scarcely to be estimated by the exclusiveness of such parallels. What is even more important, this effect could scarcely be seen in such parallels, no matter how exclusive. Not the generality, or commonplaceness, of the analogues in question, but, in a rather opposite way, their very concreteness in contrast to the generality or abstraction of Johnson's style, precludes a stylistic parallel. "Does," says Bacon, "go about nine months; mares eleven months; bitches nine weeks; elephants are said to go two years . . . those that are longer in coming to their maturity or growth, are longer in the womb." The point is worth

18. Illustrated in the Dictionary from Harris' *Lexicon Technicum* and Cheyne's *Philosophical Principles* (London, 1734), Part I, p. 330. For the *Rambler* occurrences, cf. *ante* p. 55.

19. Cf. Cheyne, *Philosophical Principles,* Part II, pp. 15, 177.

20. Cf. *idem,* Part I, p. 13.

21. For the eclipses mentioned by Johnson, see *idem,* Part I, pp. 68, 185, 238; Derham, *Physico-Theology,* Bk. I, chap. iv, n. 5; *Astro-Theology* (London, 1715), p. 193, Bk. VII, chap. vi, "Of Jupiter's Moons, Days and Seasons." For the satellites more casually mentioned and uneclipsed, see Bentley, *Works* (London, 1838), iii, 23, 69, 178, 180; Locke, *Elements of Natural Philosophy,* chap. iii, *Works* (London, 1768), iv, 538; Pope, *Essay on Man,* i, 41–42; Watts, *Improvement of the Mind,* p. 230, a passage quoted in the Dictionary, s.v. *periodical.*

22. Cf. *Gentleman's Magazine,* xx (December, 1750), 575.

23. Pliny, *Natural History,* VIII, x; X, lxxxiii. Cf. Conrad Gesner, *Historiae Animalium Liber I de Quadrupedibus Viviparis* (Zurich, 1651), pp. 417, 418. Cf. Nos. 233 and 337 in the *Catalogue of the Library of Samuel Johnson.*

emphasizing in one further and richer example. The long passage of *Rambler* 9 in praise of glass, quoted in our last chapter, is in the vein of Antonio Neri's introductory remarks to his classic *Art of Glass*, a Latin version of which appears in Johnson's library at his death.[24] On the other hand, if in the age of Newton and post-Galilean astronomy the passage need be assigned any parallels, it finds them also in the elaborate article on glass, derived partly from Neri, in Chambers' *Cyclopaedia*, in shorter passages about the composition of glass in Bacon's *Natural History* and Boyle's *Sceptical Chymist* and *Producibleness of Chymical Principles*,[25] and most clearly in a catalogue of the uses of glass in Ray's *Wisdom of God*. "Glass," says Ray,

a Material whose Uses are so many, that it is not easie to enumerate them, it serving us to make Windows for our Houses . . . for Looking-glasses, Spectacles, Microscopes and Telescopes, whereby our Sight is not only reliev'd, but wonderfully assisted to make rare Discoveries.[26]

At this point it may be illuminating to requote a part of Johnson's passage. Johnson speaks of "sand or ashes, by a casual intenseness of heat melted into a metalline form," of a "fortuitous liquefaction" by which mankind was taught to procure

a body at once in a high degree solid and transparent, which might admit the light of the sun, and exclude the violence of the wind; which might extend the sight of the philosopher to new ranges of existence, and charm him at one time with the unbounded extent of the material creation, and at another with the endless subordination of animal life; and, what is yet of more importance, might supply the decays of nature, and succour old age with subsidiary sight.

Whether or not Ray's factual allusion to glass, windows, spectacles, microscopes, and telescopes was anywhere in Johnson's mind when he wrote his *Rambler* is a biographical problem which will probably never be solved. In Johnson's heightened and thoughtful way of describing these same things, though without naming one of them [27]—in his style of periphrase, if one wishes a rhetorical or even derogatory name for it—may be seen certain limits which must be set to the enterprise of finding "sources" for the scientific

24. *Catalogue of the Library of Samuel Johnson*, No. 624, Neri de arte Vitraria, Amst. 1668. Cf. the English translation by Christopher Merret, *The Art of Glass* (London, 1662), "To the Curious Reader," pp. A–A2ᵛ.

25. Bacon, *Natural History*, Nos. 770, 779; Boyle, *Works* (London, 1772), i, 490, 656.

26. *Wisdom of God*, p. 80.

27. The word *glass* appears toward the end of Johnson's paragraph, the answer, as it were, to a poetic riddle,

allusions in the *Rambler*. Johnson's passage on glass may owe something to one or more of the sources just named, especially to Ray and Chambers, and in view of his current preoccupation with Dictionary sources, it probably does. Yet Johnson recollects and re-creates these sources at such a level of generalized elaboration that he subsumes them all and hence repudiates his dependence on any one.

One other group of *Rambler* scientific ideas, in their sources somewhat anomalous to those we have just seen, deserve special mention in this regard. The medical and physiological ideas of Johnson's *Rambler*, as we might expect from his own classical bent and from his later acknowledgment of debt to Dr. James, would seem to derive from the Hippocratic and practical medicine which he had learned while helping James with his *Medicinal Dictionary* rather than from the more pretentious mechanical and mathemati-cal theorizing, already obsolescent,[28] of which he must have had a generous smattering from such Dictionary sources as Cheyne's *Philosophical Principles*, Arbuthnot's *Essay Concerning Aliments*, and Quincy's *Lexicon Physico-Medicum*. The last, as its title pro-fesses, was dedicated to expounding the mechanical and chemical *praecognita* of medicine and to distinguishing philosophic medi-cine from the haphazard and merely empiric.[29] But Johnson's medicine looks backward.[30] A passage in *Rambler* 151 which speaks of "the several stages by which animal life makes its progress from infancy to decrepitude" might be accounted for in either Celsus or Hippocrates.[31] Another medical passage, that in *Rambler* 112, refers explicitly to Celsus. "We are taught by *Celsus* that health is best preserved by avoiding settled habits of life."[32] It will scarcely be thought incompatible with this classical and liter-

28. See the excellent account in Kurt Sprengel, *Histoire de la Médecine*, trad. A. J. L. Jourdan (Paris, 1815), v, 131–142. James's Dictionary, despite the fact that it is dedicated—by the pen of Johnson—to Richard Mead, the most important British jatromechanist of the day, is anti-mechanical. See James's comment on Boerhaave's *Oratio de Usu Ratiocinii Mechanici in Medicina* (*A Medicinal Dictionary*, Vol. i [London, 1743], Preface, p. xciv).

29. *Lexicon Physico-Medicum* (London, 1722), Preface, pp. xiii–xiv. Arbuthnot's mechanical ideas are tempered with a profound respect for the Hippocratic tradition. See *Essay Concerning . . . Aliments* (London, 1735), pp. 232, 236; Lester M. Beattie, *John Arbuthnot* (Harvard, 1935), pp. 354–376.

30. "I would bear something rather than Celsus should be detected in an error" (*Letters* i, 220, No. 310, May 23, 1773). See Johnson's opinion of the Irish mechanist Barry (*Life* iii, 34; cf. Sprengel, *op. cit.*, v, 182).

31. Celsus, *Medicinae*, II, i; Hippocrates, *Regimen*, I, xxxiii. Cf. Hale, *Primitive Origination of Mankind* (London, 1677), p. 173.

32. Celsus, *Medicinae*, I, i. Cf. *Catalogue of the Library of Samuel Johnson*, No. 259; James, *Medicinal Dictionary*, Vol. i, Preface, p. lxiii; Arbuthnot, *Essay Con-cerning . . . Aliments*, p. 217; Bacon, *Of Regiment of Health*.

ary strain of medicine that a certain confusion of sources should appear in some passages—an ambiguous and superior relation like that which we have noted in the passage on glass. We may illustrate this in a simple way by the passage in *Rambler* 156 where Johnson speaks of the tendency of the human body to a predominance of some peccant humor—a variation upon the Hippocratic doctrine of humors which by a curiously cavalier treatment of ancient history he attributes to the "methodick physicians," who were in fact noted, and censured by Galen, for their rejection of the doctrine of humors.[33] A more complex and significant example is the passage of *Rambler* 58 which dwells in a similar vein upon the innate morbidity of the corporal humors:

It is observed by those who have written on the constitution of the human body, and the original of those diseases by which it is afflicted, that every man comes into the world morbid, that there is no temperature so exactly regulated but that some humour is fatally predominant, and that we are generally impregnated, in our first entrance upon life, with the seeds of that malady, which, in time, shall bring us to the grave.[34]

This passage bears a generic resemblance to the doctrine of Hippocrates and Galen but may owe more to a passage in Arbuthnot's *Essay Concerning Aliments* which is quoted in the Dictionary under the key word *morbid*.

In some of these Senses, tho' every Human Constitution is morbid, yet are their Diseases consistent with the common Functions of Life, and leave them under their own Conduct, as to their manner of living.[35]

Or the passage may owe less to physiological than to astrological and literary sources, the classic *nascentes morimur* of Manilius' *Astronomicon* or the *prima quae vitam dedit hora, carpit* of Seneca's *Hercules Furens*,[36] or a closer source, the Popean couplets:

As Man, perhaps, the moment of his breath,
Receives the lurking principle of death;

33. In Quincy's *Lexicon*, s.v. *Methodica Medicina* and *Methodici*, methodic physicians are erroneously identified with Galen and his followers. The mistake is pointed out by Chambers, *Cyclopaedia* (London, 1741), s.v. *Methodists*. Cf. Prosper Alpinus, *De Medicina Methodica* (Leyden, 1719), pp. 96–102, Bk. II, chap. iv; James, *Medicinal Dictionary*, Vol. i, Preface, p. lv; Arbuthnot, *Aliments*, pp. 165–166; Sprengel, *op. cit.*, ii, 39–41.

34. 43, v, 276.

35. *Essay Concerning . . . Aliments*, p. 152. See this passage and the passage from the *Rambler* quoted together in the *OED*, s.v. *morbid* 1 b. Cf. Hippocrates, *Nature of Man*, chaps. iii–iv; Galen, *On the Natural Faculties*, I, ii, v; Aristotle, *On Generation and Corruption*.

36. *Astronomicon*, IV, 16; see the edition of A. E. Housman (Cambridge, 1937), pp. 3, 129, for further examples of the idea. *Hercules Furens*, III, 874.

The young disease, that must subdue at length,
Grows with his growth, and strengthens with his strength:
So, cast and mingled with his very frame,
The Mind's disease, its RULING PASSION came;
Each vital humour which should feed the whole,
Soon flows to this, in body and in soul:
Whatever warms the heart, or fills the head,
As the mind opens, and its functions spread,
Imagination plies her dang'rous art,
And pours it all upon the peccant part.[37]

Johnson's application of the principle—"This remark has been extended by others to the intellectual faculties"—brings him fairly close to the passage in Pope. In general, his use of anatomical and physiological terms in the *Rambler*, of *humour*, for example, and *peccant humour*, is at a grand and literary level of fruitful imprecision.

Johnson's use of science, even when it is correct, is on the whole far from precise. But the meaning of this for our study is not that Johnson's Dictionary has nothing to tell us about the philosophic style of the *Rambler*. Rather it is that what the Dictionary has to tell us must be sought at a different level. Occasional glimpses of the moons of Jupiter and flights of migratory birds, smatterings of technicality like the catenarian curve and quadrature of the circle, or allusions to a doctrine of the "methodick physicians" are anomalous to the prevailing generality of Johnson's conceptions —a generality which, however, readily allies itself with the broader and more easily available features of seventeenth-century and eighteenth-century science. In the philosophic similes and metaphors which we examined in the last chapter but which in our recent consideration of "sources" there has been no occasion to mention—those concerning the heterogeneous notions of old and young, the volatility of a secret, the diffusion of merit, the repulsion or attraction of human natures, to name but a few—we have seen some of the most general principles of chemistry, mechanics, optics, and astronomy assimilated to his own mind by Johnson at such a level of generality that his words find approximate echoes in the master works of all these sciences. The Nature of these sciences, as we have noticed in earlier chapters, was a "Nature frugal in her

---

37. *Essay on Man*, ii, 133–144. The term *humour* as used by the medical writers of Johnson's day "applied to any juice, or fluid part of the body," rather than to one of the four humours of the ancients (Chambers, *Cyclopaedia* [London, 1741], s.v. *humour, temperament*).

principles," [38] or as would be said today, parsimonious; and the style which describes her is one of a certain abstracted and grand parsimony. The distribution of matter through space, vacuity, or plenitude,[39] the motion of bodies (impulse, repulse, trusion, diffusion, vibration, deviation) the attraction of gravity, the diurnal rotation of the earth and its annual revolution; the vicissitudes of heat and cold, of dark and light, the refraction and reflection of light rays—these are the typical themes of Newtonian physics popularized on every page of Bentley's *Sermons* [40] or Cheyne's *Philosophical Principles,* condensed in the articles of Harris' *Lexicon Technicum,* Chambers' *Cyclopaedia,* or Quincy's *Lexicon,*[41] or expressed in the English prose of Newton himself in his *Opticks.* Bodies homogeneous and heterogeneous and the separation of compounds; [42] the force of cohesion between particles or between bodies brought into contact; the qualities of color in minute particles, and the texture of bodies under the microscope; [43] the gravity, texture, and elasticity of fluids, their ebullition and effervescence, are the master themes of Bacon or of Boyle, and are echoed in Derham, Ray, Grew, Bentley, Cheyne, or Watts. The permeation and diffusion of subtle elements in underground springs and streams of water, a general exhalation and evaporation, is a motif that runs through the sections of Woodward's *Natural History of the Earth* concerning the "Fluids of the Globe" and the "Origin and Formation of Metals and Minerals"; [44] through Ray's briefer discussion of tides, floods, vapors, rivers, springs, and mineral waters; [45] and through a chapter of Derham on "The Distribution of Earth and Waters." [46] The subtler impregnation of the air with

38. Cheyne, *Philosophical Principles* (London, 1734), Part I, p. 306; cf. p. 349.
39. Cf. Johnson's discussion of *plenum* and *vacuum, Life* i, 444.
40. Cf. *ante* p. 61, the passage from *Rambler* 8 about the diffusion of matter through space with Bentley's *Sermons, Works* (London, 1838), iii, 153: "The sum of empty spaces within the concave of the firmament is 6,860 million million million times bigger than all the matter contained in it."
41. See in Harris especially the article *mechanical philosophy* and the Preface, pp. e–f^v, Newton's *De Natura Acidorum;* in Chambers *acceleration, acid, air, animal secretion, asperity, attraction, atmosphere, atom;* in Quincy *acceleration, air, attraction, circulation, cohesion, colour, corpuscular philosophy, fluidity, light, mechanicks, opacity, particle.*
42. See Boyle, *Sceptical Chymist, Works* (London, 1772), i, 508–512; *Producibleness of Chymical Principles,* Part IV, "Of the Production of Mercury," *Works,* i, 629. Cf. *Rambler* 5, v, 31, "What is said by the chemists of their darling mercury." See Quincy, *heterogeneous, menstruum, principia.*
43. See Boyle, *Experimental History of Colours, Works,* i, 676, 682. Cf. *ante* p. 62.
44. *Natural History of the Earth* (London, 1695), Parts III and IV, pp. 115–156, 202–212.
45. *Wisdom of God* (London, 1709), pp. 89–100.
46. *Physico-Theology* (London, 1714), pp. 47–53, Bk. II, chap. v. Cf. Alan D. McKillop, *The Background of Thomson's Seasons* (Minneapolis, 1942), pp. 78–81.

noxious or beneficent particles, steams or effluvia, is the theme of
Arbuthnot's *Essay Concerning the Effects of Air on Human Bodies.*
All these ideas of natural philosophy were concentrated in a
peculiar sense in the diction of the philosophy and differed from
ordinary ideas to a great extent in the diction which conjured them
up. To use the diction, even without technical accuracy, was to
convey the tone of the philosophy.

3

A STUDY of the relations between Johnson's writing and his scientific sources may, therefore, legitimately be a search for pregnant
words and the system of ideas attached to them. "Since he was
flush of energetic and unusual words," says a critic of the Dictionary, ". . . it seemed a pity to waste them, and he poured them
twice a week into the *Rambler.*" [1] "He might write his *Ramblers*
to make a dictionary necessary," said the contemporary satirist,
"and afterwards compile his dictionary to explain his *Ramblers.*" [2]
Johnson's biographer Arthur Murphy wrote seriously:

It is remarkable that the pomp of diction, which has been objected to
Johnson, was first assumed in the Rambler. His Dictionary was going
on at the same time, and, in the course of that work, as he grew familiar
with technical and scholastic works, he thought that the bulk of his
readers were equally learned; or at least would admire the splendour
and dignity of the style.[3]

Johnson himself, in a passage of the last *Rambler,* already quoted
in this chapter, seemed conscious of the connection.

When common words were less pleasing to the ear, or less distinct in
their significance, I have familiarized the terms of philosophy, by applying them to popular ideas.

The relation between Johnson's Dictionary and his prose writing
alluded to in these passages may be further sketched in a kind of
fantasy or parable of verbal study which is provided for us through
the efforts of an early critic of Johnson's style, the Reverend Vicesimus Knox. In his *Winter Evenings,* of 1788, Knox observed the
resemblance between Johnson's *Rambler* and the prose of Browne
and quoted from the *Pseudodoxia Epidemica* seven examples of
learned diction such as he thought must have been Johnson's
model.

1. George Radford, "Johnson's Dictionary," in *Johnson Club Papers* (London,
1920), p. 116.
2. Archibald Campbell, *Lexiphanes* (London, 1767), pp. 108–109.
3. *Miscellanies* i, 466.

Intellectual acquisition is but reminiscential evocation.

We hope it will not be unconsidered that we find no constant manuduction in this labyrinth.

For not attaining the deuteroscopy, they are fain to omit the superconsequences, coherences, figures, or tropologies, and are not some time persuaded by fire beyond their literalities.

Their individual imperfections being great, they are moreover enlarged by their aggregation.

A farraginous concurrence of all conditions.

Being divided from truth themselves, they are yet further removed by advenient deception.

Deluding their apprehension with ariolation.[4]

Knox selected the first two of these examples from Browne's address "To the Reader" prefixed to the *Pseudodoxia* and the remaining five from Book iii, chapter 9, quoting all seven in the order of their occurrence, so that there can be no doubt that the *Pseudodoxia* was his first source—if indeed he consulted Johnson's Dictionary.[5] Yet each of these passages chosen by Knox to suggest Johnson's Brownism may be found one or more times in the Dictionary, under the words:

> reminiscential
> unconsidered, manuduction
> deuteroscopy, superconsequence, tropology, literality
> aggregation
> farraginous
> advenient
> ariolation

To return from these exotic Brownian examples chosen by Knox to the *Rambler* itself, we may gather from Johnson's own statement that he looked on his *Ramblers* as a kind of testing ground or supplementary illustration for the ideals of purity and canons of meaning which he was systematizing in the Dictionary.[6] At any rate the comic exaggerations which we have quoted, no less than the serious statements of Murphy and Johnson, reflect the truth that a search for the contexts of Johnson's words, their connotations or

---

4. Vicesimus Knox, *Winter Evenings* (London, 1790), i, 192. "Johnson's STYLE . . . is my Lord Bacon's; but he caught a shade of Brown's MANNER in the expression" (Mrs. Piozzi, *British Synonymy* [London, 1794], ii, 276).

5. The text of Knox's second and third quotations also precludes the Dictionary as the source.

6. The *Rambler* afforded the Dictionary illustrations under a few words: *faint* adj. (38, v, 249), *ground* v.a. (96, vi, 160), *expiration* (54, v, 347), *instillations* (72, vi, 7), *medicate* (130, vi, 378), *placability* (110, vi, 246, quoted as anonymous), *virility* (115, vi, 281). Cf. *ante* p. 48.

stylistic value, finds its appropriate guide in the collections of his own Dictionary. The philosophic words employed in various shades of metaphor by Johnson in his *Rambler* may or may not at the present day on *prima facie* examination present to us the same philosophic color as to Johnson himself or to the ideal audience among his contemporaries. In the Dictionary these words wear their color unfaded in the illustrations chosen by Johnson from classic texts of seventeenth-century and eighteenth-century philosophy. We read in the *Rambler* about an *equipoise* "between the pleasures of this life and the hopes of futurity," or "between good and ill"; or the *equipoise* "of an empty mind"; or "of desires." Or:

Every animal body, according to the methodick physicians, is, by the predominance of some exuberant quality, continually declining towards disease and death, which must be obviated by the seasonable reduction of the peccant humour to the just *equipoise* which health requires.[7]

Under *equipoise* in the Dictionary we find that the applied senses occurring in the *Rambler* have not been illustrated, but only a physical sense similar to that in the last *Rambler* quotation. Only one passage, from Glanvill's *Scepsis Scientifica,* has been selected by Johnson from his reading to illustrate this word:

In the temperate zone of our life there are few bodies at such an equipoise of humours; but that the prevalency of some one indisposeth the spirits.[8]

Or we find in the *Rambler* the word *defecate,* another word which is used in both the "natural" and the applied senses: we read of "the tenuity of a defecated air at a proper distance from the surface of the earth," and of a person who resolves "to defecate and clear" his "mind by brisker motions." [9] In the Dictionary we discover that this word is illustrated in its chemical or technical sense from Boyle, from the medical writer Gideon Harvey, and from the mock-heroical poem *Cyder* of John Philips:

> Provide a brazen tube
> Inflext; self-taught and voluntary flies
> The defecated liquor, . . .

and that the secondary or applied sense of the word is illustrated in a very metaphysical way, once more from Glanvill:

We defecate the notion from materiality, and abstract quantity, place, and all kind of corporeity from it.[10]

7. 7, v, 44; 70, v, 442; 5, v, 30; 95, vi, 157; 132, vi, 388; 156, vii, 95.
8. *Scepsis Scientifica* (London, 1665), p. 82. Cf. *ante* p. 15.
9. 117, vi, 296; 177, vii, 217.
10. *Scepsis Scientifica,* p. 17. The adjective *defecate* is illustrated from Glanvill

Or, to take a word which appears in the *Rambler* only in its applied sense, we read of *quiescent* human faculties, a *quiescent* or lethargick state of mind, and a *quiescent* or torpid state of stupidity or cowardice.[11] In the Dictionary this word is applied to physical objects, like the earth and the left side of the human body, by Glanvill, Browne, Holder, and Grew, and to a fluid medium by Newton.

Pression or motion cannot be propagated in a fluid in right lines beyond an obstacle which stops part of the motion, but will bend and spread every way into the *quiescent* medium, which lies beyond the obstacle.[12]

We have suggested above the importance of philosophic words themselves to the system of ideas and more vaguely connoted meanings which Johnson translated from the classics of natural philosophy into the imagery of his own prose. The point may be enforced by a contrast between this imagery and a scientific but less "philosophic" image which Johnson once conceived in a more offhand and less bookish context—during an actual experiment conducted at Streatham. "We were drawing Spirits over a Lamp," says Mrs. Thrale, "and the Liquor bubbled in the Glass Retort." And "there says Mr. Johnson—[Edward] Young bubbles & froths in his Descriptions like this Spirit; but Dryden foams like the Sea . . . in a Storm." [13] Here the words *bubbles* and *froths* perform the function of belittling the poetry of Young in a passage where contrasting grandeur is also expressed in the natural imagery of *foam, sea,* and *storm.* But another kind of dignity, half ironic indeed, might be attached to bubbles, by another word. In the *Life of Young* Johnson attributes to one of Young's tragedies "the greatest ebullitions of imagination." [14] In the *Rambler* the same larger word occurs in contexts of a similar half-disparaged dignity: we have imagination "heated . . . to such a state of activity and ebullition, that . . . it fumed away in bursts of wit, and evaporations of gaiety"; [15] we have "temerity . . . the *ebullition* of genius." [16] We have fear which is necessary "to allay the *effervescence* of an agitated fancy." [17] In the Dictionary *ebullition* is il-

(in the spiritual sense) and from Boyle (in the chemical), and the noun *defecation* from Harvey.

11. 49, v, 314; 103, vi, 205; 183, vii, 250.

12. *Opticks* (New York, 1931), p. 362. Cf. *Rambler* 137, vi, 417, "gloomy quiescence of astonishment," and the illustration from Glanvill in the Dictionary, s.v. *quiescence.*

13. *Thraliana* (Oxford, 1942), i, 174.

14. *Lives* iii, 397.

15. 101, vi, 189.

16. 129, vi, 372.

17. 43, v, 281.

lustrated from Bacon, Browne, Quincy, Arbuthnot, and Newton; *effervescence* is illustrated from Arbuthnot, Grew, and Woodward.

> When aqua fortis, or spirits of vitriol, poured upon filings of iron, dissolves the filings with a great heat and ebullition, is not the heat and ebullition effected by a violent motion of parts?
>
> *Newton.*[18]

> Hot springs do not owe their heat to any colluctation or effervescence of the minerals in them, but to subterranean heat or fire.
>
> *Woodward's Nat. Hist.*[19]

It may be desirable at this point to indicate by some gesture of enumerative analysis the importance of such examples in the background of *Rambler* philosophic vocabulary. In Appendix A of this study will be found an alphabetized list of about 380 *Rambler* philosophic words which in Johnson's Dictionary are the keys to a profusion of examples from Bacon, Browne, Arbuthnot, and other philosophic writers. Bacon is the single author most often quoted. From Bacon's *Natural History,* in Johnson's eyes the parent and sufficient authority for English philosophic diction, Johnson drew about 75 illustrations for a somewhat smaller number of the *Rambler* words. He illustrated, for example, the following mechanical terms of motion and causation:

accelerate, attraction, compression, diffusion, dissolution, dissipation, emission, percussion, relaxation, repercussion, resilience, resistance, rotation, trepidation.[20]

The chemical terms:

adulteration, assimilate, corrosion, ingredient, liquefaction, metalline, precipitation, sediment, volatility.

The medical and physiological terms:

acrimony, contagion, exacerbation, hypochondriacal, infection, irritate, mortification.

From Bacon's *Physiological Remains* he illustrated *ebullition* and *volatility, mortification* and *mortify;* from the *New Atlantis, composition, radiation, resuscitate.* From Sir Thomas Browne, an author whom Johnson was to credit with having "augmented our philosophic diction," [21] or rather from the *Pseudodoxia Epidemica,*

18. *Opticks,* p. 377.
19. *Natural History* (London, 1695), p. 144.
20. See Appendix B for a full account of Johnson's illustration of *Rambler* philosophic words from Bacon and from the other authors to be named.
21. *Life of Browne, Works* iv, 612.

the only work of Browne's which he used for the Dictionary, he illustrated more than 50 of the *Rambler* philosophic words. Such mechanical terms of motion and cause as:

actuate, attraction, eccentricity, emanation, emission, equilibrium, gravity, progression, progressive, quiescent, recess, reciprocation.

The more miscellaneous terms:

> interstitial, involution, tortuosity
> frigidity, irradiation, scintillation
> magnetism, meridian, meteorological.

And a rather rococo medical collection:

alexipharmick, antidotal, antidote, chronical, ebriety, inebriation, mortify, narcotick, noxious, preservative, suffocate, valetudinary, vulnerable, vulnerary.

From the more specialized works of John Arbuthnot, Johnson, in accord perhaps with his own introspective and hypochondriac interest, and because he considered Arbuthnot "the first man" among the writers of the reign of Queen Anne,[22] drew even more heavily than from Browne. The Explanation of Chemical Terms prefixed to Arbuthnot's *Essay Concerning Aliments* was an especially rich area, from which Johnson drew definitive illustrations for the *Rambler* words *acrimony, ebullition, effervescence, volatility*. Elsewhere in the same *Essay* he found such words as:

accelerate, adherence, elastick, influx, mechanism, ramification, relaxation, tenuity, vacuity.

cordial, emollient, excoriation, flatulency, medicate, morbid, palpitation, peccant, phlegmatick, putrefaction, restorative.

And in the companion work, Arbuthnot's *Practical Rules of Diet:*

circumvolution, evacuate, flaccid, inflation.

anodyne, apoplexy, balsamick, delirium, exacerbation, inoculation, irritation, lethargick, palliative, paroxysm, stimulate, suffocation.

One other work, Newton's *Opticks,* one of the purest fountainheads of the stream of scientific ideas and diction which we seek to trace in Johnson's writing, deserves to be signalized at this point. From about 30 speculative pages at the end of the *Opticks* [23] Johnson illustrated the words:

---

22. *Life* i, 425. Cf. *Lives* iii, 177, *Life of Pope*, Par. 213.
23. Bk. III, Part i, Quest. 31.

assimilate, attraction, coruscation, ebullition, elastic, ingredient, texture, volatile.

From the rest of the *Opticks* such words as:

accelerate, ambient, compression, ether, flexibility, gravity, quiescent, percussion, progression, resistance, rotation, vibration.

For illustrations of the same *Rambler* words Johnson drew only less heavily upon various essays of Boyle, especially his *History of Fluidity and Firmness* and *Sceptical Chymist;* upon Glanvill's Brownian *Scepsis Scientifica,* Locke's *Essay,* Watts's *Logic* and *Improvement of the Mind,* and Quincy's *Lexicon Physico-Medicum;* upon the teleologists Ray and Bentley, the chronologist Hale and the fossilist Woodward, and upon the philosophic poets Milton and Thomson. He drew more lightly on yet other philosophic authorities—Burnet, Cheyne, Derham, Grew among the religio-scientific writers; Sharp, Wiseman, and Gideon Harvey among the surgeons and physicians; Holder in his *Elements of Speech* and *Discourse Concerning Time.* Despite the fact that he chose a good many illustrations for the same words from Shakespeare or Dryden or Swift and from a few religious writers, Johnson found in the philosophic writers just cited a preponderant context for that part of his *Rambler* vocabulary which we have described as philosophic.[24]

4

THE sort of analysis which we have just offered might be said, with some fairness, to tend toward biography or the history of Johnson's mind rather than toward the objective or public history of English words. Yet for a reader of so wide a scope and of such accurate discrimination as Johnson, and when our appeal is to a philological monument of such dimensions as his *Dictionary of the English Language,* the privately biographical approaches the public. A comparison of the philosophical sources which we have just surveyed with other works to be found in the same area of literature —the philosophic works of Hobbes, for example, those of the practically minded Robert Hooke, or of the popularizing Desaguliers, or even the papers in the *Philosophical Transactions*—will, I believe, convince a curious student that our induction (or, as

24. For relevant meanings of the 380 select words in Appendix A, there are about 200 Dictionary illustrations from Shakespeare, Dryden, Pope, and other nonphilosophic poets, about 120 from Addison, Swift, and other literary prose authors, about 100 from religious writers, chiefly Hooker and South, about 95 from the philosophic poets Milton, Thomson, Blackmore, and Philips, and from various scientific and technical writers, chiefly those mentioned above, about 570. See Appendix B.

Browne might have put it, manuduction) from the vocabulary of Johnson's *Rambler* through his Dictionary has led us to the classical and most concentrated efflorescences of philosophic words in the history of the English language. In this respect the works of Bacon, Browne, Arbuthnot, Newton, and a few others are more exclusive Johnsonian sources than the passages about moons, magnets, birds, and elephants which we have cited in an earlier part of this chapter. Even more important for our purpose, a study of Johnson's philosophic mind is a study of objective language values because of the combined accuracy, originality, and authority of his prose usage. It is true, as we might have expected from our earlier discussion of philosophic diction in the seventeenth century, that most of the words which we have so far examined as typical of Johnson's philosophical bent had been used in their applied or immaterial senses by earlier authors. Johnson is scarcely, in the starkest sense of the word, an innovator. Yet Johnson's philosophic style, in its general tenor, in the frequency of his engagement in the process of transferring the literal and philosophic into the metaphoric and psychological, is distinctly a creative and progressive style. The progressive tendency of such a style may, moreover, be estimated in a certain selection of words in which a degree of innovation does appear. *Frigorifick,* says the *Rambler* in his own Dictionary, "Causing cold. A word used in science," with an illustration from Quincy's *Lexicon:* "Frigorifick atoms or particles mean those nitrous salts which float in the air in cold weather, and occasion freezing." In the *Rambler* we find the "frigorifick torpor" of death, the "frigorifick power" of bashfulness, and the "fatal influence of frigorifick wisdom." [1] The history of the language as recorded in Johnson's most comprehensive successor, the *Oxford English Dictionary,* does not contradict our impression that in these uses Johnson made an original metaphoric transfer. Here the earliest figurative use recorded is the very *Rambler* phrase about the power of bashfulness. Another word of the same quality, *colorifick,* is defined by Johnson in his Dictionary as: "That which has the power of producing dyes, tints, colours, or hues," with an illustration from Newton's *Opticks,* but in the *Rambler* the word is used in a literary way to mean something vaguely but impressively like "colorful." "This month," he says of May, ". . . covers the meadow with verdure, and decks the gardens with all the mixtures of colorifick radiance." [2] And this phrase again is the first example of the meaning quoted in the *Oxford Dictionary.* At the opposite end of a modern scale of ex-

1. 120, vi, 315; 129, vi, 371; 159, vii, 115.
2. 124, vi, 342.

pectancy about Johnson's vocabulary might come two such words as *acrimonious* and *repulsion,* which in his Dictionary are defined and illustrated (from Gideon Harvey on *Consumptions* and Arbuthnot on *Air*) in the physical senses, but in the *Rambler* are used in transferred senses now familiar but illustrated in the *Oxford Dictionary* no earlier than from Johnson himself.

The resentment . . . will regularly be more acrimonious as pride is more immediately the principle of action.[3]

There are many natures which . . . seem to start back from each other by some invincible repulsion.[4]

The following selection of figurative or transferred uses from the *Rambler* includes only examples which are not anticipated in either Johnson's Dictionary or the *Oxford Dictionary.* All but seven are quoted in the *Oxford Dictionary.* To various modern readers they will perhaps testify Johnson's originality in various degrees.

It had been a task worthy of the moral philosophers to have considered . . . the *climactericks* of the mind.[5]

This natural and necessary *comminution* of our lives . . . often makes us insensible of the negligence with which we suffer them to slide away.[6]

The antidotes with which philosophy has medicated the cup of life . . . have allayed its bitterness, and *contempered* its malignity.[7]

Scarce any man now peruses it [a passage from *Macbeth*] without some disturbance of his attention from the *counteraction* of the words to the ideas.[8]

The writer . . . receives little pleasure or advantage from the *diffusion* of his name.[9]

Nothing can so much disturb the passions, or perplex the intellects of man, as the *disruption* of his union with nature.[10]

Those . . . who want not inclination to wisdom or virtue, though they have been *dissipated* by negligence, or misled by example.[11]

3. 40, v, 258. See the two Johnsonian illustrations in *OED,* s.v. *asperity* 4, in a sense anticipated, however, by illustrations in Johnson's Dictionary. Cf. the Johnsonian illustrations, s.v. *asperity* 3, 5, and 6.
  4. 160, vii, 119.
  5. 151, vii, 63.
  6. 108, vi, 234.
  7. 130, vii, 58.
  8. 168, vii, 166; cf. 29, vi, 191.
  9. 101, vi, 190.
  10. 78, vi, 44.
  11. 124, vi, 342; cf. *OED,* s.v. *dissipated* 2, from Johnson's *Life of Savage;* and *dissipated* 1, *dissipate* 6, other quotations from Johnson. Cf. Johnson's *Dictionary,* s.v. *dissipate.*

Who . . . endeavour to lose their sense of danger in the *ebriety* of perpetual amusement.[12]

They . . . will not suffer more fear to intrude into their contemplations than is necessary to allay the *effervescence* of an agitated fancy.[13]

The tardy *emission* of *Pope's* compositions.[14]

These papers of the day, the *Ephemerae* of learning, have uses more adequate to the purposes of common life than more pompous and durable volumes.[15]

The great principles of truth . . . like light transmitted from room to room, . . . lose their strength and splendour, and fade at last in total *evanescence*.[16]

Different poets . . . lament the deceitfulness of hope, the *fugacity* of pleasure, the fragility of beauty.[17]

Against the *instillations* of this frigid opiate [the desire to stop working], the heart should be secured.[18]

Steadily and resolutely assign to any science or language those *interstitial* vacancies which intervene in the most crowded variety of diversion or employment.[19]

The antidotes with which philosophy has *medicated* the cup of life.[20]

At this time of universal *migration*, when almost everyone . . . has retired . . . into the country.[21]

He that finds the frigid and *narcotick* infection of vain imagination beginning to seize him, should turn his whole attention against it.[22]

He who endeavours the cure of our intellectual maladies, mistakes their cause; . . . his *prescriptions* avail nothing.[23]

To give those faculties which cannot lie wholly *quiescent*, some particular direction.[24]

12. 167, vii, 160.
13. 43, v, 281.
14. 169, vii, 173.
15. 145, vii, 32.
16. 156, vii, 95.
17. 143, vii, 16.
18. 207, vii, 384. In *OED*, s.v. *instillation* 1 *transf.* and *fig.* this passage and *Rambler* 72, vi, 7, are the only examples. In Johnson's Dictionary, s.v. *instillation*, *Rambler* 72, vi, 7, is the only example.
19. 108, vi, 235.
20. 130, vii, 58. Cf. Johnson's Dictionary, s.v. *medicate*, the example from *Rambler* 130, vi, 378.
21. 135, vii, 406; cf. 138, vi, 423.
22. 89, vi, 112.
23. 87, vi, 98.
24. 49, v, 314.

Social life is perpetually branched out into minuter subdivisions, till it terminates in the last *ramifications* of private friendship.[25]

Active employment . . . is generally a necessary part of this intellectual *regimen.*[26]

These rules corrupted by fraud . . . have, by the common *resiliency* of the mind from one extreme to another, incited others to an open contempt of all subsidiary ordinances.[27]

Less frequently, and perhaps more surprisingly, the Rambler seems to slip into novelty in a shade of technically applied or literal philosophic meaning. Thus: *animation* [28] of the magnetic needle (rather than of vegetables or of metals simply considered), the *armature* [29] of the magnet (rather than of a shelly or prickly animal), and to *concentrate* [29] the virtue of a magnet; *indissoluble* [30] in the sense of not fusible (rather than of inseparable or indestructible); *gregarious,*[31] of savages (a sense between that of the earlier application to animals and a social metaphor of Mrs. Piozzi's in 1789); *biennial,*[32] recurring every two years (rather than lasting two years); *symmetrical* [33] and *untransposed,*[34] both used by the Rambler in criticism of versification and each the earliest recorded use of the word in any sense. In an even simpler way the style of the Rambler shows a certain originality of philosophic color in his occasional use of very technical words, found in earlier medical writers or in scientific lexica, but anomalous in so literary a context. Thus: *abscind,*[35]

25. 99, vi, 180. Cf. the conspicuously repeated and gruesome use of the word *ramification,* of veins in corpses injected with coloring fluid, in Johnson's life of Frederic Ruysch for Dr. James's *Medicinal Dictionary.* Cf. Johnson's *Preface* to the Dictionary (*Works* ix, 210) and Coleman's parody: "In vain may the laborious Lexicographer boast of having traced every radical word through a collateral series of Parallel Ramifications" (*Prose on Several Occasions* [London, 1787], ii, 92).

26. 89, vi, 112.

27. 110, vi, 249. See some further Johnsonian earliest examples in the *OED,* s.v. *projection* 4 (*Adventurer*); *compression* 2 b, *concentrate* 4, *subduct* 3 (*Idler*); *intumescence* 1 b (*Taxation No Tyranny*); *effusion* 4, *emit* 5 (*Lives of the Poets*). Under *flexible* 3 b (the absolute sense) the earliest quotation is from the legal argument about Hastie the schoolmaster which Johnson wrote for Boswell in 1772. See Johnson's *Preface to Shakespeare* (*Works* ix, 300), *refrigerate,* a metaphor of which there are no examples in *OED; Debates in Parliament* (*Works* xiii, 282), the noun *soporific* in a sense that antedates by about seventy years the earliest *OED* example.

28. 61, v, 393.

29. 199, vii, 344; cf. *OED, armature* 6 and *concentrate* 2.

30. 174, vii, 200; cf. *OED, indissoluble* 2 b.

31. 99, vi, 178.

32. 61, v, 389; cf. *OED, biennial* 2.

33. 94, vi, 146; cf. *OED, symmetrical* 1.

34. 86, vi, 93; cf. *OED, untransposed.* The word does not appear in Johnson's Dictionary.

35. 90, vi, 118.

abscission,[36] *detruncation* [36] (further terms of prosodic criticism), *barometrical* and *flaccid* in a discussion of the effects of atmosphere on the human mind,[37] the medical terms *discuss,*[38] *essential,*[39] *morbid,*[40] and *vulnerary,*[41] *inhibition* [42] of sleep, and the mathematical terms *mensuration* [43] and *incommensurate.*[44] The word *electrify* may be found in electrical papers read before the Royal Society at least as early as 1745 and published in the *Philosophical Transactions,* but Johnson's use of the word in the *Rambler* seems to have a peculiar timeliness in that it appeared within a few weeks of Cave's publication in April, 1751, of Franklin's *Experiments and Observations on Electricity.*[45] Finally it is worth noticing that the *Oxford Dictionary* often draws upon Johnson for the illustration of words which are recorded as common in the seventeenth century or marked *obsolete, archaic,* or *rare,* for example:

athanor, coactive 1, copulation 1, discrimination 2, discuss 2, excrescence 1 c, expiration 4, flux 6, infusion 2 b, inject 2, latitude 2, luminary 3 (of things), momentaneous, morbid 1 b, papilionaceous, progression 2, recession 2, respiration 3, sensible 8 b, stimulation 1, superstruct, temperature 5 (of humours), tumour 4.

And the spacing of the illustrations sometimes indicates that these words had attained or approximated their archaic status at the date when Johnson used them. In Johnson's day his friend Arthur Murphy noticed a "scholastic" coloring in his prose, a "tincture from the writers of the last century." It must of course remain doubtful in the case of any given philosophic word that Johnson was either the first by whom the new was tried, or the last to lay the old aside. Johnson himself told Boswell that he had not taken upon himself to add more than four or five words to the English language, and he said that he disapproved of linguistic license,[46] a statement am-

36. 88, vi, 107.
37. 117, vi, 296–297.
38. 130, vi, 378.
39. 120, vi, 314.
40. 43, v, 276.
41. 47, v, 314.
42. 79, vi, 51.
43. 103, vi, 204.
44. 127, vi, 362. For some other technical illustrations from Johnson, see *OED,* s.v. *excision, lacteal, metallic* 4, *turbinated* (*Idler*); *emersion* 2 b, *tenuity* (*Rasselas*).
45. *Rambler* 118, vi, 304. The word was used figuratively by Chesterfield in 1752. See *ante* p. 31; *OED,* s.v. *electrify;* Franklin, *Experiments and Observations* (London, 1769), Letter to Collinson, July 11, 1747, p. 11. Cf. *Rambler* 199, vii, 339, "wheels of electricity."
46. *Life* i, 221. Boswell later heard Johnson coin *peregrinity* and *depeditation,* and Johnson admitted having "made" three or four words in his Dictionary (*Life* v, 130).

ply corroborated by the general tenor of his criticism and his lexicography. Yet a study of Johnson's words in the *Oxford Dictionary* affords support for the generalization which is the theme of this study, that Johnson in his creative prose was engaged in a persistent process of metaphoric transfer from the realm of the philosophic to that of the psychological, a fact which, along with the occasional and quite harmonious archaism of his vocabulary, has been obscured by the very success of his style and his literary and lexicographic authority.[47]

47. Johnson's role in the history of the philosophic words collected in this study (cf. Appendix A) is broadly indicated in the fact that he is represented under these words in the *Oxford Dictionary* by about 150 quotations besides those already cited. For some *Rambler* figurative uses see especially *assimilate* 2 b, *balsamick* 5, *concentration* 1 *fig.*, *corrosion* 2, *evacuation* 4, *flexibility* 3, *immerge* 2, *maturation* 4, *opiate* b, *palliative* 2, *putrefaction* 4, *ventilation* 1 *fig.* See the examples from Johnson's *Letters* under *ferment* 1 b, *lacerate* 2.

A few nonphilosophic words in the *Rambler* seem to be innovations, the most significant for students of Johnson's literary mind being perhaps *colloquial. Rambler* 101, vi, 190, "the colloquial wit," is the earliest example in *OED*, s.v. *colloquial* 1 (conversational). Cf. 14, v, 94, "colloquial entertainment." *Rambler* 208, vii, 395, "colloquial barbarisms," is the earliest example in *OED*, s.v. *colloquial* 2 (of common speech). The word does not appear in the first three editions of Johnson's Dictionary. In the fourth edition it appears without illustration. See *OED*, *compact* 1 b, *depreciated* 2 *absol.*, *inadequate* b, *insusceptive* (= insusceptible), a word illustrated only from Johnson, *irascibility*, *officinal*, *vagrance*.

CHAPTER V

Some Stylistic Values

1. Corpuscular Epistemology

AN ancient distinction between the primary and the secondary qualities of bodies, with a preference for the former as objective and reliable, was revived in the sixteenth century and impressively developed at the outset of the seventeenth in the writings of Galilei.[1] Thereafter the distinction is characteristic of both empiricist and rationalist philosophy during the period when the main sources of Johnson's Dictionary were being written. It is the epistemological key to a pervasive system, the point of view from which looking outward we see a universe much more refined, barren, and strict, in fact much more universal than our ordinary perceptions would indicate; and looking inward, we begin to find either literally or by shades of analogy, a determinate account of our ideas and emotions as motions of something physical.[2] "We cannot," says Glanvill, "know any thing of *Nature* but by an *Analysis* of it to its *true initial causes:* and till we know the first springs of natural motions, we are still but Ignorants."

It is conceived to be as certain, as our faculties can make it, that the same qualities, which we resent within us, are in the object, their Source. And yet this confidence is grounded on no better foundation, then a delusory prejudice, and the vote of *misapplyed sensations,* which have no warrant to determine either one or other. I may indeed conclude, that I am formally *hot* or *cold;* I feel it. But whether these qualities are *formally,* or only *eminently* in their producent; is beyond the knowledge of the *sensitive.*[3]

It is possible to produce passages of this tenor from almost any of the scientific sources of Johnson's Dictionary, and many of them passages quoted in the Dictionary. Thus Newton:

For a sound in a Bell or musical String, or other sounding Body, is nothing but a trembling Motion, and in the Air nothing but that Motion propagated from the Object, and in the Sensorium, 'tis a Sense of that

---

1. Edwin A. Burtt, *Metaphysical Foundations of Modern Physical Science* (New York, 1925), pp. 56, 73–80.
2. Cf. Descartes, *Les Passions de l'Ame,* I, vii, xxvii, xxxi, xxxvi.
3. *Scepsis Scientifica* (London, 1665), pp. 154, 65–66.

Motion under the Form of Sound; so Colours in the Object are nothing but a Disposition to reflect this or that sort of Rays more copiously than the rest; in the Rays they are nothing but their Dispositions to propagate this or that Motion into the Sensorium, and in the Sensorium they are Sensations of those Motions under the Forms of Colours.[4]

And Locke, especially, is quoted throughout the Dictionary in passages that epitomize his characteristic doctrine of knowledge. Thus:

impression 1.
> Sensation is such an *impression* or motion, made in some part of the body, as produces some perception in the understanding.

obliterate 2.
> These simple ideas, the understanding can no more refuse to have, or alter, or blot them out, than a mirror can refuse, alter, or *obliterate* the images which the objects set before it produce.

operate.
> Bodies produce ideas in us, manifestly by impulse, the only way which we can conceive bodies *operate* in.

snowball.
> A *snowball* having the power to produce in us the ideas of white, cold, and round, the powers, as they are in the *snowball*, I call qualities; and, as they are sensations in our understandings, ideas.[5]

The work of Locke alone would have been enough to insure a thorough immersion of Johnson's mind in empirical epistemology. Johnson excluded Hobbes from the Dictionary, no doubt because of his impiety.[6] Berkeley he quoted only eight times, five times from a letter to Pope and three from Berkeley's religious writings.[7]

4. *Opticks* (New York, 1931), p. 125. Cf. Dictionary, s.v. *sensorium*. Cf. Boyle, *Experimental History of Colours, Works* (London, 1772), i, 664, 671, 676, 693, and Dictionary, s.v. *adventitious, taffeta,* and *thread;* Bentley, *Sermons, Works* (London, 1838), iii, 38, 71, 148; Cheyne, *Philosophical Principles* (London, 1734), Part I, pp. 269, 313.

5. Cf. Locke, *Essay Concerning Human Understanding,* II, i, 23; II, i, 25; II, viii, 11; II, viii, 8. Cf. Dictionary, s.v. *duration, effect, extraneous, extrinsical, impulse, operation, reflection, sensation, soft, soporifick, succession, superinduce, support.* For some evidence of Johnson's general epistemological interest, see Dictionary, s.v. *seeing, species, specifick, symbol, symbolize, tang, tower, think, trigger, troop, turn* v.n. 1, *vividly, unvarying, warn, waste* 1, *way* 15, *wipe* 6, *yield.*

6. "He has quoted no authour whose writings had a tendency to hurt sound religion and morality" (*Life* i, 189).

7. Cf. *Works of Alexander Pope,* ed. Elwin and Courthope, ix (London, 1886), 3–5, Berkeley to Pope, Naples, October 22, 1717, and Johnson's Dictionary, s.v. *few* 1, *go* v.n. 63, *hedge-row, throw* v.a. 2, and *worth* adj. 2; Berkeley's *A Word to the Wise* in *A Miscellany* (London, 1752), p. 98, and Dictionary, s.v. *hand* 1; A

And one remembers Johnson's *argumentum ad lapidem* or kick-the-brick refutation of Berkeley's idealist resolution of the dualism of primary and secondary qualities.[8] Locke was evidently the British philosopher chosen to represent his kind in the Dictionary. He is pre-eminently the philosopher of the Dictionary, one of its most important prose sources.[9] There is also Isaac Watts, whose *Logic* and *Improvement of the Mind* are Dictionary sources from which Johnson chose epistemological passages, and whom Johnson in his *Life of Watts* correctly considers as both critic and disciple of Locke.[10] A recent study has pointed out Johnson's interest, expressed at various times, in such current epistemological themes of a Lockean cast as the distinction of colors by touch, simple ideas and undefinable names, the innate equality of minds, the limitations of human knowledge, and the uncertainty of history.[11] Locke is the philosopher of Johnson's conversation and of his prose writings, of *Rasselas*, for example, where the fine philosophic passage in chapter XLVIII shows Johnson (or Imlac among the Egyptian tombs) at grips with the Lockean heresy that God might if He pleased "superadd to matter a faculty of thinking." [12] In the *Rambler* Johnson alludes to Locke by name five times,[13] and in a passage where he refers to a blind man who identified the color scarlet with the "clangour of a trumpet," he is indebted, probably at first hand, to the *Essay Concerning Human Understanding*.[14] "Ideas not represented by sensible objects are fleeting, variable, and evanescent," laments the Rambler in another place,[15] and "Every idea is obliterated with less difficulty, as it has been more slightly impressed." [16]

Discourse Addressed to the Magistrates in A *Miscellany*, p. 71, and Dictionary, s.v. *run* v.a. 12; *The Analyst or a Discourse Addressed to an Infidel Mathematician* (Dublin, 1734), in Berkeley's *Works* (London, 1898), iii, 24, and Dictionary, s.v. *science* 2. Johnson alludes to Berkeley in *Idler* 10, viii, 38. Contrast the Berkeleyan cast of Ephraim Chambers' *Cyclopaedia*, e.g., the long quotations from the *Principles of Human Knowledge*, s.v. *body, matter, existence, external world*.

8. *Life* i, 471. For a more refined interpretation of Johnson's meaning, see H. F. Hallett, "Dr. Johnson's Refutation of Bishop Berkeley," *Mind*, lvi (April, 1947), 132–147.

9. Quoted some 1,674 times in the first volume (*ante* p. 34, n. 17).

10. *Lives* iii, 308–309. See the recommendation of Locke and Watts in Johnson's Preface to Dodsley's *Preceptor*, *Works* ix, 416. Cf. *Logick* (London, 1745), p. 40, *Improvement of the Mind* (London, 1741), p. 311, and Dictionary, s.v. *meridian* and *vellication*.

11. Kenneth MacLean, *John Locke and English Literature of the Eighteenth Century* (New Haven, 1936), pp. 27, 40–41, 59, 73, 81, 106, 108, 127, 150, 159–161.

12. *Works* xi, 141 (chap. xlviii).

13. 85, vi, 87; 89, vi, 109; 137, vi, 418; 154, vii, 84; 160, vii, 118. Cf. Locke, *Conduct of the Understanding*, §§ 28, 38.

14. 94, vi, 147 and *Essay*, iii, iv, 11; cf. *Life* ii, 190; *Tatler*, No. 227; and Marjorie Nicolson, *Newton Demands the Muse* (Princeton, 1946), pp. 83–85.

15. 110, vi, 248.

16. 185, vii, 261.

The parents of Captator "took care that the blank" of his "understanding should be filled with impressions of the value of money." [17] The following more developed social image centers upon the Lockean doctrine of essences and their impressions upon our senses:

Few have strength of reason to over-rule the perceptions of sense; and yet fewer have curiosity or benevolence to struggle long against the first impression. He therefore who fails to please in his salutation and address, is at once rejected, and never obtains an opportunity of showing his latent excellencies, or essential qualities.[18]

Certain passages which we have already quoted as more abstracted instances of Johnson's mechanical imagery may be re-examined with relevance at this point.

No man can at pleasure obtund or invigorate his senses, prolong the agency of any impulse, or continue the presence of any image traced upon the eye, or any sound infused into the ear.[19]

The works and operations of nature are too great in their extent, or too much diffused in their relations . . . to be reduced to any determinate idea. It is impossible to impress upon our minds an adequate and just representation of an object.[20]

This utter exemption from restraint leaves every anomalous quality to operate in its full extent, and suffers the natural character to diffuse itself to every part of life.[21]

Certain key words in these passages, *agency, impulse, impress, impression, operate, operation,* and related words constitute one of the most frequent and variously modulated motifs in the *Rambler*. We find mournful ideas violently *impressed*,[22] thoughts not immediately *impressed* by sensible objects,[23] *impressions* of dread,[24] *impressions* of precept (set against the inclinations of nature),[25] the violence of *impression* made by elephants upon enemy troops confronting them; [26] human glory or the memory of happiness

17. 197, vii, 328.
18. 166, vii, 154. Cf. Nehemiah Grew, *Cosmologia Sacra* (London, 1701), Bk. II, chap. vi, "Of Wisdom," the four Cardinal Efficients, Body, Sense, Phancy, Reason, and the four ways of Operation of each, e.g., Body upon Body, Body upon Sense, Body upon Phancy, Body upon Reason.
19. 78, vi, 42.
20. 125, vi, 344.
21. 138, vi, 425. Cf. *ante* p. 66. Cf. 137, vi, 417, "Wonder is a pause of reason. . . ."
22. 47, v, 304.
23. 143, vii, 20.
24. 126, vi, 354.
25. 129, vi, 272.
26. 21, vi, 138.

obliterated; [27] the *operation* of flattery, of genius, of remedies, of nature; [28] magnets which *operate* upon the thoughts; [29] vanity, patronage, mischief, predominant appetite, and external accidents [30] which do likewise, and petty qualities, like imperceptible instillations, which *operate* upon our lives unseen and unregarded; [31] the *impulse* of malice or benevolence, of covetousness, of curiosity; [32] the slow succession of soft *impulses* which keep the thoughts of a good-humored man in motion; [33] a secret *impulse* by which Papilius has been kept in motion from his earliest years; [34] a lady who languishes for want of some external *impulse;* [35] the *agency* of magnets [36] and the *agency* of beauty; [37] readers susceptible of pain and pleasure only from powerful *agents;* [38] men *actuated* by natural desires, by various purposes, and by passions; [39] and authors who *actuate* their languor by taking a turn in a garret.[40]

The Lockean stage of epistemology at which Johnson with most of his contemporaries rested was a convenient stage; it supported a distinct way of imagining and using words. Berkeley by saying *Esse* is *percipi*—primary qualities, as well as secondary, are in the perceiver—closed a great imaginative gap no less effectively than if he had affirmed the outside reality of both kinds of qualities. The vividness with which the gap had been imagined may be shown in a passage from one of Addison's *Spectators*—on the Pleasures of the Imagination:

Things would make but a poor Appearance to the Eye, if we saw them only in their proper Figures and Motions: And what Reason can we assign for their exciting in us many of those Ideas which are different from any thing that exists in the Objects themselves, (for such are Light and Colours) were it not to add Supernumerary Ornaments to the Universe, and make it more agreeable to the Imagination? . . . what a rough unsightly Sketch of Nature should we be entertained with, did all

27. 48, v, 309; 103, vi, 205. "Every idea is obliterated with less difficulty, as it has been more slightly impressed" (185, vii, 261).
28. 155, vii, 89; 117, vi, 296; 52, v, 332; 125, vi, 418. Cf. *post* Appendix A.
29. 199, vii, 345. Cf. *post* Appendix A.
30. 135, vi, 406; 146, vii, 38; 118, vi, 302; 131, vi, 384; 128, vi, 365.
31. 72, vi, 7.
32. 115, vi, 278; 131, vi, 387; 132, vi, 391.
33. 72, vi, 8.
34. 141, vii, 2.
35. 42, v, 275.
36. 199, vii, 344.
37. 92, vi, 128.
38. 98, vi, 173.
39. 151, vii, 68; 131, vi, 383; 56, v, 358.
40. 117, vi, 298. Cf. *post* Appendix A.

her Colouring disappear, and the several Distinctions of Light and Shade vanish? [41]

This of course is only a naïve literary man's conception—that it might be possible to strip the world of its secondary qualities, so that it could be *seen* as it really *is*, a bare construct of mechanical operations and mathematical laws, a plain museum of the six simple machines.[42] Yet we may wonder whether this is not the most natural way in which to realize the philosophy. A recent critic has conferred upon the fundamental dogma of the philosophy the name "Postulate of an Impoverished Reality." [43] In the world of this postulate one was, as Addison said, "every where entertained with pleasing Shows and Apparitions." One was surrounded by unseen corpuscular forces which *operated* upon one's nerves. It was a world where Burke might speculate: "beauty acts by relaxing the solids of the whole system"; [44] where Lessing might be interested in marble sculpture, but was capable of thinking that it might be better if oil painting had never been invented—that "mere color and transitory expression have no ideal because Nature has proposed to herself nothing definite in them." [45] It was a very abstract world and so it harmonized readily with certain neo-classic esthetic principles. Buffon, a natural historian, would recommend "care in . . . expressing things only in the most general terms." [46] Johnson would neglect the streaks of the tulip and, while rejecting the overparticular and accidental diction of trades and "arts," would make notable use of the general and more readily extensible diction and ideas of those physical and mathematical sciences that were branches of "philosophy."

A concomitant of abstraction was regularity and predictability. "At this time of day," said one of Johnson's Dictionary sources, ". . . all the general powers and capacities of matter are . . . clearly understood." [47] This regularity had for a century found

41. *Spectator*, No. 413, June 24, 1712. Addison refers the reader to the Eighth Chapter of the Second Book of Mr. Locke's *Essay*.

42. Or, in the last analysis, as a later philosopher has phrased it, an "unearthly ballet of bloodless categories" (F. H. Bradley, *Principles of Logic*, Bk. III, Part II, chap. iv, § 16). Cf. A. N. Whitehead, *Science and the Modern World* (New York, 1925), p. 80.

43. Iredell Jenkins, "The Postulate of an Impoverished Reality," *Journal of Philosophy*, xxxix (September, 1942), 533–547.

44. *Philosophical Inquiry into . . . the Sublime and Beautiful*, IV, xix.

45. *Laokoön*, ed. Hugo Blümner (Berlin, 1880), pp. 469, 399, Lessing's ms. remains. Cf. F. O. Nolte, *Lessing's Laocoön* (Lancaster, 1940), p. 37.

46. *Address Delivered before the French Academy upon the Day of His Reception*, August 25, 1753.

47. Bentley, *Sermons, Works* (London, 1838), iii, 71. "All the established laws of nature, are constituted and preserved by gravitation alone" (*idem*, p. 75).

various parallels, both more and less metaphoric, in the movements of man and in his fabrications: in the automata ambulatory and volant, for example, of Bishop Wilkins' *Mathematical Magic* [48] and the toy coach and horses that are said to have run on the table for Louis XIV; [49] in the absolute state (if a degree of *Geistesgeschichtlich* exaggeration is excusable), in the machinelike precision of its army marching on the broad axial boulevard of its planned city, in the science of human society and the Lockean theory of constitutionalism. [50] The metaphoric and imaginative value of the new science in such realms may be summed up in the title of a poem published in 1728 by Newton's friend J. T. Desaguliers: *The Newtonian System of the World, the Best Model of Government.* More recently, after the crude animal spirits of Descartes, the train of imaginations of Hobbes, and the "moral Gravitation" of Shaftesburyan litterateurs, [51] a more refined psychology of association had made a subtler entrance for the laws of regularity into the human mind. It is not certain—perhaps not even likely—that Johnson read Hume's *Treatise of Human Nature*, [52] but the program conceived by Hume was characteristic of the age. In the speculative passage at the close of the *Opticks* Newton had suggested:

If natural Philosophy, in all its Parts, by pursuing this the inductive Method, shall at length be perfected, the Bounds of Moral Philosophy will be also enlarged.

The laws of association (of resemblance, of contiguity in place or time, of cause and effect), [53] says Hume, with an eye on Newton,

are therefore the principles of union or cohesion among our simple ideas, and in the imagination supply the place of that inseparable connexion, by which they are united in our memory. Here is a kind of ATTRACTION, which in the mental world will be found to have as extraordinary

---

48. *Mathematical Magic* (London, 1691), pp. 172–173. Cf. Johnson's Dictionary, s.v. *ambulatory.*

49. David Brewster, *Letters on Natural Magic* (New York, ca. 1832), pp. 241–242.

50. See John H. Randall, Jr., *The Making of the Modern Mind* (Boston, 1940), chaps. xiii and xiv, and the highly suggestive synthesis by Lewis Mumford, *The Culture of Cities* (New York, 1938), chap. ii, "Court, Parade, and Capital," esp. pp. 77, 88, 91–97.

51. James Thomson, *Liberty*, V, 1. 257. Cf. *Spectator*, No. 120, *Guardian*, No. 126, and Alan D. McKillop, *The Background of Thomson's Seasons* (Minneapolis, 1942), pp. 31–41.

52. Cf. *Life* ii, 236.

53. Reduced to a single association of contiguity in time by Hartley's theory of vibrations in the medullary substance (*Observations on Man* [London, 1749], i, 65–72; I, ɪ, 10–11).

effects as in the natural, and to shew itself in as many and as various forms.[54]

And Hume looked on the systematic study of these mental principles as a specially English, specially eighteenth-century program, following the physical empiricism of Bacon at about the same interval as that between Thales and Socrates.[55] It is true that by temperament and religious conviction Johnson resisted the new regularizing of the human soul. In a later political pamphlet he was to write:

It seems to be almost the universal error of historians to suppose it politically, as it is physically true, that every effect has a proportionate cause. In the inanimate action of matter upon matter, the motion produced can be but equal to the force of the moving power; but the operations of life, whether private or publick, admit no such laws. The caprices of voluntary agents laugh at calculation. It is not always that there is a strong reason for a great event. Obstinacy and flexibility, malignity and kindness, give place alternately to each other, and the reason of these vicissitudes, however important may be the consequences, often escapes the mind in which the change is made.[56]

But there were many ways of participating in the spirit of the age. There was, notably for Johnson, the stylistic way of mechanical metaphor and diction—not to elaborate here on the implications of his persistent parallel, balance, and precise antithesis. It has been said of Johnson that the temper that made other men of his age deists, made him the kind of rational classicist in criticism that he was. The same temper had also much to do with the style of his moral writings. Even in a series of essays like the *Rambler*, where Johnson spoke for the spiritual nature of man, the will and its responsibilities, he yielded to his century in his imaginative idiom, the language of mechanical philosophy which he found, both literal and metaphoric, in writers from Bacon to Locke and which he applied to psychology in a metaphoric way that was in degree of abstraction and pervasiveness peculiarly his own.

The Cartesian separation of spirit from matter and insistence upon the thinking self has been considered one of the causes of literary introspection and self-analysis at the end of the seventeenth

54. *Treatise of Human Nature*, I, i, iv. Cf. Ernest Mossner in *PQ*, xxv (April, 1946), 138.

55. *Treatise* (Oxford, 1888), Introduction, pp. xx–xxi. Cf. *Rambler* 24, v, 157; *Preface to Shakespeare*, ix, 272; MacLean, *op. cit.*, p. 12.

56. *Falkland's Islands*, x, 54. Cf. Johnson's humorous description of the mind as a mechanical tool—vice, file, or razor—(Boswell's *Journal of a Tour to the Hebrides*, ed. Pottle and Bennett [New York, 1936], p. 20).

century and the later self-glorification of pre-romanticism.[57] In the Lockean psychology, as its implications unfolded, man's conscious self or his soul, a kind of anomalous prisoner in an invisible world of matter, received through the operations upon it of corpuscular agents many and vivid reports of its milieu but all indirect, and the most vivid having a low degree of reliability. Living within the integument of a body no more securely known than the bodies outside it, the soul in its isolation was the passive receiver of many impressions, upon which at a second stage it thought much, inferred and constructed the multitude of elaborate things which constitute the world. The soul was empty and abstract, yet center and protagonist of all that is known and all knowing. A recent writer has traced the working of these concepts from the philosophy of Locke through the structure of American democracy into such esthetic expressions as the blank and unrewarded independence of three "Daughters of Revolution" in the painting by Grant Wood.[58] In the present context it seems relevant to say at least that the morally introspective bent of Samuel Johnson, no less than the hypochondriac, was highly compatible with the kind of medical, chemical, and mechanical philosophy from which he drew the images characteristic of his prose style. At a slightly earlier date Pope in his philosophic poetry had drawn on teleological applications of the new science to convey the concept of presiding and providential Deity that lives in all things and makes one universe—"Spreads undivided, operates unspent,"—or his editor Warburton had quoted Newton's *Opticks* in a footnote to show how Nature (in the motion of comets) sometimes deviates from law.[59] And Thomson in his *Seasons* had fused philosophic diction with more highly colored pictures of nature within the same frame of reference.

> Lo! from the dread immensity of space
> Returning with accelerated course,
> The rushing comet to the sun descends.[60]
>
> Hail, Source of Being! Universal Soul. . . .
> At thy command the vernal sun awakes
> The torpid sap, detruded to the root
> By wintry winds, that now in fluent dance

57. Marjorie Nicolson, "The Early Stage of Cartesianism in England," SP, xxvi (1929), 356–374. For some objections, see the review in PQ, ix (April, 1930), 179.

58. F. S. C. Northrop, *The Meeting of East and West* (New York, 1946), pp. 55, 160, and Plate IX.

59. *Essay on Man*, i, 150, 274.

60. *Summer*, ll. 1703 ff.

And lively fermentation mounting spreads
All this innumerous-coloured scene of things.[61]

As certain sciences developed in the course of the eighteenth century and became more subtle, they lent themselves even more to deistic, to pantheistic, or to Platonic outward lookings through poetic imagery. Electricity, for example, something mysterious, a coruscant blue and green flame, elusively and unpredictably spirit-like, was more to the mind of an Erasmus Darwin or a Shelley than the colorless mechanics which Addison had supposed to be reality.

> And from a star upon its forehead shoot,
> Like swords of azure fire or golden spears . . .
> Vast beams like spokes of some invisible wheel
> Which whirl as the orb whirls, swifter than thought,
> Filling the abyss with sun-like lightnings,
> And perpendicular now, and now transverse,
> Pierce the dark soil, and as they pierce and pass
> Make bare the secrets of the earth's deep heart.[62]

Newton's hypothesis of an ether as primordial essence from which proceed both matter and force seemed to imaginative scientists in the early nineteenth century on the way to verification. And romantic poets, by a parallel imaginative process, were busy putting back into nature the soul which the school of Descartes had taken out.[63] But the scientific imagery of Johnson, coming chronologically between that of Thomson and Pope and that of Shelley and written in the moral spirit of an earlier era, works in an opposite way. It conveys partly social ideas (the annual migration of pleasure seekers to the country, the tribes of human pests like insects), but mostly psychological and moral ideas (the impressions made by things upon the mind, the operation or impulse of motives, the attraction of desires and repulsion of fears, or the equilibration of

61. *Spring*, ll. 556 ff. Cf. Johnson's Dictionary, s.v. *accelerate, adhesive, agglomerate, congeal, delirious, disease, fermentation, irritate, palpitation, putrefaction, rotation, suffocate, sulphur, torpid, vegetation, vibration.* Cf. Herbert Drennon, "James Thomson's Contact with Newtonianism and His Interest in Natural Philosophy," *PMLA,* xlix (March, 1934), 71–80; McKillop, *The Background of Thomson's Seasons,* chaps. i and ii.

62. *Prometheus Unbound*, IV, 270–279. Shelley describes the Spirit of the Earth, in terms strongly suggestive of discoveries announced by Humphrey Davy in 1807 and 1808, the electro-chemical analysis of earths into potassium, barium, magnesium, and other new elements (Carl Grabo, "Electricity, the Spirit of the Earth, in Shelley's *Prometheus Unbound*," *PQ,* vi (April, 1927), 133–150.

63. Barfield, *History in English Words* (New York, 1926), p. 201. Cf. Hoxie N. Fairchild, *The Romantic Quest* (New York, 1931), p. 145; Mark Schorer's account of Blake's antipathy to Bacon, Newton, and Locke in "Blake and the Cosmic Nadir," *Sewanee Review,* xliii (April–June, 1935), 219.

the two, the ebullition or effervescence of genius or of fancy, the analysis of primogeneal mental qualities, ideas homogeneous and heterogeneous); never the mystery of any presence "whose dwelling is the light of setting suns." Johnson's *Ramblers,* as a plausible outcome of the very abstraction, simplification, and systematization of the world seen by the mechanical science, exhibit perhaps the most concentrated use in English literature of mechanical imagery turned inward to the analysis of the soul.

2. *Philosophic Diction Extended*

"POWERFUL preservatives" which in one *Rambler* hinder a prejudice from spreading its infection [1] have a less metaphoric parallel in another where "many who have laid down rules of intellectual health, think preservatives easier than remedies," [2] or in others where *preservatives* against evil counteract one another, or where we find *preservatives* against the infection of the writer's malady, against the vanities and vexations of the world, and against temptations to falsehood.[3] In the same way, the *palliatives* of incurable miseries [4] and the cure for human miseries which is not *radical* but *palliative* [5] have less metaphoric echoes in *palliation* of faults, failings, and occurrences,[6] the *palliating* of wickedness, failings, absurdities, remote evils, and faults.[7] In one passage we find "physicians who, when they cannot *mitigate* pain, destroy sensibility, and endeavour to conceal by *opiates* the inefficacy of their other medicines"; [8] in others, the *mitigation* of pain or of duty,[9] miseries, pain, a sentence, or penalties *mitigated.*[10] We find the words *malignity* and *malignant* in contexts of a highly medical flavor. "Infatuation strengthens by degrees, and, like the poison of opiates, weakens without any external symptom of malignity." [11] "The particles that impregnate the air" are known only "by their salutary or malignant effects." [12] But *malignity* and *malignant*

1. 58, v, 373.
2. 47, v, 304.
3. 126, vi, 353; 2, v, 11; 6, v, 37; 96, vi, 158.
4. 143, vii, 16.
5. 32, vi, 209.
6. 54, v, 348; 65, v, 415.
7. 8, v, 49; 28, vi, 185; 31, v, 201; 41, v, 266; 76, vi, 31.
8. 150, vii, 57.
9. 47, vi, 305; 65, vi, 416.
10. 32, v, 208; 49, v, 314; 114, vi, 274, 276.
11. 89, vi, 111.
12. 72, vi, 7.

have many less physical uses [13] and with their cognates *malice*,[14] *malevolence*,[15] *malevolent*,[16] *maliciousness*,[17] form one of the largest families of moral words in the *Rambler*. *Torpid* is a word which, when applied to wasps, in a passage which contains the words *papilionaceous* and *ephemera*, has the color of natural history,[18] but is a term of physical description which applies metaphorically to persons who languish in anxieties, to the polite and gay during the months of summer, to human faculties, and to risibility.[19] The spiritual sin of *acedia* finds many other ways into the Rambler's meditations: in such physical versions as *stagnation*,[20] *languor*,[21] *languishment*,[22] and *lassitude;* [23] in the moral forms of *dejection*,[24] *despondency*,[25] *indolence*,[26] and *procrastination*.[27] The *diseases, infections, maladies,* and *symptoms* [28] of the soul have their more abstract representatives in *debility*,[29] *infirmity*,[30] and *imbecility*.[31]

A simply mechanical meaning for the word *asperity* appears in a passage where "angular bodies and uneven surfaces lose their points and asperities by frequent attrition against one another," [32] and in another where unpolished gems are not correctly valued "till their asperities are smoothed and their incrustations rubbed away," [33] or in the oxymoronic phrase "asperities of smoothness." [34] But a physiological conception, the irritation of living tissue, is present when disease and infirmity are *exasperated* by luxury,[35]

13. *Malignity*, e.g., 4, v, 26; 9, v, 55; 11, v, 67; 112, vi, 262; 114, vi, 273; 119, vi, 308; *malignant*, e.g., 2, v, 15; 149, vii, 53; 177, vii, 216; 183, vii, 249, 251.
14. e.g., 22, v, 147; 32, v, 211; 46, v, 299; 56, v, 357.
15. e.g., 3, v, 19; 5, v, 31; 10, v, 62; 11, v, 66.
16. e.g., 3, v, 19.
17. e.g., 20, v, 136.
18. 82, vi, 67.
19. 134, vi, 402; 124, vi, 340; 83, vi, 72; 125, vi, 349.
20. 124, vi, 304; 198, vii, 336.
21. 77, vi, 40; 178, vii, 223.
22. 124, v, 343.
23. 207, vii, 390.
24. 133, vi, 396; 141, vii, 5; 176, vii, 213.
25. 25, v, 164.
26. 127, vi, 360; 130, vi, 377; 350, vii, 61.
27. 155, vii, 90; 134, vi, 403.
28. See *post* Appendix A.
29. 48, v, 307.
30. 58, v, 374.
31. 48, v, 307; 148, vii, 49; 176, vii, 213. Cf. Quincy's *Lexicon Physico-Medicum*, s.v. *debility, imbecility, lassitude, malignant*.
32. 138, vi, 424.
33. 166, vii, 154.
34. 122, vi, 327.
35. 58, v, 274.

when tenderness is irritable to the smallest *asperity*,[36] or in the *exasperating* of difficulty by remedies.[37] Thirdly, the meaning tends to be literally social or psychological in *asperity* of sarcasm, of misfortune, or of contradiction.[38] Johnson's fondness for the conception appears in such related expressions as *acrimony* of malice or of evil,[39] *acrimonious* resentment,[40] *acerbity* of exclamation,[41] and *exacerbation* of diseases, human misery, or hatred.[42]

The very abstractness of Johnson's philosophic imagery lent itself to extensions, from the richest and nearly colorful cores of metaphor to certain more pervasive and sinewy, if almost transparent, qualities of diction. A Derham in his *Physico-Theology* might write of the man "whose ardour of inclination eggs him forward, and buoys him up under all opposition." [43] Or a better stylist, Watts, might write more vividly: "Children . . . perceive and forget a hundred things in an Hour; the Brain is so soft that it receives immediately all Impressions like Water or liquid Mud." [44] Or, in another vein, literal and imageless, yet correct, Cheyne in a passage quoted by Watts might refer to studies that have "no Tendency to rectify the Will, to sweeten the Temper, or mend the Heart." [45] It is characteristic of less imaginative writers that their imagery does not tend to affect more abstract parts of their discourse; when brief essays in metaphor are made, they produce solid, homely, and vivid metaphors like that of Watts, or they end in bungles like that of Derham. Johnson rightly objected to the parody of his style attempted by Blair in the phrases "perturbation of vice" and "vacuity of folly." He said "the Imitators of his style had not hit it." [46] A nice discrimination of the etymological sense of learned words and so of the images latent in them was one of Johnson's chief talents—a management of very generalized philosophic words so as not to lose the logic of their images and an extension of the principle of this imagery into a precise and quiet use of many even more transparent words. In Johnson's prose the lexicographer joins the stylist in an accuracy both of under-

36. 112, vi, 259.
37. 66, v, 420.
38. 26, v, 170; 32, v, 210; 74, vi, 21.
39. 144, vii, 23; 32, v, 209.
40. 40, v, 258.
41. 200, vii, 347.
42. 32, v, 211; 114, vi, 272; 185, vii, 261. See *post* Appendix A, *acerbity, acrimony, asperity,* and their cognates.
43. *Physico-Theology* (London, 1714), p. 275; V, i.
44. *Improvement of the Mind* (London, 1741), p. 255.
45. *Idem,* p. 328. Cf. George Cheyne, *Essay of Health and Long Life* (London, 1725), Preface, p. v.
46. *Boswell Papers* xiii, 40–41, Ashbourne, 19 September 1777.

standing and of imagination. Examples of more abstract yet physical imagery, of a wide range, might be multiplied from the *Rambler* almost indefinitely:

It has been usual in all ages for moralists to repress the swellings of vain hope . . . by instances of . . . sudden subversions of the highest eminences of greatness.[47]

In proportion as those who write on temporary subjects are exalted .above their merit at first, they are afterwards depressed below it.[48]

The care . . . has been, that whenever they decline into obliquities, they should tend towards the side of safety.[49]

There is always room to deviate on either side of rectitude without rushing against apparent absurdity.[50]

There is in his negligence a rude inartificial majesty, which . . . swells the mind by its plenitude and diffusion.[51]

Lest the superfluities of intellect run to waste, it is no vain speculation . . . how we may govern our thoughts, restrain them from irregular motions, or confine them from boundless dissipation.[52]

Experience soon shows us the tortuosities of imaginary rectitude, the complications of simplicity, and the asperities of smoothness.[53]

The most forcible arguments [should] be produced in the latter part of an oration, lest they should be effaced or perplexed by supervenient images.[54]

We hourly find such [narrators] clouding the facts which they tend to illustrate.[55]

Whoever aspires to the notice of the publick . . . must quicken the frigid and soften the obdurate.[56]

Curiosity . . . makes us taste everything with joy, however otherwise insipid, by which it may be quenched.[57]

Johnson reminds us that *rectitude* is straight, *simplicity* simple, *asperity* rough, the *obdurate* hard, the *insipid* tasteless; that *superfluities* run, and that *plenitude* is full. The physical images that lie

47. 29, v, 191.
48. 106, vi, 224.
49. 129, vi, 372.
50. 129, vi, 372.
51. 122, vi, 331.
52. 8, v, 48.
53. 122, vi, 327.
54. 207, vii, 390.
55. 122, vi, 328.
56. 127, vi, 361.
57. 103, vi, 204.

inconspicuous in Latin derivatives—*repress, subversions, eminences, exalted, depressed, decline, obliquities, deviate, rectitude,
superfluities, effaced, supervenient, plenitude, diffusion*—are
brought into relief through his exactitude either in matching these
words with one another or in interlocking and contrasting them
with plainer and more concrete words—*swellings, run, smoothness,
swells, clouding, soften, taste*. He galvanizes a curious vitality from
the rigidities of Latin abstraction. At other places in Johnson's
writing the same realization of meaning may be observed in the
application of abstract words to quite solid or concrete descriptions—"At last the green path began to decline from its first
tendency," "What arts of cultivation can elevate a shrub?" [58]—
or, on the other hand, where the Latin or Greek name of a thing
is established or stereotyped, in the reversal of this name into
plain English. Johnson once in speaking of a bulldog changed the
word *tenuity* to "thin part"; [59] in the *Rambler* he speaks of "the
dreadful symptom of canine madness, termed by physicians the
dread of water"; [60] and there seems something eminently Johnsonian in the fact that while Boswell wrote a *Tour to the Hebrides*,
Johnson, avoiding a Latin proper and concrete name without any
abstract depths of meaning, wrote a *Journey to the Western Islands*,
or that throughout the Dictionary he refers to the *Pseudodoxia
Epidemica* by the plainer, if Latin, name *Browne's Vulgar Errours*.

Johnson's innocence about English etymologies ("May not
spider be *spy dor*, the insect that watches the *dor*," [i.e., the bumble-
bee]? "I have sometimes derived it [*lattice*] from *let* and *eye; leteys*,
that which *lets* the eye.") has been a stock source of amusement
to critics of the Dictionary, but some of the Dictionary definitions
show his persistent realization of another class of etymologies.

autopsy.   Ocular demonstration; seeing a thing one's self.

insult.   1. The act of leaping upon anything. . . .
          2. Act or speech of insolence or contempt.

polite.   1. Glossy; smooth.
          2. Elegant of manners.

result.   1. Resilience; act of flying back.
          2. Consequence; effect. . . .

58. 65, v, 413; 25, v, 163. Cf. *Debates in Parliament, Works* xiii, 514, malt *exalted*
in the still; xiii, 4, Mr. Onslow *exalted* to the chair; xii, 121, a lieutenant *exalted* to a
captain; xii, 156, *degradation* of a man who was *exalted*.
59. *Life* iii, 190.
60. 6, v, 35. Until the 4th edition of 1756 the text read "the hydrophobia, or
dread of water." Cf. *post* pp. 123, 134.

version. 1. Change; transformation.
2. Change of direction.
3. Translation.[61]

For words which have the credit of antiquity in their roots Johnson's method is that of rigorous etymology and exhaustive analogy. He is a connoisseur of meanings thus deduced. A closely related phenomenon of his prose style is the homogeneity of texture created by the use of certain generic ideas of motion and space in a wide variety of contexts. Thus, in the *Rambler: abstracted* philosophy and *abstraction* from common occurrences; [62] ideas *conjoined, conjunction* of pride and want; [63] a mind *contracted* by solitude, *contraction* of income, *contraction* of the channel of a current; [64] hearts or syllables *dilated;* [65] meteorous pleasures *dissipated, dissipation* of understanding; [66] *dissolution* of ice and of gay societies; [67] *incursions* of disease, of appetite, and of error; [68] *exuberance* of money, of inhabitants, of faculties, and of pride; *exuberant* eulogies; [69] to *intercept* sympathy, *interception* of beams; [70] officious *interposition* of matchmakers, *interposition* of darker bodies to invigorate the luster of diamonds; [71] principles of vegetation *obstructed, obstruction* of happiness; [72] *obtrusion* of new ideas, lectures which *obtrude* themselves upon the unwilling; [73] to preclude liberty, *preclusion* of adventitious amusements; [74] to *propagate* panic, scandal, or virtue; [75] to *repress* a rival, *repression* of eagerness; [76] disputes or precepts *transmitted* to posterity.[77] The span

61. See the longer analysis s.v. *prejudice* and the discussion of the word *arrive* in the *Plan* (*Works* ix, 183); the use of *ingredient* in the passage from Browne (*Pseudodoxia*, III, xxiii) quoted in the Dictionary, s.v. *alexipharmick;* Pope's use of *result* (*Odyssey*, XI, 735–738) quoted by Johnson in the *Life of Pope*, Par. 332; *Lives* iii, 231; and Woodward, *Natural History* (London, 1695), p. 54, "furious and impetuous insults of the sea."
62. 18, v, 118; 175, vii, 205.
63. 143, vii, 19; 149, vii, 54.
64. 177, vii, 216; 26, v, 171; 108, vi, 237.
65. 27, v, 175; 92, vi, 132.
66. 68, v, 430; 85, vi, 87.
67. 186, vii, 268; 124, vi, 340.
68. 33, v, 217; 70, v, 444; 129, vi, 371.
69. 26, v, 169; 154, vii, 87; 173, vii, 198; 56, v, 360; 136, vi, 415.
70. 149, vii, 52; 86, vi, 90.
71. 115, vi, 278; 150, vii, 60.
72. 159, vii, 115; 123, vi, 334.
73. 103, vi, 205; 196, vii, 322.
74. 93, vi, 141; 135, vi, 410.
75. 25, v, 165; 183, vii, 251; 49, v, 318.
76. 21, v, 139; 116, vi, 287.
77. 40, v, 258; 129, vi, 370. See the *Rambler passim* for similar subdued expressions of physical relation in more uniform contexts; see, for example, *post* Appendix A, *aberration, abscission, adhesion, attraction, collision, diffusion, dissipation, dissolution, infusion, revolution.*

or scope of Johnson's usage is of basic and primitive meanings—
ideas which join ice and gay societies, dark bodies and matchmakers, principles of vegetation and of happiness. If one were to
select some single word as the type of Johnson's diction, it might
be from the series just quoted, *dissipation, exuberance,*[78] *propagate,*[79] or *transmit,* bridges of the most abstract and essential sort
between the mechanical and socio-mental realms, and among
the most frequently used words in Johnson's writing. The vocabulary of "hard" words is a kind of basic English, like the language
of integers and particles proposed by Bishop Wilkins. Some of the
expressions may strike us as odd—to *obtund* remorse,[80] to *effuse*
social luster,[81] to *object* the indecency of encroaching upon some-
one's life [82]—but such expressions are functions of the extreme
ductility of the pristine Latin roots, and as such enjoy a guaranteed
meaning.

We have often been told of the generality and abstraction of
Johnson's style. It is worth while to notice the structure of that
abstraction, the quality of the generalities or schemata which con-
stantly overshadow his argument. Generality in a strictly logical
sense is not equivalent to magnificence, universality, or cosmology,
but in a Platonic sense, conveyed perhaps better by stylistic implication than by logical precision, it is. There are the abstractions
of mathematics, logic, and metaphysics, or on the other hand the
generalities of evasion, ambiguity, vagueness, and redundancy,
but there is also—perhaps somewhere between these other
two kinds—what was called by Johnson the "grandeur of generality."

As we read Johnson, we are continually reminded:

Not only (I), as we have recently seen, of motion and rest, cause
and effect, *operation, impulse, agitation,*[83] *incursion, interception,
propagation,* and *transmission* in their most attenuated and variously applicable forms; but: (II) Of time and space in their most
universal, spatial, spacious, and chronological implications. We
find *periodical* remorse, tortures, vicissitudes, eulogies—*periodical*

78. Cf. "exuberate into an atheist," *Life* iv, 98.
79. Cf. "propagate procerity," *Works* iv, 532; *Life* i, 308.
80. 72, vii, 198.
81. 124, vi, 341.
82. 5, v, 27.
83. *Agitation* of the passions, 156, vii, 98; of the spirits, 117, vi, 297; of the water
during a storm, 103, vi, 202; of a coach, 133, vi, 394. Cf. *excursion,* 180, vii, 233;
118, vi, 304; 137, vi, 418; 119, vi, 309; 147, vii, 40.
Cf. *post* Appendix A, *accelerate, actuate,* and cognate words listed under these,
and *velocity.*

writers and sheets.[84] *Adjacent* is applied to villages and to difficulty; [85] the lands of an heiress are *contiguous* to those of a young gentleman.[86] Migrations, visits, excursions are *annual, biennial, nocturnal,* and *momentaneous.*[87] One thinks upon *duration, perpetuation, perpetuity,*[88] *alternation, succession,* and *vicissitude*—especially *vicissitude,*[89] stock idea of the cosmological and teleological writers,[90] for seasons, satellites, and planets, employed no less frequently by Johnson for the ups and downs of the human *terrestrial* existence, the lot of man upon the *terraqueous globe.*[91] (III) Of quantity and degree, increase and decrease, all the more and less of human experience in terms of largest implication. *Abatement,* one of the most frequently used words in the *Rambler,* is of character, of hope, of confidence—of a way of living, of expenses, and of rent.[92] On all sides we encounter the versatile words *diminution, deduction, deficience,* or *addition, superaddition, aggravation, augmentation, multiplication,* and *plenitude.* (IV) Of likeness and difference, distinctions and antitheses—a category of meaning which has the closest affinity for Johnson's moral interest in what is right, normal, or standard, and the deviations from it and for larger considerations of teleological harmony. *Heterogeneous* applies to sciences, principles, notions, ideas, and bodies.[93] *Accommodate, accommodation,* and *commodious,* prime terms of the teleological writers,[94] are encountered throughout in social and literary contexts—to *accommodate* disputes, dress *accommodated* to fortune, *accommodation* of sound to sense.[95] The

84. 155, vii, 94; 85, vi, 86; 21, v, 142; 193, vii, 306; 193, vii, 308; 23, v, 151.

85. 135, vi, 409; 146, vii, 35; 66, v, 419.

86. 34, v, 220.

87. See *post* Appendix A, *annual, biennial, nocturnal, momentaneous;* cf. *coeval, diurnal, perennial, chronological.*

88. Cf. 67, v, 428; 89, vi, 112, *perpetual* motion.

89. See *post* Appendix A, *vicissitude.*

90. Bentley, *Sermons, Works* (London, 1838), iii, 121, 158, 162, 185, 189; Cheyne, *Philosophical Principles* (London, 1734), Part I, pp. 207, 245, 247; Hale, *Primitive Origination of Mankind* (London, 1667), p. 96; Ray, *Wisdom of God in the Creation* (London, 1709), pp. 77, 229; Woodward, *Natural History of the Earth* (London, 1695), pp. 248, 267, 270.

91. 24, v, 157; cf. Derham, *Physico-Theology* (London, 1714), *passim,* chapter headings.

92. 188, vii, 278; 115, vi, 278; 130, vi, 382; 26, v, 171; 132, vi, 389; 35, v, 231.

93. See *post* Appendix A, *heterogeneous.*

94. Bentley, *Sermons, Works,* iii, 19, 55, 59; Cheyne, *Philosophical Principles,* Part I, pp. 146, 170, 240, 316, 332; Hale, *Primitive Origination of Mankind,* p. 1; Ray, *Wisdom of God in the Creation,* p. 103; Derham, *Physico-Theology,* pp. 39, 73, 79, 100, 201, 275, 293, 294, 305, 412, n. 6.

95. 142, vii, 8; 149, vii, 54; 92, vi, 129. Cf. *Letters* i, 329; ii, 367, 394; *Life* v. 310, n. 3.

Rambler presents a constant texture of *congruity, parity, diversity, contrariety, obliquity, opposition, repugnance;* of what is *symmetrical, commensurate, incommensurate,*[96] *consistent, equal, equivalent.* (V) In like manner, finally, of substance and essence and more frequently their opposites, the accidental, superficial, or unnecessary. "The essential and necessary substance," says the Rambler, "of which only the form is left to be adjusted by choice." [97] *Adventitious,* a characteristic Johnsonian word, applies to gladness, miseries, motives, amusements, decorations and disguises, pain, and beauty.[98] The notorious word *adscititious* means almost the same and applies to happiness, qualities, character, passions, and excellence.[99] *Supernumerary* applies to gratuities, moments, distress, and a bottle.[100] In various contexts appear *appendages, concomitants, superficies, superfluities;* what is *elemental, essential, intrinsick,* or on the other hand *accidental, collateral, external, extraneous, extrinsick, fortuitous, secondary, subaltern, subsidiary, superficial,* and *supplemental.*

It is worth recalling that Boswell, speaking of a quality of Johnson's prose which may be less perceptible to the twentieth century, his "splendour of images," mentions at the same time his "comprehension of thought," and in another place joins Johnson's "brilliancy of fancy" with "force of understanding," and in yet another alludes to a "union of perspicuity and splendour." [101] A perceptive modern critic, remarking that in Johnson's day there had arisen a vague suspicion that prose literature ought to go deeper than the Addisonian conversation, and that Johnson, harking back to Sir Thomas Browne, attempted to restore to prose certain of its lost powers, speaks of Johnson's "chiaroscuro," his "evident effort to suggest something more than can be defined." [102] The quality of Johnson's prose which the critic discerned is perhaps also indefinable but may be suggested in the statement, summarizing our argument of the last few pages, that Johnson is continually metaphoric and hence abstract and generic on a grand scale. "Animals are . . . analogous to Vegetables in many things," wrote Johnson's contemporary, the associationist Hartley, "and

96. See *post* Appendix A, *commensurate, incommensurate, symmetrical.*
97. 131, vi, 384.
98. See *post* Appendix A, *adventitious.*
99. See *post* Appendix A, *adscititious.*
100. 190, vii, 290; 108, vi, 234; 126, vi, 353; 109, vi, 241.
101. *Life* ii, 335; iv, 116, 366; cf. iii, 317; iv, 428; and i, 40, n. 3, Miss Seward's opinion.
102. P. H. Frye, "Dryden and the Critical Canons of the Eighteenth Century," *The University Studies of the University of Nebraska,* vii (Lincoln, 1907), 17–19.

Vegetables to Minerals: So that there seems to be a perpetual Thread of Analogy continued from the most perfect Animal to the most imperfect Mineral, even till we come to elementary Bodies themselves." [103] If we add to Hartley's scale the realm of mind, we have the universe of analogy within which Johnson moves. Johnson matches the physical scale of analogy, but especially the lower, mechanical, and elemental end of it, against the realm of mind. The two halves of experience, the mechanical outer, the vital, spiritual, and voluntary inner, with their partial resemblances (the mechanics of psychology) are his theme. And as he has the terms of either realm at his command, so he has the terms of the more transparent, algebraic realm where mechanics and psychology and all things else are subsumed. The thoughtful imagery of which Boswell spoke is an imagery of high shadows on the screen of the categories, of lengthened metaphysical implications.

3. Philosophic Humor

A STRAIN of gross humor in technical Latin and Latinate grandiloquence had been demonstrated by the pompous gulls and mock pedants of Ben Jonson [1] and in the satire on words in his *Poetaster*,[2] where imitating the vomit of words in Lucian's Dialogue he anticipated *Lexiphanes,* the loudest satire on the words of Samuel Johnson. In the early days of the Royal Society, Shadwell's virtuoso Sir Nicholas Gimcrack had spoken of "Emittent and Recipient," of the "Superficies or surface" of the "humid Element," of the "follicular impulsion of Air." [3] More recently Pope, Swift, and Arbuthnot in their satirical and burlesque sketches had taken pleasure in a similar bumptious overpiling of words. Dr. Robert Norris, on being called to treat the "Strange and Deplorable Frenzy of Mr. J——N D——IS," inquires:

What Regimen have you observ'd since he has been under your Care? You remember, I suppose, the Passage of *Celsus,* which says, if the Patient, on the third Day, have an Interval, suspend the Medicaments at Night? let Fumigations be used to corroborate the Brain; I hope you have upon no Account promoted Sternutation by Hellebore.[4]

103. David Hartley, *Observations on Man* (London, 1749), i, 294. Cf. the quotations in Johnson's Dictionary from Watts, s.v. *sound* and *sweet.*
1. See *Epicoene*, IV, iv, 68, the speech of Daw on mania; V, iii, Cutbeard and Otter on the impediments to valid marriage.
2. V, iii, 465–530.
3. Duncan, *The New Science and English Literature in the Classical Period* (Menasha, 1913), pp. 74, 79, 108.
4. Pope and Swift, *Miscellanies in Verse and Prose* (London, 1744), "The Narra-

And the *Memoirs of Martinus Scriblerus*—"infatuated scholar" [5]—
was a natural ground for a more pointed form of such pleasant-
ries.

In pursuance of his Theory, he supposed the constrictors of the Eyelids
must be strengthened in the supercilious, the abductors in drunkards and
contemplative men, who have the same steady and grave motion of the
eye. That the buccinators or blowers up of the Cheeks, and the dilators
of the Nose, were too strong in Choleric people; and therefore Nature
here again directed us to a remedy, which was to correct such extraordinary dilatation by pulling by the Nose.[6]

During Johnson's later years the method is illustrated in Sterne's
Tristram Shandy. "If 'tis wrote against anything," says the author
of his book:

'tis wrote, an' please your worships, against the spleen; in order, by a
more frequent and a more convulsive elevation and depression of the
diaphragm, and the succussations of the intercostal and abdominal
muscles in laughter, to drive the *gall* and other *bitter juices* from the gall
bladder, liver and sweet-bread of his majesty's subjects, with all the in-
imicitious passions which belong to them, down into their duodenums.[7]

A large part of Smollett's talent for the disgusting consists in a
coarse blend of everyday rankness, sores, and sweat with the
vaguer horrors of laboratory and medical terminology. "The inhabitants of Madrid and Edinburgh found particular satisfaction
in breathing their own atmosphere, which was always impregnated with stercoraceous effluvia." [8]

At a later and more metaphysical stage in the history of philosophic diction, the big words appear with a certain transcendental
facetiousness, a Burtonian and Shandeyan flourish, in so different
a work as the *Biographia Literaria* of Coleridge and are grossly
caricatured in the Coleridgean Panscope and Flosky of Peacock's
satirical fantasies. The outline of an era and a movement is crudely
sketched in this passage from *Headlong Hall*.

Mr. Panscope. The *authority*, sir, of all these great men, whose works, as
well as the whole of the Encyclopedia Britannica, the entire series of the
Monthly Review, the complete set of the Variorum Classics, and the
Memoirs of the Academy of Inscriptions, I have read through from be-

---

tive of Dr. Robert Norris," p. 12. Cf. p. 28, the quotation from Blackmore in "A
Further Account of the most Deplorable Condition of Mr. Edmund Curll."
    5. *Lives* iii, 182; *Life of Pope*, Par. 222.
    6. Chap. x. Cf. Arbuthnot's *Humble Petition of the Colliers, Cooks, Cook-Maids,
Blacksmiths, Jack-makers, Braziers, and Others* (George A. Aitkin, *Life and Works
of John Arbuthnot* [Oxford, 1892], protest against a proposal to make use of the
sun's rays for "catoptrical" cooking.
    7. *Tristram Shandy*, iv, 22.
    8. *Humphry Clinker*, Bath, May 8. Cf. Hot-well, April 18.

ginning to end, deposes, with irrefragable refutation, against your ratiocinative speculations, wherein you seem desirous, by the futile process of analytical dialectics, to subvert the pyramidal structure of synthetically deduced opinions, which have withstood the secular revolutions of physiological disquisition, and which I maintain to be transcendentally self-evident, categorically certain, and syllogistically demonstrable.

Squire Headlong said, "Bravo! Pass the bottle. The very best speech that ever was made." Mr. Escot said acidly, "It has only the slight disadvantage of being unintelligible." And Mr. Panscope:

I am not obliged, sir, as Dr. Johnson observed on a similar occasion, to furnish you with an understanding.[9]

The fortune of big words in English had undergone changes since the day of Johnson. Though we think of Johnson's *Rambler* as a primary instance of magniloquence and Campbell's *Lexiphanes* as adscititious ridicule which existed and survives only for its wry reflection of a distinguished original, we have to admit, on the other hand, that the most notable loci of magniloquence in the nineteenth century are in the opposite mode, the ridiculous. The instances adduced by Jespersen in his *Growth and Structure of the English Language* indicate that philosophic words, or more accurately now, merely big words, became increasingly known as the vehicles of a kind of elephantine playfulness. "Iniquitous intercourses contaminate proper habits." "Cryptogamous concretion never grows on mineral fragments that decline repose." [10] "The sense of the Comic," Meredith was to say in his *Essay*, "is much blunted by habits of . . . using humouristic phrase: the trick of employing Johnsonian polysyllables to treat of the infinitely little." [11]

But Johnson himself, one should not forget, was humorous— with a humor which consisted partly in an awareness of his own peculiarities, among those peculiarities his way with words. Perhaps no other man was ever so persistently discussed and praised

9. Chap. v, in *Headlong Hall and Nightmare Abbey* (Everyman's Library), p. 90. Cf. pp. 97, 115, 128, 190, 278, and especially p. 239, Mr. Flosky in chap. viii of *Nightmare Abbey*.

10. Jespersen, *Growth and Structure of the English Language* (New York, 1923), p. 150. Oliver Wendell Holmes in his verses entitled *Aestivation* showed how far the Latinization of English might be carried.

In candent ire the solar splendor flames;
The foles, languescent, pend from arid rames;
His humid front the cive, anheling, wipes
And dreams of erring on ventiferous ripes.
(From the *Autocrat of the Breakfast Table*, in *Poems* [Cambridge, 1895], p. 158.)

11. *An Essay on Comedy* (New York, 1913), p. 59,

and even imitated within his own hearing or just out of his hearing. There can be little question that in his later years Johnson was acutely conscious of the role he played among his many friends, of how he looked and talked, how he impressed them.[12] His self-consciousness sometimes took the form of "complacency," an amused acceptance of his own worth,[13] sometimes the form of an ironic humor by which he claimed for himself softer virtues than he had.

> Then, shaking his head and stretching himself at his ease in the coach, and smiling with much complacency, he turned to me and said, 'I look upon *myself* as a good humoured fellow.' [14]

Sometimes that of a flattered amusement at caricature of himself or a conscious burlesque of his own stylistic and conversational idiosyncrasy.[15] He smiled when he said that a certain man "might have *exuberated* into an Atheist." [16] "He seemed," says Boswell, "to take a pleasure in speaking in his own style; for when he had carelessly missed it, he would repeat the thought translated into it." [17]

All this, it is true, represents a Johnson whose character and reputation had been formed by the work of the *Rambler* and other writing of his early middle age. Yet one may not be surprised to find something analogous in Mr. Rambler himself, the protagonist of the essays, or in the correspondents who furnish him with billets. We have kept our faces very straight in the discussion of Johnson's philosophic diction, exploring its character as a pervasive meta-phoric vehicle of psychological discourse. There is no reason to think that for the most part philosophic diction did not come spontaneously and seriously to Johnson's mind—as the leaves to the tree. The Rambler is noted for the moral profundity of his character. Yet, as with all such classics, it is possible that there are more smiles upon the face of seriousness than a posterity of students will notice. If he wrote of little fishes, said Goldsmith, Dr. Johnson would make them talk like whales,[18] and as a matter of fact Johnson might have constructed a very pleasant fable on this principle. It is a very light twist of humor that one may detect

12. "He helped me to fill up blanks which I had left in first writing it [Boswell's *Journal of a Tour to the Hebrides*], when I was not quite sure of what he had said, and he corrected any mistakes that I had made" (*Life* v, 307; cf. 245, n. 2, 253, 279).
13. *Life* i, 443; cf. ii, 66; iii, 7, 405; iv, 179; *Letters* ii, 313–314.
14. *Life* ii, 362; cf. *Life* iv, 166, 280; *Miscellanies* i, 167, Piozzi, *Anecdotes*.
15. *Life* iii, 255–256.
16. *Life* iv, 98.
17. *Life* iv, 320.
18. *Life* ii, 231.

here and there in the *Rambler*, much more restrained than the lavished pedantry of Slawkenbergius in Sterne, or the Smelfungian technicalities of Smollett; a certain mild contrast, and at the same time a metaphorical juncture, between gravity of diction and homeliness of content, a shade of grimace at some meanness or pretense. It is a humor that often involves the bigness of legal, political, or social vocabulary. Squire Bluster as a boy was taught to exercise a petty surveillance over his household, so that by the age of eighteen he was

a complete master of all the lower arts of domestic policy, had on the road detected combinations between the coachman and the ostler, and procured the discharge of nineteen maids for illicit correspondence with cottagers and charwomen.[19]

A lover in the *Rambler* has "frequent interviews" [20] with his mistress at her "habitation," [21] is "admitted" [22] to her presence, or "dismissed." [23] In the world of thrift and finance, a haberdasher's apprentice learns to "make up parcels with exact frugality of paper and pack thread," [24] returns home to the country and is considered "a master of pecuniary knowledge," [25] desires to clear himself from the "adhesion of trade," and looks back on his "officinal state." [26] The same person tries to become a gentleman by frequenting the public walks but on being recognized by a lady, says, "Here was an end of all my ambulatory projects." [27] A young lady who is ten weeks past sixteen thinks herself "exempted from the dominion of a governess"; [28] spinsterhood is "antiquated virginity"; [29] matchmakers are "hymeneal solicitors"; [30] the authors of journals and gazettes are "diurnal historiographers." [31]

It is a form of exaggeration that unites readily with the philosophic and of which we have already seen some simpler instances

19. 142, vii, 11. Cf. *Debates in Parliament, Works* xii, 45, "plots of the colliers and . . . combinations of the weavers." Cf. other accounts of country life in *Ramblers* 61, v, 389; 66, v, 421; 116, vi, 285–286; 198, vii, 335; and especially 147, vii, 43, "villatick bashfulness."

20. 186, vii, 267.

21. 103, vi, 204. Cf. 117, vi, 299, the "author's habitation," a garret.

22. 182, vii, 246; 40, v, 259.

23. 119, vi, 311, "three I dismissed." Cf. 109, vi, 242, "dismission" of a tutor.

24. 116, vi, 288.

25. 116, vi, 288.

26. 123, vi, 333–334. Cf. Quincy's *Lexicon*, s.v. *officinal.*

27. 123, vi, 336. Cf. *Idler* 48, viii, 192, "ambulatory students."

28. 84, vi, 82.

29. 39, v, 253; 119, vi, 307.

30. 115, vi, 284.

31. 145, vii, 32. Cf. 141, vii, 3, "evening compotations"; 199, vii, 344, widows "confederated."

in the dismal literalities of pedantry with which the portraits of Gelidus and Gelasimus were embellished—the quadrature of the circle, the catenarian curve, and the satellites of Jupiter. The metaphoric shade, of a semi-philosophic sort, may be detected in some other portraits, in that of Gulosulus, for instance, who is "venerated by the professors of epicurism," and who whenever any innovation is "made in the culinary system . . . procures the earliest intelligence, and the most authentick receipt"; [32] in that of the unfortunate beauty Victoria who was never permitted to sleep till she "had passed through the cosmetic discipline, part of which was a regular lustration performed with bean-flower water and May-dews"; [33] or in the portrait of the country housewife, who seems resolved that her secret of making English capers "shall perish with her, as some alchymists have obstinately suppressed the art of transmuting metals." [34] The alchymical humor appears in the same portrait, less obtrusively, but more richly in the use of the word *projection*. This arcanic philosophical word, occurring in the *Rambler* three times [35] in its literal chemical or alchemical sense—the crisis of an operation, the moment of transmutation—suffers a certain bathos when we are told that among the worries of the country housewife was

to watch the skillet on the fire, to see it simmer with the due degree of heat, and to snatch it off at the moment of projection.[36]

The same treatment is accorded two even less obtrusive words—*event* and *register*—in the story of an adventurer in lotteries. In a more serious context we hear of "experiments of which the event has been long registered," [37] but the adventurer in lotteries bought forty tickets and in order to estimate his chances beforehand—in a ridiculous parallel of scientific experiment—wrote the numbers upon dice and threw them for five hours every day in a garret,

And examining the event by an exact register, found on the evening before the lottery was drawn, that one of . . . [his] numbers had been

32. 206, vii, 384.
33. 130, vi, 378, ". . . my hair was perfumed with variety of unguents. . . . The softness of my hands was secured by medicated gloves, and my bosom rubbed with a pomade prepared by my mother, of virtue to discuss pimples, and clear discolorations." Cf. 133, vi, 395, "cosmetic science." Cf. the philosophic parallel between punch and conversation in *Idler* 34, quoted *ante* p. 68. Cf. *Adventurer* 115, ix, 119, "epidemical conspiracy for the destruction of paper."
34. 51, v, 329. Cf. 103, vi, 208, Nugaculus the gossip who was "obliged to traffick like the chymists, and purchase one secret with another."
35. 67, v, 425; 111, vi, 254; 199, vii, 340, "whole weeks without sleep by the side of an athanor, to watch the moment of projection."
36. 51, v, 328. Cf. Quincy's *Lexicon*, s.v. *projection*.
37. 154, vii, 86.

turned up five times more than any of the rest in three hundred and thirty thousand throws.[38]

We may conclude this chapter and our study of Johnson's philosophic diction with one further example of philosophic humor, the most extended in the *Rambler* and the mellowest. The letter of Hypertatus in *Rambler* 117, on the advantages to an author of living in a garret, blends philosophic metaphor with a characteristic Johnsonian subject and attitude. It was considered by the satirist Campbell "one of Mr. J——n's *chef d'oeuvres,* both for stile and matter." [39] "That the professors of literature generally reside in the highest stories, has been immemorially observed." The garret is the "usual receptacle of the philosopher and poet," the "aerial abode" or "habitation" of literature.[40] Because:

It is universally known that the faculties of the mind are invigorated or weakened by the state of the body, and that the body is in a great measure regulated by the various compressions of the ambient element. . . . I have discovered, by a long series of observations, that invention and elocution suffer great impediments from dense and impure vapours, and that the tenuity of a defecated air at a proper distance from the surface of the earth, accelerates the fancy, and sets at liberty these intellectual powers which were before shackled by too strong attraction, and unable to expand themselves under the pressure of a gross atmosphere. I have found dulness to quicken into sentiment in a thin ether, as water, though not very hot, boils in a receiver partly exhausted; and heads, in appearance empty, have teemed with notions upon rising ground, as the flaccid sides of a football would have swelled out into stiffness and extension.

Another cause of the gaiety and sprightliness of the dwellers in garrets is probably the increase of that vertiginous motion, with which we are carried round by the diurnal revolution of the earth . . . he that towers to the fifth story, is whirled through more space by every circumrotation, than another that grovels upon the ground-floor.

38. 181, vii, 240. Cf. *Debates in Parliament, Works* xiii, 492, the *event* of an adventure in lotteries, in a short discourse on the evil of lotteries; and xiii, 499, law an *experiment* of which the *event* is uncertain. The *OED* records the later standard use of *event* in the science of probabilities. For its application to scientific experiment see the quotation from Boyle in Johnson's Dictionary.

Philosophic humor, in its most labored and frigorifick form, appears throughout *Rambler* 199, in which Hermeticus dilates upon the virtues of Rabbi Abraham's magnet for detecting infidelity in wives.

39. *Lexiphanes* (London, 1767), p. 16.

40. 117, vi, 293–295. Professor Curtis Bradford, in his Yale doctoral dissertation "Samuel Johnson's 'Rambler,' " (1937), p. 111, has pointed out an analogue for this *Rambler* in an anonymous leaflet *An Essay on the Antiquity, Dignity, and Advantages of Living in a Garret* (London, 1751), which was quoted at length in the *Newcastle General Magazine,* iv (February, 1751), 97–101, and hence antedates *Rambler* 117, the date of which is April 30, 1751.

Hypertatus, in the tide of his enthusiasm for the idea, would propose:

that there should be a cavern dug, and a tower erected, like those which *Bacon* describes in *Solomon's* house, for the expansion and concentration of understanding, according to the exigence of different employments, or constitutions.

Perhaps some that fume away in meditations upon time and space in the tower, might compose tables of interest at a certain depth; and he that upon level ground stagnates in silence, or creeps in narrative, might, at the height of half a mile, ferment into merriment, sparkle with repartee, and froth with declamation.

"As it seldom happens," says Hypertatus in his confident vein,

that I do not find the temper to which the texture of . . . [each man's] brain is fitted, I accommodate him in time with a tube of mercury, first marking the point most favourable to his intellects, according to rules which I have long studied, and which I may, perhaps, reveal to mankind in a complete treatise of barometrical pneumatology.[41]

After pausing to notice Solomon's house, that academy of science and laboratory which Johnson had discovered when he read Bacon's *New Atlantis* for the Dictionary, and which Glanvill in the Address prefixed to his *Scepsis Scientifica* had called "a Prophetick Scheam of the Royal Society," [42] a student of Johnson's philosophic ideas might focus his attention upon the pregnant phrase *barometrical pneumatology*—a science of the soul, that is, or a psychology, in terms of atmospheric pressure.[43] In the *Plan of an English Dictionary* Johnson had discussed the gradations of meaning from the literal through shades of analogy and metaphor to the facetious. Here in *Rambler* 117 are the two sides of human experience of which we have said so much, the outer mechanical and the inner spiritual, brought together not in metaphor but in a playful exaggeration of causal relation. Or, if we look more closely at the whole passage, the exaggeration of literal science will be seen to verge on metaphor and turn into it. The mind affected by compres-

41. 117, vi, 296–299.
42. *Scepsis Scientifica* (London, 1665), p. c^v.
43. The *OED*, quoting from Campbell's *Lexiphanes* a verbatim burlesque of Johnson's phrase, places it under definition 3 of *pneumatology*: "The science or theory of air or gases; pneumatics." *Pneumatology* had meant also in the seventeenth century, and still meant, something quite different, the doctrine of spiritual beings, meaning 1 of the *OED*, under which Johnson's *Preface to Shakespeare* is quoted. But again *pneumatology* in the rationalistic age of Johnson meant psychology, and though the *OED* fails to illustrate this meaning as early as 1751, there can be no doubt that this is the meaning the word conveys in *Rambler* 117. The *Rambler* phrase is quoted in the *OED* under *barometrical*.

sions of the ambient element, invention and elocution impeded by
dense and impure vapors, fancy accelerated by the tenuity of a
defecated air—"as water, though not very hot, boils in a receiver
partly exhausted"—are the serious analogies of other *Rambler*
passages turned into the fun of exaggerated literalism. The step
to analogy or metaphor is but a short one and is taken almost immediately. We fume away in meditations, stagnate in silence, ferment
into merriment, sparkle with repartee, froth with declamation—as
in so many other *Rambler* passages we talk of the ebullition and
effervescence of fancy or genius, lament the evaporation of a secret,
or analyze the impulse of desire and the counteraction of fear.
Hypertatus, if he ever got round to it, meant to favor mankind
with "a complete treatise of barometrical pneumatology." This
project (or visionary "projection," as Johnson in a more sober mood
would have called it) [44] is an epitomized and facetiously literal
analogue of the broader treatise in metaphoric psychology which
Johnson himself was writing in some of the most characteristic
Ramblers.

44. *Adventurer* 108, ix, 107; *Rambler* 48, v, 309, "projects" ["projection" in Folio
text].

APPENDICES

Appendix A
Index of Philosophic Words in The Rambler

THE flexibility or extensibility of philosophic meaning (see esp. *ante* pp. 104–113) or, if one insists, a necessary vagueness in the concept, precludes the aim of completeness in this index. Many marginal words have been admitted only in a selection of better examples. Certain other abstract terms which might be claimed for the philosophic vocabulary in its fullest extension and some common and easy terms, chiefly medical (as *disease, malady, remedy*) have been altogether omitted. The index aims, however, at being a complete guide to more specific, technical, and esoteric literal terms of science and to clearly scientific metaphors and similes, in short to the markedly philosophic loci in the *Rambler*. Through contrast of examples it aims, wherever possible, to show the relation between literal philosophic terms and metaphors. The names of authors which appear under most entries (e.g., Bacon, Browne, South, Shakespeare) are inserted as a guide to the identifications of Dictionary examples grouped according to authors in Appendix B. See the introduction to Appendix B (*post* p. 146).

Through the kindness of Professor Curtis B. Bradford in lending me a copy of the *Rambler* annotated with his painstaking collations of the several texts,[1] I am able to say that Johnson's revisions of the *Rambler* in 1751–52 (for the first collected duodecimo edition of 1752) and in 1754 (for the "fourth" edition of 1756) had a very slight effect upon the philosophic vocabulary of the received text from which (in the edition of 1787) this index is derived. In all, about 28 examples under 22 words disappeared in the revisions and have been restored within square brackets in the index. Under *celestial, hydrophobia,* and *hypothesis,* the lost examples are unique. Under *lenitive* (*antidote*) and *mechanist* (*mechanician*) appear instances where Johnson changed one philosophic word

---

1. See his Yale doctoral dissertation "Samuel Johnson's 'Rambler'" (1937), chap. ii and Appendix II, and his article "Johnson's Revisions of The Rambler," RES, xv (July, 1939), 302–314.

for another. The unique example under *abscission* first appears in the second revision, in place of the more literary word *elision*. *Philosophical* appears in a phrase added to the text in the first revision.

A careful reading of the *Debates in Parliament* has failed to discover some 311 of the 380 words distinguished in the index by capital letters as the main entries. This fact, or the countable difference between the philosophic vocabulary of the *Rambler* and that of the *Debates,* is indicated by the insertion of select references to the *Debates* for the remaining 69 words. The comparison of vocabulary may be rounded out here in a small collection of philosophic words which have been found in the *Debates* but not in the *Rambler: amputation,* xii, 75; *appendant,* xii, 178; xiii, 141, 298; *concussion,* xiii, 222; *conflagration,* xiii, 182; *corpulence,* xiii, 300; *counterbalance,* xiii, 224, 239; *diffusive,* xii, 182; *distillation,* xiii, 391; *equilibrium,* xii, 221, 236; xiii, 150, 236; *evaporate,* xii, 30; *flux,* xii, 124; *foment,* xii, 168; *inebriate,* xiii, 432; *intoxicate,* xiii, 54, 169, 391, 453; *intoxication,* xiii, 250; *soporific* n., xiii, 282; *subterraneous,* xii, 44; xiii, 252. And see *primogenial, Plan of a Dictionary,* ix, 179; *intumescence, Preface,* ix, 223.

The *Rambler* index is followed (p. 145) by a short list of philosophic words which appear, though not in the *Rambler,* in some of Johnson's later writings.

ABERRATION. of . . . example, 70, v, 446; from the rule in . . . verse, 86, vi, 95; from the laws of medicine, 112, vi, 258. Glanvill. Cf. *erratick,* 117, vi, 294; gratifications (i.e., pleasures of wandering), 124, vi, 339; industry (i.e., wandering among coffee-houses to pick up jokes), 141, vii, 5.

ABSCIND. syllables, 90, vi, 118. ABSCISSION. of a vowel, 88, vi, 107 [*elision* in Folio]. Browne, Wiseman. Cf. *rescind,* 131, vi, 387.

ABSORB. time . . . in sleep, 108, vi, 233; diffidence . . . in the sense of danger, 129, vi, 373. Burnet, Harvey, Philips.

ACCELERATE. descent to life merely sensual, 7, v, 43; effects [of time], 47, v, 306; 60, v, 383; [alchymical] projection, 111, vi, 254; executions, 114, vi, 273; tenuity of . . . air . . . accelerates the fancy, 117, vi, 296; manhood, 151, vii, 63; effects of time, 159, vii, 116. Arbuthnot, Bacon, Newton, Thomson, Watts. Cf. *celerity,* 19, v, 124; 117, vi, 298; 131, vi, 385; 177, vii, 216. Cf. RETARD.

ACCRETION. of matter stored in the mind, 184, vii, 254. Arbuthnot, Bacon.

ACERBITY. of exclamation, 200, vii, 347. Cf. EXACERBATION.

ACRIMONY. of evil, 32, v, 209; of malice, 144, vii, 23; 46, v, 296; 64, v, 409; 77, vi, 41; 93, vi, 141; 121, vi, 325; 144, vii, 23; 173, vii, 196; 183, vii, 251; (*Debates*, xiii, 52, 120, 176, 497). Arbuthnot, Bacon, South. ACRI-MONIOUS. 40, v, 258; 121, vi, 320; (*Debates*, xiii, 118). Harvey.

ACTUATE. man . . . actuated by passions, 56, v, 358; wings . . . by the perpetual motion, 67, v, 428; [bodily] exercises . . . to actuate . . . the mind, 89, vi, 113; actuate . . . languor, 117, vi, 298; purposes which actuate mankind, 131, vi, 383; men . . . actuated . . . by natural desires, 151, vii, 68; 206, vii, 280. Browne. Cf. *agency*, 78, vi, 44; 92, vi, 128; 199, vii, 344; *agent*, 98, vi, 173; 137, vi, 417; *coactive*, 57, v, 366; *cogency*, 70, v, 343; 76, vi, 31; *cogent*, 99, vi, 178; virtues . . . in *act*, 76, vi, 31.

ADHESION. of trade, 123, vi, 333; extraneous to character, 166, vii, 157; (of extraneous substances to . . . ship, *Debates*, xiii, 197). Boyle, Locke. ADHESIVE. appetites, 155, vii, 93. Thomson. Cf. *adhere*, 7, v, 40; 64, v, 406; *adherence*, 168, vii, 164; *adherent*, 43, v, 277. (*Adhere, adherence, adherent* occur *passim* in *Debates*.)

ADJACENT. difficulty, 66, v, 419; villages, 135, vi, 409 and 146, vii, 35. Bacon, Newton.

ADSCITITIOUS. happiness, 20, v, 137; passions, 49, v, 315; character, 123, vi, 336; excellence, 155, vii, 89; qualities, 179, vii, 228; (treasures, *Debates*, xiii, 356).

ADULTERATE. officiousness and liberality . . . adulterated, 74, vi, 19. Boyle, Glanvill. Cf. *unadulterated*, 33, v, 213. ADULTERATION. [of] promiscuous dedication, 136, vi, 413. Bacon.

ADUMBRATION. of . . . images by . . . sound, 94, vi, 147. Bacon, Glanvill, Hale.

ADVENTITIOUS. secondary and adventitious gladness, 36, v, 234; and artificial miseries, 37, v, 251; and separable decorations and disguises, 60, v, 382; or foreign pain, 69, v, 435; beauty of *Aeneas*, 94, vi, 145; amusements, 135, vi, 410. Bacon, Boyle, Woodward.

AERIAL. abode, 117, vi, 295. Arbuthnot, Locke, Milton, Newton.

AGGLOMERATE. moments . . . into days and weeks, 108, vi, 235. Thomson.

AGGREGATE. of knowledge and happiness, 129, vi, 375. Bentley, Glanvill.

AGRICULTURE. the first and noblest science, 145, vii, 29. Browne, Woodward.

ALEXIPHARMICK. 120, vi, 314. Browne.

AMALGAMATE. bodies of heterogeneous principles, 25, v, 166.

AMBIENT. element, 117, vi, 296. Bentley, Milton, Newton. Cf. *ambulatory, ante* p. 117.

ANATOMY. 19, v, 125; of an insect, 138, vi, 423. Bacon, Shakespeare. ANATOMICAL. enquiries, 85, vi, 84. Locke, Watts. ANATOMIST. 45, v, 292; 140, vi, 437.

ANIMATION. [of] the magnetic needle, 61, v, 393. Bacon. Cf. *animate,* fury, 18, v, 118; hopes, 62, v, 399; efforts, 145, vii, 31; the timorous, 147, vii, 41; industry, 150, vii, 58 and 187, vii, 273; magnets, 199, vii, 345. Cf. *reanimate, Debates,* xii, 140; *Adventurer* 69, ix, 52.

ANNUAL. flights of human rovers, 135, vi, 407; migrations of . . . mankind, 138, vi, 423; (payment, *Debates,* i, 235).

ANODYNE. 120, vi, 314; 202, vii, 359. Arbuthnot.

ANTIDOTAL. writing, 109, vi, 240. Browne. ANTIDOTE. [to passion, 2, v, 11], *lenitive* in revision of 1754; to fear and to hope, 29, v, 191; against sorrow, 47, v, 306; to indulgence, 110, vi, 251; 150, vii, 58; 199, vii, 342. Browne, Quincy, Shakespeare.

APOPLEXY. 149, vii, 53. Arbuthnot, Locke, Quincy, Shakespeare.

APPROXIMATION. desire . . . invigorated by . . . approximation of . . . object, 58, v, 370. Browne, Grew, Hale. Cf. *approximate* v., 60, v, 381.

ARMATURE. [of] the magnet, 199, vii, 344. Ray.

ASCENDANT. n. [of] *Eumathes* over his friend, 181, vii, 242. Locke. ASCENDANT. adj. desire . . . in the mind, 207, vii, 388. Browne, South.

ASPERITY. and intricacies [in the path of study], 25, v, 167; of sarcasm, 26, v, 170; of misfortune, 32, v, 210; of contradiction, 74, vi, 21; of the wintry world, 80, vi, 55; of our language, 88, vi, 107; irritable by the smallest asperity, 112, vi, 259; habitual, 119, vi, 307; of smoothness, 122, vi, 327; censured with great asperity, 126, vi, 353; angular bodies and uneven surfaces lose . . . points and asperities by . . . attrition, 138, vi, 424; men of learning and asperity, 141, vii, 5; of reply, 176, vii, 213; surliness and asperity, 195, vii, 321; (of resentment, *Debates,* xiii, 289; of sentiment, xiii, 299). Boyle. Cf. ASPER. correspondent, 200, vii, 350; *exasperate,* 20, v, 131; 58, v, 374; 66, v, 420, 421; 73, vi, 14; 74, vi, 19; 185, vii, 262; (*Debates,* xii, 86 and *passim*).

ASSIMILATE. falsehood . . . to the mind, as poison to the body, 95, vi, 157. Bacon, Milton, Newton.

ASTRONOMER. 99, vi, 181; 113, vi, 268; 117, vi, 292; 118, vi, 304. Bacon, Blackmore, Locke. Cf. *astrologer,* 201, vii, 353.

ATHANOR.   whole weeks without sleep by the side of, 199, vii, 340. Quincy.

ATOM.   atoms we cannot perceive, till . . . united into masses, 108, vi, 235. Quincy, Ray.

ATTRACTION.   contrary attractions [to holy life], 7, v, 44–5; [of example, 50, v, 322], omitted in revision of 1754; contrariety of, 153, vii, 76; mutual attraction of natures, 160, vii, 119; of example, 188, vii, 280; increased by the approach of the attracting body, 207, vii, 389. Bacon, Browne, Newton.

ATTRITION.   [of] angular bodies and uneven surfaces . . . against one another, 138, vi, 424. Arbuthnot, Woodward.

BALANCE.   trepidations of, 1, v, 5; adjust every day by, 112, vi, 258; (*Debates, passim;* cf. *ante* p. 63). Chambers, Shakespeare. Cf. *overbalance,* 150, vii, 57.

BALSAM.   120, vi, 314. BALSAMICK.   202, vii, 359. Arbuthnot, Hale.

BAROMETER.   adjust every day by, 112, vi, 258. Arbuthnot, Harris. BAROMETRICAL.   pneumatology, 117, vi, 297. Derham.

BIENNIAL.   visit, 61, v, 389. Ray.

BOTANIST.   118, vi, 304. Thomson, Woodward. BOTANY.   19, v, 125.

CANINE.   madness, 6, v, 35.

CATENARIAN.   curve, 179, vii, 228. Cheyne, Harris.

CATHARTICK.   of vice, 2, v, 11; of the soul, 87, vi, 98. Garth, Quincy.

CELESTIAL.   [observations, 8, v, 47], omitted in revision of 1754. Browne, Shakespeare. The word appears in moral and theological senses in 4, v, 263; 91, vi, 343; 118, vi, 301; 124, vi, 343.

CHEMIST.   5, v, 31; 68, v, 430; 99, vi, 181; *chymists,* 103, vi, 208; 139, vi, 430. Cf. *alchymists,* 51, v, 329. CHEMISTRY.   19, v, 125; 25, v, 166. Arbuthnot, Boerhaave.

CHRONICAL.   diseases, 85, vi, 86. Browne, Quincy. CHRONOLOGICAL.   series of actions, 60, v, 385; memorials [i.e., histories], 122, vi, 329; local or chronological propriety, 140, vi, 437. Hale. CHRONOLOGY.   exact, 62, v, 397; celestial, 118, vi, 301. Holder.

CIRCULATION.   of . . . productions, 106, vi, 224; of . . . copies, 146, vii, 36; of infamy, 183, vii, 251; (of coin, *Debates,* xii, 362; of intelligence, xiii, 206). Arbuthnot, Burnet.

CIRCUMROTATION.   of the earth, 117, vi, 297.

CIRCUMVOLUTION.   [of] a river, 65, v, 414; of the gulph of INTEMPERANCE, 102, vi, 199. Arbuthnot, Wilkins.

CLIMACTERICK. of the mind, 151, vii, 63. CLIMACTERICAL. year, 59, v, 377. Browne.

COALITION. of common sentiments, 143, vii, 20; (of dominions, *Debates,* xiii, 374). Bentley, Glanvill, Hale.

COEVAL. rules . . . with reason, 156, vii, 96. Bentley, Hale.

COHABIT. wit . . . with malice, 22, v, 147; [48, v, 310], omitted in revision of 1751–52; animals . . . by pairs, 99, vi, 178. South.

COHERE. natures . . . which immediately cohere, 160, vii, 119. Cheyne, Woodward.

COLLISION. [of] flint [to produce fire], 25, v, 116; of parties, 61, v, 387; of consonants, 88, vi, 106; of happy incidents, 154, vii, 85; (of parties, *Debates,* xiii, 175). Bentley, Milton.

COLORIFICK. radiance, 124, vi, 342. Newton.

COMMENSURATE. duties of life . . . to its duration, 71, vi, 6. Bentley, Glanvill. Cf. INCOMMENSURATE, MENSURATION.

COMMINUTION. of our lives, 108, vi, 234. Bacon, Bentley, Ray.

COMPOSITION. of the pudding, 51, v, 329. Bacon.

COMPRESS. all matter to perfect solidity, 8, v, 46; affections . . . into a narrower compass, 99, vi, 179. COMPRESSION. of the ambient element, 117, vi, 296. Bacon, Newton.

CONCATENATE. propositions . . . into arguments, 151, vii, 66. CONCATENATION. of society, 24, v, 148; [of] events, 41, v, 266; of causes and effects, 54, v, 345; [of] rhyme, 121, vi, 326; of effects, 137, vi, 418; [of cause and effect in the fable], 139, vi, 429; (of blunders, *Debates,* xii, 163; of enormities, xiii, 388; of society, xiii, 389). South.

CONCENTER. views, 19, v, 127; great qualities . . . in Mr. Frolick, 61, v, 391. Hale, Wotton. Cf. *concentrate* [the virtue of magnets], 199, vii, 344; *concentration* of ideas, 80, vi, 57; of understanding, 117, vi, 298.

CONCOMITANT. of good or bad actions, 8, v, 51; of virtue, 52, v, 337; of misery, 74, vi, 20; of guilt, 79, vi, 51; of great events, 152, vii, 72; of our undertakings, 207, vii, 388; (*Debates,* xiii, 146). Bacon, Harvey, Philips, South, Watts, Wotton.

CONDENSATION. [of atmosphere], 117, vi, 297. Bentley, Browne. Cf. *condense, False Alarm,* x, 26.

CONFLUENCE. of visitants, 147, vii, 40. Bacon, Bentley, Shakespeare. CONFLUX. of men, 53, v, 338. Milton. Cf. *flux, Debates,* xii, 124; *Preface to Shakespeare,* ix, 240.

CONGEAL. curiosity . . . by indolence, 118, vi, 304; mind in perpetual inactivity by the fatal influence of frigorifick wisdom, 129, vi, 371;

knowledge and virtue . . . by . . . frigorifick power [of diffidence], 159, vii, 115. Burnet, Thomson. Cf. *congelation, Western Islands*, x, 376.

CONGRUITY. of truth to . . . faculties of reason, 20, v, 131; (of principles, *Debates*, xiii, 64). Glanvill.

CONSTELLATE. scattered graces, 201, vii, 353. Glanvill. CON-STELLATION. of great qualities, 61, v, 391. Milton.

CONTAGION. of example, 14, v, 91; of misery, 59, v, 376; of impatience, 73, vi, 12; of vanity, 95, vi, 154; of felicity, 148, vii, 47; of peculiarities, 164, vii, 144; 50, v, 320; ([in a pest house], *Debates*, xii, 76; of venality, xiii, 157; of bribery, xiii, 236). Bacon, Milton, Shakespeare.

CONTEMPER. [antidotes have contempered malignity], 150, vii, 58. Ray.

CONTEXTURE. of principal story, 122, vi, 331; of continued dialogues, 140, vi, 441; of events, 145, vii, 30; [of narrations, 176, vii, 214], omitted in revision of 1754. Blackmore, Philips, Wotton. Cf. *intertexture, Adventurer* 58, ix, 37. Cf. TEXTURE.

CONTIGUOUS. heiress, whose land lies contiguous to mine, 34, v, 220; (countries, *Debates*, xiii, 308). Bacon, Milton, Newton.

COPULATION. wit . . . the unexpected copulation of ideas, 194, vii, 314.

CORDIALS. 120, vi, 314; (*Debates*, xiii, 440). Arbuthnot.

CORROSION. of envy, 17, v, 112; [of] happiness [by] ill-humour, 74, vi, 19; of idle discontent, 133, vi, 399; of inveterate hatred, 185, vii, 262. Bacon, Quincy, Woodward. Cf. *corrode, Rasselas*, xi, 88.

CORUSCATION. of declining day, 135, vi, 409. Bacon, Garth, Newton.

COUNTERACT. our own purpose, 29, v, 193; passion . . . to counteract its own purpose, 53, v, 340; [providence, 76, vi, 35], omitted in edition of 1754; appetites, 77, vi, 38; happiness, 83, vi, 72; [sound] ought never to counteract [meaning], 94, vi, 150; one terror . . . another, 126, vi, 353; [avarice or malice, 148, vii, 46], omitted in revision of 1751–52; force of external agents [by] superior principal, 151, vii, 63; (*Debates*, xiii, 97, 113). South. COUNTERACTION. stratagems of, 29, v, 191; of . . . motive, 70, v, 443; [of] infection, 89, vi, 112; of a false principle, 93, vi, 138; of the words to the idea, 168, vii, 166.

CRUCIBLE. some bodies . . . set the . . . crucible at defiance, 174, vii, 200; melting . . . estates in, 199, vii, 340.

CULINARY. sciences, 51, v, 328; system, 206, vii, 384. Arbuthnot, Newton.

DECLINATION. [of] the sun, 137, vi, 422. Browne, Woodward. Cf. *declension* of character, 32, v, 212; of . . . influence, 130, vi, 381.

DEFECATE. air, 117, vi, 296; mind, 177, vii, 217. Boyle, Glanvill, Harvey, Philips.

DELIRIUM. argumental, 95, vi, 158. Arbuthnot. DELIRIOUS. lethargick or delirious, 198, vii, 336. Thomson.

DETRUNCATION. of . . . syllables, 88, vi, 107.

DIFFUSION. of water, 36, v, 237; [of liberality, 64, v, 407], omitted in revision of 1751–52; of his name, 101, vi, 190; [of Clarendon's style], 122, vi, 331; (*Debates*, xiii, 42). Bacon, Boyle. Cf. *diffuse* (adj.), 140, vi, 441; (verb), 20, v, 131; 40, v, 257; 78, vi, 46; 106, vi, 224; 125, vi, 344; 126, vi, 356; 138, vi, 425; 144, vii, 24; 183, vii, 250; 190, vii, 289; 203, vii, 395; (*passim* in *Debates*). Cf. *diffusive*, *Debates*, xii, 182; *Adventurer* 50, ix, 23.

DISCUSS. a pomade . . . of virtue to discuss pimples, 130, vi, 378.

DISRUPTION. of . . . union with physical nature [i.e., death], 78, vi, 44. Blackmore, Ray, Woodward.

DISSIPATE. man of letters . . . dissipated by the awe of company, 14, v, 93; genius, 17, v, 115; veneration, 50, v, 322; attention, 52, v, 335; meteorous pleasures, 68, v, 430; gratifications, 78, vi, 43; thoughts . . . are dissipated, 113, vi, 267; persons by negligence, 124, vi, 342; resolution, 134, vi, 401; visions of calamity, 134, vi, 403; attention, 137, vi, 419; gloom of collegiate austerity, 141, vii, 3; application, 153, vii, 76; 155, vii, 90; fear, 159, vii, 114; anxiety, 159, vii, 116; unwilling or dissipated auditor, 196, vii, 322; difficulty, 196, vii, 324; and relieve [vexation], 204, vii, 371; attention, 208, vii, 395; (*Debates*, xii, 258 and *passim*). Thomson, Woodward. DISSIPATION. of great abilities, 17, v, 115; of . . . industry, 71, vi, 4; of understanding, 85, vi, 87; the true purpose of human existence, 100, vi, 188; of the fortunes, 203, vii, 366. Bacon, Hale, Milton, Woodward.

DISSOLVE. pearls of the ocean [to make medicine], 120, vi, 314; (union, *Debates*, xii, 150; a contract, xii, 302). Bacon, Milton, Shakespeare, Woodward. DISSOLUTION. of close alliances, 47, v, 303; [of ourselves], 85, vi, 86; of gay societies [in summertime], 124, vi, 340; of the ice, 186, vii, 268; (of government, *Debates*, xii, 115; xiii, 118). Bacon, Bentley, Milton, Shakespeare, South. Cf. INDISSOLUBLE. Cf. *dissoluble*, *Preface to Shakespeare*, ix, 251.

DISTEMPER. 74, vi, 20; (*Debates*, xii, 47, 328; xiii, 412). Bacon, Shakespeare, South. DISTEMPERED. mind, 58, v, 372. Boyle, Shakespeare.

DISTIL. v.a. leaves and flowers, 51, v, 327; spices of Arabia, 120, vi, 314; (spirits, *Debates*, xiii, 405, 409; liquors, xiii, 408, 409). Boyle, Shakespeare. DISTIL. v.n. drops of lethe distil from the poppies and cypress, 3, v, 18. DISTILLER. of washes, 51, v, 301; ([of spirits], *Debates*, xii, 436). Boyle. Cf. *distillation, Idler*, 31, viii, 124.

DIURNAL. writers, 1, v, 5 and 169, vii, 173; revolution of the earth, 117, vi, 297; historiographer, 145, vii, 32.

DUCTILE. the future . . . pliant and ductile, 41, v, 266; minds, 50, v, 321. Bacon, Philips. DUCTILITY. of mind, 112, vi, 262; sprightliness and ductility, 180, vii, 235; of obedience, 197, vii, 330. Watts.

EBRIETY. 167, vii, 160. Browne. Cf. INEBRIATION.

EBULLITION. [of] imagination, 101, vi, 189; of genius, 129, vi, 372. Arbuthnot, Bacon, Browne, Newton, Quincy. Cf. *boil*, 66, v, 419; 74, vi, 19; 117, vi, 296.

ECLIPSE. n. of the moons of Jupiter, 24, v, 159. Locke,* Milton, Shakespeare. ECLIPSE. v. virtues, 54, v, 348; splendor, 73, vi, 14; [beauties, 87, vi, 100], omitted in revision of 1754. Shakespeare.

EFFERVESCENCE. of an agitated fancy, 43, v, 281; of the fancy, 101, vi, 195; of contrary qualities, 167, vii, 162. Arbuthnot, Grew, Woodward.

EFFICIENT. n. accidental causes, and external efficients, 63, v, 402. Hale.

EFFLORESCENCE. mirth . . . as the efflorescence of a mind, 141, vii, 6. Bacon.

EFFULGENCE. [of] TRUTH, 96, vi, 163. Blackmore, Milton.

EFFUSE. water, 71, vi, 126; [social] lustre, 124, vi, 341. Milton. Cf. *effusion*, 122, vi, 330; 139, vi, 432; 194, vii, 314. Cf. difference . . . between evaporation and *effusion, Western Islands*, x, 480.

ELASTICK. springs of motion, 48, v, 307. Arbuthnot, Bentley, Blackmore, Newton.

ELECTRICITY. wheels of, 199, vii, 339; shock of, 199, vii, 339. Quincy. ELECTRIFY. a bottle, 118, vi, 304.

EMANATION. good-humour . . . the emanation of a mind, 72, vi, 8. Browne, South.

EMISSION. of the breath, 88, vi, 104; [of] honour, 146, vii, 38 and 169, vii, 173; of *Pope's* compositions, 169, vii, 173. Bacon, Browne, South. EMIT. light [from a star], 61, v, 388. Arbuthnot.

EMOLLIENTS. 133, vi, 395. Arbuthnot, Quincy.

EPHEMERA. 82, vi, 67; of learning, 145, vii, 32.

EPIDEMICAL. infatuation, 10, v, 64; (discontent, *Debates*, xii, 142; weakness, xiii, 390; diseases, xiii, 402; fury, xiii, 421). Bacon, Graunt, South.

EQUILIBRATION. of undetermined counsel, 111, vi, 254; (war continued in an equilibration, *King of Prussia*, iv, 578).

EQUIPOISE. of an empty mind, 5, v, 30; between the pleasures of this life, and the hopes of futurity, 7, v, 44; between good and ill, 70, v, 442; of the mind, 95, vi, 157; [of] desires, 132, vi, 388; [of] the peccant humour, 156, vii, 95; (*Debates*, xii, 364, 371, 378; xiii, 96, 227, 326, 361, 373, 468 and *passim;* cf. *ante* pp. 63–64, 83). Glanvill.

EQUIPONDERANT. reasons, 1, v, 5; nothing equiponderant to the security of truth, 20, v, 137. Locke, Ray.

ESSENTIAL. virtues, 120, vi, 314; substance, 131, vi, 384; (and constituent, *Debates*, xii, 120; xii, 61, 204, 214; xiii, 153, 162). Arbuthnot, Bacon, Bentley. Cf. *inessential,* 98, vi, 175.

ETHER. dulness to quicken into sentiment in a thin ether, 117, vi, 296. Locke, Newton.

EVACUATE. streets, 171, vii, 187; (towns of Flanders, *Debates*, xiii, 302). Boyle. EVACUATION. of all duties, 31, v, 203. Hale. Cf. VACUITY.

EVANESCENCE. [of] principles of truth, 156, vii, 95; of . . . reward, 163, vii, 137. Arbuthnot, Thomson. EVANESCENT. incidents, 60, v, 386; ideas, 110, vi, 248.

EVAPORATION. [of] affections, 99, vi, 179; of gaiety, 101, vi, 189; of wit, 187, vii, 279. Quincy, Woodward. Cf. *vapour,* 133, vi, 398; *fumes,* 77, vi, 39.

EVENT. [of] experiments, 1, v, 6; 157, vii, 86; [of throwing dice], 181, vii, 240; ([of] an experiment, *Debates*, xiii, 499; [of an adventure in lotteries], xiii, 492).

EXACERBATION. in diseases, 32, v, 211; of human misery, 114, vi, 272; of hatred, 185, vii, 261. Arbuthnot, Bacon.

EXCENTRICITY. from the general round of life, 151, vii, 65. Browne, Harris, Holder, Wotton.

EXCORIATIONS. artificial, 133, vi, 395. Arbuthnot.

EXCRESCENCES. [on melted sand or ashes], 9, v, 56; [on] the softest bloom of roseate virginity, 112, vi, 260; ([on] the monarchy, *Debates*, xii, 272).

EXHALE. kindness, 64, v, 408. Shakespeare. EXHALATION. of spices, 78, vi, 43. Burnet, Milton, Shakespeare.

EXHAUST. [topicks of amusement, 23, v, 154], omitted in revision of 1754; fortune, 63, v, 403; past, 69, v, 440; treasure, 72, vi, 11; life, 87, vi, 101; a receiver, 117, vi, 296; powers of modern wit, 136, vi, 412; persuasions, 139, vi, 433; expedients, 141, vii, 6; description and sentiment, 143, vii, 14; any single subject, 150, vii, 59; radical vigour, 178, vii, 223; [children] exhaust . . . by their profusion, 196, vii, 325; (*Debates*, xii, 9; xiii, 44, 76 and *passim*). Bacon, Locke, Philips, Wiseman. Cf. *unexhausted* fountain of tears, 141, vii, 4; surfeit with *unexhausted* variety, 206, vii, 381.

EXPAND. seminal idea . . . into flowers, 184, vii, 254; beauty, 196, vii, 324. EXPANSION. of understanding, 117, vi, 299. Bentley, Blackmore, Grew, Locke.

EXTRANEOUS. separate . . . real character from extraneous adhesions and casual circumstances, 166, vii, 157. Locke, Woodward.

FECUNDITY. exuberance and fecundity of . . . seasons, 111, vi, 253. Bentley, Ray, Woodward.

FERMENT. into merriment, 117, vi, 299; heterogeneous sciences fermenting in the mind, 154, vii, 84. FERMENTATION. [of] a secret, 13, v, 82; of . . . mind, 74, vi, 19. Boyle, Harris, Thomson.

FLACCID. sides of a football, 117, vi, 296. Arbuthnot, Bacon, Holder. Cf. *flaccidity, Idler* 17, viii, 64.

FLATULENCE. of pride, 75, vi, 28. Arbuthnot, Glanvill.

FLEXIBLE. [persons], 64, v, 407; minds, 110, vi, 249; temper, 132, vi, 390; mind, 133, vi, 399; to arguments, 203, vii, 366. Bacon, Locke, Shakespeare. FLEXIBILITY. of language, 92, vi, 132; of submission, 109, vi, 242; (and complaisance, *Debates*, xiii, 465). Newton, Woodward. FLEXURE. of *Meander*, 117, vi, 293. Shakespeare. Cf. *inflexible*, 79, vi, 52; 124, vi, 343; 125, vi, 346.

FLUCTUATION. of will, 63, v, 404; of uncertainty, 95, vi, 157 and 137, vi, 419; of chance, 99, vi, 179 and 174, vii, 199; of . . . wishes, 102, vi, 195; (of counsels, *Debates*, xiii, 71; of measures, xii, 77). Boyle, Browne. Cf. *fluctuate*, 2, v, 13; 132, vi, 388.

FLUID. resistance of, 179, vii, 228. Arbuthnot.

FRIGID. judge, 18, v, 117; villainy, 77, vi, 41; infection, 89, vi, 112; critick, 106, vi, 224; [persons], 127, vi, 361; indifference, 128, vi, 366; reception, 149, vii, 53; graciousness, 165, vii, 151; neutrality, 190, vii, 288; opiate, 207, vii, 389. Cheyne. FRIGIDITY. of age, 111, vi, 255; (of old age, *Debates*, xii, 78). Browne, Glanvill. FRIGORIFICK. torpor, 120, vi, 315; wisdom, 129, vi, 371; power [of bashfulness], 159, vii, 115. Quincy.

FUGACITY. of pleasure, 143, vii, 16. Boyle.

GENERATE. obstructions to the vital powers, 85, vi, 86. Arbuthnot, Bacon, Milton. Cf. *generation*, 59, v, 380.

GEOMETRICIAN. 54, v, 345; 113, vi, 268. Browne, Watts. Cf. *geometrical* (in a quotation from Pascal), 92, vi, 128.

GRAVITY. [of] liquors, 69, v, 438. Browne, Newton, Quincy.

GREGARIOUS. savages . . . never, 99, vi, 178. Ray.

HETEROGENEOUS. bodies, 14, v, 94; ideas, 23, v, 151; principles [in chemistry], 25, v, 166; notions, 141, vii, 4; sciences fermenting in the mind, 154, vii, 85. Woodward.

HUMOUR. fatally predominant, 43, v, 276; peccant, 156, vii, 95. Milton. Ray.

HYDROPHOBIA. [6, v, 35], omitted in revision of 1754. Quincy.

HYPOCHONDRIAC. dejection, 73, vi, 16. Bacon.

HYPOTHESIS. [24, v, 157; 31, v, 201], omitted in revision of 1754. South.

IMMERGE. ourselves in luxury, 65, v, 416. Cf. *immerse*, 2, v, 13; 70, v, 442; *immersion*, 103, vi, 205.

IMPREGNATE. with the seeds of malady, 43, v, 276; the air with particles, 72, vi, 7; thoughts with various mixtures, 167, vii, 162; 96, vi, 160; 193, vii, 308. Browne. Cf. *pregnant*, 177, vii, 215.

INCLINATION. of [a] carriage, 34, v, 222; wealth . . . the general center of inclination, 131, vi, 382; [of magnets], 199, vii, 341; 100, vi, 183; 129, vi, 372; 135, vi, 408; (*inclinations* to the balance of power, *Debates*, xiii, 304). Newton, Shakespeare, South.

INCOMMENSURATE. 127, vi, 362. Holder. Cf. COMMENSURATE, MENSURATION.

INDISSOLUBLE. union [in marriage], 100, vi, 183; bodies, indissoluble by heat, 174, vii, 200; (friendship, *Debates*, xii, 144). Boyle, South, Thomson.

INEBRIATION. 153, vii, 78. Browne. Cf. EBRIETY. Cf. *inebriating*, *Debates*, xiii, 432; *inebriated*, *False Alarm*, x, 33.

INFECT. with the waters of lethe, 3, v, 19; with enthusiasm, 5, v, 28; [66, v, 421], omitted in revision of 1751–52; with regard for trifling accomplishments, 66, v, 422; with the jargon of a particular profession, 99, vi, 182; 71, v, 4; (*Debates*, xii, 46 and *passim*). Milton, Shakespeare.
INFECTION. of the writer's malady, 2, v, 11; of prejudice, 58, v, 373; of the intellect, 89, vi, 112; greater part of mankind . . . gay or serious by infection, 188, vii, 280; of uneasiness, 204, vii, 371; (of vice, *Debates*, xiii, 406). Bacon, Quincy. INFECTIOUS. 31, v, 204. Bacon, Shakespeare.

INFLATION. of his heart, 154, vii, 84; of spirits, 195, vii, 320. Arbuthnot.

INFLUX. of corruption, 201, vii, 354. Arbuthnot, Hale, Ray.

INFUSE. any wish, 4, v, 24; malignity, 56, v, 358; poison of discord, 64, v, 410; diffidence which . . . disappointments . . . infuse, 69, v, 437; tendencies . . . which nature infuses, 69, v, 438; poison, 77, vi, 41; despair of success, 134, vi, 402; (discipline, *Debates*, xii, 52; xiii, 43). Milton, Shakespeare. INFUSION. of dissimilar ideas, 101, vi, 195; of imagery, 124, vi, 342; of wisdom, 135, vi, 410; in the current of . . . ideas, 141, vii, 2; [in thought], 167, vii, 162; of . . . new ideas, 169, vii, 171; (cooling and diluting infusion, *Debates*, xii, 361).

INGREDIENT. in orange pudding, 51, v, 329; chemical, 68, v, 430; (*Debates*, xii, 114). Arbuthnot, Bacon, Milton, Newton.

INHIBITION. terror and, 25, v, 165; of sleep, 79, vi, 51.

INOCULATION. benefits of early inoculation, 133, vi, 397.

INSIPID. common pleasures of life, 74, vi, 20; 103, vi, 204; common amusements, 132, vi, 390. Boyle, Floyer. INSIPIDITY. 18, v, 121; 176, vii, 212.

INSTIL. mean notions . . . into . . . children, 18, v, 122; desires . . . by imperceptible communications, 141, vii, 2. INSTILLATION. [in] the draught of life, 72, vi, 7; of . . . frigid opiate, 207, vii, 389.

INSTRUMENT. optical, 105, vi, 219; of steerage, 175, vii, 208; of mental vision, 176, vii, 213; (of tyranny, *Debates*, xii, 204; of French policy, xii, 150). Blackmore, Mortimer.

INTERMEDIATE. variations [between summer and winter], 80, vi, 55; hour, 115, vi, 283; space, 127, vi, 359; gradations from . . . first agent to . . . last consequence, 137, vi, 417; passages, 139, vi, 429. Arbuthnot, Newton, Watts.

INTERMIX. histories, 84, vi, 81. Milton. INTERMIXTURE. of subjects, 107, vi, 227; of an unseasonable levity, 125, vi, 346. Bacon, Boyle.

INTERSTITIAL. spaces, 8, v, 46; vacancies, 108, vi, 235. Browne. Cf. *interstice, Preface to Shakespeare*, ix, 294.

INVOLUTION. of infernal darkness, 168, vii, 167. Browne, Glanvill. Cf. *involve*, 64, v, 407; 68, v, 431.

IRRADIATION. from above, 7, v, 45; of knowledge, 108, vi, 236; of intelligence, 154, vii, 83. Browne, Digby, Hale.

IRRITATE. curiosity, 124, vi, 343; admirers, 140, vi, 436; virulence, debtors, 142, vii, 11, 12; [an] adversary, 206, vii, 384; (opponents, *De-*

bates, xiii, 104; wit, xiii, 379). Bacon, Thomson. IRRITATION. 74, vi, 19; 183, vii, 251. Arbuthnot.

LACERATE.   a story, 122, vi, 331; the heart, 128, vi, 367; (by sorrow, *Letters* i, 212; the mind, ii, 67; continuity of being, *Life* iii, 419). Mrs. Piozzi, *British Synonymy* (1794), i, 345, comments on the surgical character of the word. See *laceration* of an idea, *Rasselas,* xi, 141; of mind, *Letters* i, 383; *Life* ii, 106.

LATITUDE.   [and] longitude, 197, vii, 331.

LAX.   faculties, 85, vi, 86; definitions, 143, vii, 15. Holder, Milton, Quincy, Woodward. LAXITY.   [of the atmosphere], 117, vi, 297; of a rustick life, 138, vi, 425. Bentley, Quincy, Wiseman. Cf. RELAX.

LENITIVE.   of passion, 2, v, 74 [*antidote* in Folio and revision of 1751–52]; by which the throbs of the breast are assuaged, 76, vi, 33. South. Cf. *lenient,* 47, v, 305; *lenity,* 12, v, 74.

LETHARGY.   111, vi, 256; 118, vi, 304; (powers of the continent . . . benumbed by a *lethargy, Debates,* xiii, 343). Arbuthnot, Shakespeare. LETHARGICK.   103, vi, 205; 198, vii, 336. Arbuthnot.

LEVITY.   of . . . lines [of verse], 94, vi, 149. Cf. *levity* [of wings], *Rasselas,* xi, 19, chap. vi; [of manners], xi, 52, chap xvii. Bentley, Milton, Shakespeare.

LIQUEFACTION.   [of] sand or ashes, 9, v, 56. Bacon, Burnet.

LONGEVITY.   [of] animals, 169, vii, 169. Arbuthnot, Ray.

LONGITUDE.   67, v, 426; 197, vii, 331. Arbuthnot.

LUMINARY.   of life, 2, v, 12. Bentley, Milton, Wotton. LUMINOUS. 20, v, 137. Bacon, Bentley, Milton, Newton.

LUNAR.   world, 105, vi, 219; mountains, 117, vi, 292. Cf. *sublunary* hopes, 28, v, 187; transactions, 49, v, 316 (added in revision of 1751–52); power, 114, vi, 274. Bacon, Browne.

MAGNET.   160, vii, 121; 199, vii, 341–345. Locke. MAGNETICK. 61, v, 393; 199, vii, 344. -ICAL.   199, vii, 342. Blackmore, Newton. MAGNETISM.   199, vii, 339–341. Browne, Glanvill.

MATHEMATICIAN.   103, vi, 205.

MATURATION.   of . . . schemes, 111, vi, 254; of a plan, 156, vii, 99. Bacon, Bentley. Cf. *mature* v. 122, vi, 327; *maturity,* 169, vii, 169.

MECHANICAL.   operation, 85, vi, 87. Newton. MECHANICK.   [i.e., mechanical philosopher], 153, vii, 76; ([i.e., workman], *Debates,* xii, 100). MECHANISM.   degraded animals to, 95, vi, 155. Arbuthnot, Bentley. MECHANIST.   117, vi, 292; 173, vii, 197 [*mechanician* in Folio].

MEDICAL. refinements, 85, vi, 84; axiom, 167, vii, 160. Browne. MEDICATE. gloves, 130, vi, 378; the cup of life, 150, vii, 58. Arbuthnot, Graunt. MEDICINAL. springs, 83, vi, 73; spring, 142, vii, 7. Quincy, Milton, Shakespeare. MEDICINE. of the mind, 17, v, 113 and 52, v, 333; 47, v, 306; 87, vi, 98; 105, vi, 219; 112, vi, 258; 150, vii, 58; 151, vi, 63; (efficacy [of spirits] in medicine, *Debates*, xiii, 507; laws . . . the medicines of a state, xii, 303; and *passim*). Shakespeare.

MEDIUM. resistance of, 127, vi, 359; (between . . . interests, *Debates*, xii, 305; [which transmits sensations], xiii, 92). Bacon, Holder, Newton.

MENSURATION. of time, 103, vi, 204. Arbuthnot. Cf. COMMENSURATE, INCOMMENSURATE.

MERCURY. 5, v, 31; 67, v, 425. Arbuthnot, Hill.

MERIDIAN. 65, v, 412; 197, vii, 331. Browne, Watts.

METALLICK. composition, 199, vii, 344. Blackmore, Wotton. METALLINE. form, 9, v, 56. Bacon, Boyle.

METEOROLOGICAL. observations, 24, v, 159. Browne. METEOROUS. pleasures, 68, v, 430. Milton. Cf. *meteor*, 184, vii, 258; 203, vii, 367; 208, vii, 393.

MICROSCOPE. 112, vi, 260; of criticism, 176, vii, 213. Bentley.

MIGRATION. into the country, 135, vi, 406; of the gay and busy, 138, vi, 423. Browne, Woodward.

MOMENTANEOUS. excursions, 2, v, 11. Bacon.

MORBID. every man comes into the world morbid, 43, v, 276. Arbuthnot.

MORTIFICATION. 15, v, 96; of enemies, 16, v, 106; 203, vii, 365; (of insult and neglect, *Debates*, xii, 392; of losses, xiii, 203). Arbuthnot, Bacon, Milton. MORTIFY. pride of wit and knowledge . . . mortified, 6, v, 35; one . . . mortified in full assemblies, 119, vi, 307; childhood not easily . . . mortified, 149, vii, 54; Diogenes . . . [not] mortified, 202, vii, 361. Bacon, Boyle, Browne, Shakespeare.

NARCOTICK. infection, 89, vi, 112. Browne, Quincy.

NATURALIST. 118, vi, 304. Cf. *natural historian*, 169, vii, 169.

NOXIOUS. plants, 108, vi, 238. Browne.

NUTRIMENT. 85, vi, 85. Shakespeare, South.

OBTUND. remorse, 72, vii, 192; senses, 78, vi, 44. Harvey.

OPERATE. petty qualities operate unseen, 72, vi, 365; neither benefit nor mischief operate, 118, vi, 302; external accidents operate variously upon different minds, 128, vi, 365; predominant appetite . . . operated, 131, vi, 384; vanity . . . to operate, 135, vi, 406; every anomalous quality to operate, 138, vii, 425; neither fortune nor patronage operated, 146, vii, 38; (*Debates,* xii, 158 and *passim*). Locke, Watts. OPERATION. passions of . . . forcible operation, 18, v, 117; [of remedies], 52, v, 333; mechanical operation, 85, vi, 87; of genius, 117, vi, 296; of nature, 125, vi, 344; 137, vi, 418; [of a chemist], 139, vi, 430; [of] flattery, 155, vii, 89; (*Debates,* xiii, 72 and *passim*). Bacon, Bentley, Boyle, Locke, Milton.

OPIATE. 89, vi, 111; 150, vii, 57; of irreligion, 171, vii, 182; [of] flattery, 172, vii, 192; 207, vii, 389; (of another expedient, *Debates,* xiii, 78). Bentley.

OPTICAL. instrument, 105, vi, 219. Boyle.

OSCILLATION. of a beam charged with equal weights, 63, v, 404.

PALLIATIVE. n. of incurable miseries, 143, vii, 16. PALLIATIVE. adj. cure for human miseries, 32, v, 209. Arbuthnot. Cf. *palliate,* 8, v, 49; 28, v, 185; 31, v, 201; 32, v, 209; 41, v, 266; 54, v, 348; 65, v, 415; 68, v, 433; 96, vi, 159; 143, vii, 16; 195, vii, 321; (*Debates,* xii, 237; xiii, 79); *palliation,* 76, vi, 31.

PALPITATION. of a champion on the day of combat, 101, vi, 192; [on seeing a dead rat], 126, vi, 352; [of the] breast, 156, vii, 99; 181, vii, 241. Arbuthnot, Harvey, Thomson.

PAPILIONACEOUS. tribe, 82, vi, 67. Quincy. Cf. PAPILIUS. correspondent, 141, vii, 6.

PAROXYSM. of corporal pain, 52, v, 335; of outrage, 74, vi, 19; of violence, 112, vi, 261. Arbuthnot, Harvey.

PARTICLE. particles that impregnate [the air], 72, vi, 7; of time, 108, vi, 235; of knowledge, 121, vi, 321; of our duration, 178, vii, 223. Blackmore, Newton.

PECCANT. humour, 156, vii, 95; (peccant part, *Life* ii, 100). Arbuthnot.

PERCUSSION. [of rhyme], 86, vi, 93. Arbuthnot, Bacon, Newton, Shakespeare.

PERENNIAL. constant and perennial softness of manner, 72, vi, 7; verdure, 80, vi, 55; happiness, 178, vii, 223. Cheyne, Harvey.

PERIODICAL. vicissitudes, 21, v, 142; sheets, 23, v, 151; tortures, 85, vi, 86; remorse, 155, vii, 94; eulogies, 193, vii, 306; writers, 193, vii, 308. Bentley, Browne, Derham, Watts. Cf. *period,* 54, v, 345.

PERPETUAL. [wings actuated] by the perpetual motion, 67, v, 428; curiosity in perpetual motion, 89, vi, 112; (drudgery, *Debates,* xii, 292). Arbuthnot, Milton, Wilkins. *Perpetuate, perpetuation, perpetuity* occur *passim.*

PETRIFY. [parts of the earth] petrified with perpetual frost, 108, vi, 233. Woodward.

PHILOSOPHER. [i.e., astronomer or microscopist], 8, v, 46 and 9, v, 57; [i.e., meteorologist], 103, vi, 205. Locke, Milton, South. PHILO-SOPHICK. 105, vi, 218. -ICAL. 83, vi, 73, added in revision of 1751–52; 138, vi, 423. Milton, Shakespeare. PHILOSOPHY. [experimental], 31, v, 201; 137, vi, 420; 150, vii, 57; [moral], 191, vii, 294. Shakespeare.

PHLEGMATICK. sediment of weariness, 69, v, 438. Arbuthnot, Harvey, Shakespeare.

PHYSICK. of the mind, 2, v, 11; [to the soul, 47, v, 302], omitted in revision of 1754; 85, vi, 84; 96, vi, 159; 120, vi, 314; ([for a tainted imagination], Debates, xii, 47). Locke. Cf. physician, 6, v, 35; 118, vi, 304; 120, vi, 314; 150, vii, 57; 156, vii, 95; (Debates, xiii, 392).

PHYSIOGNOMY. 23, v, 154. Bacon, Locke.

PHYSIOLOGY. 151, vii, 63. Bentley, Glanvill.

PNEUMATOLOGY. treatise of barometrical, 117, vi, 297.

POSTULATE. 13, v, 82; 155, vii, 88; settled principle or self-evident postulate, 158, vii, 107. Browne, Watts.

PREPONDERATE. present objects falling . . . into the scale . . . preponderate, 7, v, 44; faults . . . preponderate, 78, vi, 33; (Debates, xii, 299; xiii, 199, 291, 513; cf. ante p. 64). Bentley, Glanvill, Locke, Watts. PREPONDERATION. of . . . motives, 131, vi, 387. Watts. Cf. EQUIPONDERANT.

PRESCRIPTION. [for] intellectual maladies, 87, vi, 98. Shakespeare.

PRESERVATIVE. 2, v, 11; against vanities, 6, v, 37; [for] intellectual health, 47, v, 403; [against] prejudice, 58, v, 373; against the temptations of falsehood, 96, vi, 158; from evil, 126, vi, 353; [of] caution, 126, vi, 353. Bacon, Browne, Harvey. Cf. preserve, 2, v, 12; 45, v, 292; health, 112, vi, 258; (Debates, xiii, 19, 20, 22, 33, 38, 42); preservation, 126, vi, 353; (Debates, xiii, 29).

PROGRESSION. 108, vi, 236; 127, vi, 360. Browne, Locke, Newton, Shakespeare. PROGRESSIVE. motion [of Truth] . . . perpetually progressive, 96, vi, 160; [fortune, 165, vii, 148], omitted in revision of 1754. Bacon, Browne, Milton, Ray.

PROJECTION. [in cooking with a skillet], 51, v, 328; [chemical or alchemical], 67, v, 425; 111, vi, 254; 199, vii, 340. Bacon.

PROPERTY. of the catenarian curve, 179, vii, 228; of . . . magnets, 199, vii, 345. South, Watts.

PUTREFACTION. of stagnant life, 47, v, 307; (putrefaction and stench . . . the causes of pestilential distempers, Debates, xii, 207).

Arbuthnot, Bacon, Quincy, Thomson. Cf. *putrid,* 165, vii, 148. Cf. *putrefy, Falkland's Islands,* x, 68.

QUADRATURE. of the circle, 179, vii, 229. Watts.

QUIESCENCE. of astonishment, 137, vi, 417. Glanvill. QUIESCENT. faculties, 49, v, 314; state, 103, vi, 205; 183, vii, 250. Browne, Glanvill, Grew, Holder, Newton.

RADIATION. of understanding, 29, v, 189; of hope and comfort, 128, vi, 364. Bacon. Cf. *radiance,* 77, vi, 39. Cf. IRRADIATION.

RADICAL. cure, 32, v, 209; worth, 70, v, 444; postulate, 156, vii, 96; corruption, 171, vii, 183 and 175, vii, 208; vigour, 178, vii, 223; (hatred, *Debates,* xii, 143). Arbuthnot, Bacon, Bentley, Wilkins. RADICATE. disease of the intellect . . . radicated, 89, vi, 112. Browne, Glanvill. Cf. *eradicate,* 58, v, 370; 126, vi, 354; *eradication,* 183, vii, 252.

RAMIFICATION. of private friendship, 99, vi, 180; cf. *ante* p. 91, n. 25. Arbuthnot, Hale.

RAREFACTION. [of atmosphere], 117, vi, 297. Burnet, Wotton.

RECEIVER. partly exhausted, 117, vi, 296. Bentley.

RECESS. of . . . sun from northern climes, 188, vii, 277. Browne. RECESSION. from temerity, 76, vi, 34; migration . . . [or] stated recession, 135, vi, 407. Cf. *secession* from sport and noise, 110, vi, 250.

RECIPROCATION. of pleasure, 101, vi, 191; of beneficence, 104, vi, 209; of civility, 106, vi, 221 and 108, vi, 233; of benefits, 137, vi, 422; of mischief, 185, vii, 261. Bacon, Browne, Ray. Cf. *reciprocal,* 91, vi, 124; 172, vii, 192; *reciprocally,* 26, vi, 171; marriage thus reciprocally fraudulent, 197, vii, 327.

REGIMEN. [prescribed, 5, v, 28], omitted in revision of 1754; intellectual, 89, vi, 112; [for] intellectual health, 112, vi, 259; ([i.e., diet], *Debates,* xiii, 490).

REGISTER. n. [of the event in throwing dice], 181, vii, 240. Bacon, Boyle, Shakespeare. REGISTER. v. event [of] experiments, 154, vii, 86. Milton.

REGULATE. temperature, 43, v, 276; [life] by passion, and by fancy, 63, v, 402; 66, v, 422; superintending what he cannot regulate, 69, v, 438; the body . . . by various compressions of . . . ambient element, 117, vi, 296; choice, 130, vi, 380 and 184, vii, 255; opinion, 136, vi, 411; enquiries, 147, vii, 41; punishments, 148, vii, 48; [desire, 165, vii, 146], omitted in revision of 1751–52; books, 181, vii, 240; measures, 185, vii, 263; conduct, 190, vii, 290; precedence, 192, vii, 301; [165, vii, 146; 184, vii, 256], omitted in revision of 1751–52; [5, v, 28; 180, vii, 233; 207, vii, 388], omitted in revision of 1754; (trade, *Debates,* xiii, 80; opinions, xiii, 380). Locke, Wiseman.

RELAX. [moments, 6, v, 37], omitted in revision of 1754; rules of politeness, 75, vi, 30; the mind, 85, vi, 87; muscles of disciplinarian moroseness, 141, vii, 3; [vigilance, 165, vii, 149], omitted in revision of 1754; (embargo, *Debates*, xii, 17; severity, xiii, 474). RELAXATION. of metrical rigour, 88, vi, 109; of the law, 114, vi, 274; of vigilance, 123, vi, 333; ease [and], 127, vi, 359; [in eulogistic dedications], 136, vi, 415; of . . . gravity, 168, vii, 167; [of vigilance, 184, vii, 256], omitted in revision of 1751–52; (of orders, *Debates*, xiii, 190; of discipline, xiii, 194; of cares, xiii, 514). Arbuthnot, Bacon, Burnet. Cf. LAX.

REMISSION. of his ardour, 65, v, 413; though some remission may be obtained, a complete cure will scarcely be effected, 89, vi, 112. Bacon, Locke, Woodward. Cf. *remit*, 17, v, 111; 26, v, 172; 113, vi, 266; 127, vi, 361; 137, vi, 422; 171, vii, 182; 185, vii, 261; 207, vii, 390; (*Debates*, xii, 31, 240).

REPERCUSSION. [of] sounds . . . from one coxcomb to another, 23, v, 152; [of] precepts . . . from one author to another, 129, vi, 370; of communicated pleasure, 148, vii, 47. Bacon, Blackmore.

REPULSION. of [natures], 160, vii, 119. Arbuthnot.

RESILIENCY. of mind from one extreme to another, 110, vi, 249. Bacon.

RESISTANCE. of fluids, 179, vii, 228. Bacon, Locke, Newton.

RESOLVABLE. bodies . . . into the same elements, 68, v, 430. Arbuthnot, South.

RESTORATIVE. n. 120, vi, 314. Arbuthnot, Mortimer, Shakespeare, South.

RESUSCITATE. the powers of digestion, 48, v, 311; the vital functions, 85, vi, 87. Bacon. RESUSCITATION. of first principles [of] government, 156, vii, 95; of desires, 207, vii, 388.

RETARD. death, which . . . we may precipitate, but cannot retard, 17, v, 114; 60, v, 383; to forward or retard, 69, v, 437; application [of justice], 81, vi, 62; [speed, 87, vi, 100], omitted in revision of 1754; progress, 96, vi, 162; in their designs, 118, vi, 302; progress of life retarded by the *vis inertiae*, 134, vi, 402; hastened or retarded the revolutions of empire, 141, vii, 1; old age, 151, vii, 63; effects of time may . . . be accelerated or retarded, 159, vii, 116; (justice, *Debates*, xiii, 143; 261, 263). RETARDATION. latent inequalities of the smoothest surface . . . by continued retardation wholly overpower [a moving body], 127, vi, 359; of . . . pupil's progress, 132, vi, 391. Bacon.

REVOLUTION. of the stars, 8, v, 47; [of] events, 26, v, 168; of the gay world, 42, v, 271; diurnal revolution of the earth, 117, vi, 297; 122, vi, 332; of empire, 141, vii, 1; of ancient kingdoms, 145, vii, 32; [of a]

house, 161, vii, 124; of sentiment, 196, vii, 322; of opinion, 203, vii, 367; ([political], *Debates*, xii, 276; in the empire, xii, 383). Milton, Watts. Cf. *revolve*, 54, v, 348; 60, v, 384.

ROTATION.   [of a vessel in] the gulph of *Intemperance*, 102, vi, 200; of petty cares, 108, vi, 234; (of parties, *Debates*, xii, 77; of power, xiii, 166, 293; of affairs, xiii, 175, 327). Bacon, Hale, Newton, Thomson.

ROTUNDITY.   of bodies, 138, vi, 424. Bentley, Grew, Shakespeare.

SALUBRITY.   of admonitions, 14, v, 91; 150, vii, 58.

SALUTARY.   remonstrances, 40, v, 262; effects [of] pain, 47, v, 302; [counsels, 50, v, 320], omitted in revision of 1754; arts, 57, v, 366; effects [of] . . . particles [in] . . . air, 72, vi, 7; plants, 83, vi, 73; precepts, 87, vi, 97; custom, 100, vi, 187; cautions, 108, vi, 239; remarks, 129, vi, 371; purposes, 155, vii, 92; sorrow, 195, vii, 320; (measures, *Debates*, xii, 23; coercions, xii, 292; restraints, xiii, 92; law, xiii, 444). Bentley, Ray.

SATELLITE.   [of] Jupiter, 99, vi, 181. Bentley, Locke.

SCINTILLATION.   of conceit, 141, vii, 4. Browne, Glanvill.

SEDIMENT.   phlegmatick sediment of weariness and deliberation, 69, v, 438. Bacon, South, Woodward.

SEMINAL.   idea, 184, vii, 254. Glanvill.

SENSORY.   78, vi, 43. Bacon, Newton. Cf. *sensation*, 78, vi, 42; (*Debates*, xiii, 247); *sensibility*, 78, vi, 42, 46; 150, vii, 57; *sensible*, 102, vi, 201.

STIMULATE.   perseverance, 207, vii, 389. Arbuthnot, Sharp. STIMULATION.   of necessity, 145, vii, 30. Watts.

SUBDUCT.   from the number of . . . encomiasts, 118, vi, 304; (Austrians . . . subducted to garrison the frontier, *Debates*, xiii, 302). Milton.

SUBLIME.   the spirits of youth sublimed by health, 69, v, 438. Glanvill, Milton.

SUBMARINE.   voyage, 105, vi, 219. Ray, Wilkins.

SUBSIDIARY.   sight [i.e., spectacles], 9, v, 57; ordinances, 110, vi, 249; strength, 154, vii, 83. Arbuthnot.

SUBTILIZE.   the art of thievery, 114, vi, 273. Glanvill, Grew, Ray.

SUFFOCATE.   by a poisonous vapour, 183, vii, 250. Browne, Shakespeare, Thomson. SUFFOCATION.   [by drowning], 38, v, 249; in a quicksand, 61, v, 390. Arbuthnot, Bacon, Cheyne.

SULPHUR.   99, vi, 181. Milton, Thomson, Woodward.

SUPERFICIES. of life, 128, vi, 364 and 196, vii, 323. Cf. *superficial,* 72, vi, 11.

SUPERINDUCE. habits may superinduce inability to deny . . . desire, 64, v, 406; (habits superinduced, *Debates,* xiii, 460). Bacon, Locke, South.

SUPERVENIENT. images, 207, vii, 390. Browne.

SYMMETRICAL. elegance, 94, vi, 146.

SYMPTOMS. of the writer's malady, 2, v, 11; of canine madness, 6, v, 35; of some deeper malady, 74, vi, 19; of malignity, 89, vi, 111; of an intellectual malady, 95, vi, 152.

TELESCOPE. 24, v, 157; 61, v, 388; [of] criticism, 176, vii, 214. Watts.

TEMPERATE. v. fear . . . by this universal medicine of the mind, 17, v, 113. Bacon, Browne, Milton, Shakespeare, Wiseman. TEMPERATURE. [of] the human body, 43, v, 276. Bacon, Watts, Woodward. Cf. *temper* v., 87, vi, 104.

TENSION. [of the atmosphere], 117, vi, 297. Blackmore, Holder.

TENUITY. of a defecated air, 117, vi, 296. Arbuthnot, Bacon, Bentley, Glanvill.

TEPIDITY. [of] the body, 80, vi, 55.

TERRAQUEOUS. globe, 24, v, 157. Woodward.

TEXTURE. of liquors, 69, v, 438. Milton, Newton. Cf. CONTEXTURE.

THEOREM. 179, vii, 228. Graunt.

TINCTURE. sceptre tinctured with ambrosia, 3, v, 16. Blackmore, Watts. Cf. *tinct, Preface to Shakespeare,* ix, 251.

TORPID. comfort, 48, v, 311; wasps, 82, vi, 67; faculties, 83, vi, 72 and 85, vi, 86; 124, vi, 340; risibility, 125, vi, 349; generation, 134, vi, 402. Ray, Thomson. Cf. *torpescence, Letters* ii, 441, App. D.

TORTUOSITY. of imaginary rectitude, 122, vi, 327. Browne.

TRANSFUSION. of blood, 199, vii, 340. Boyle.

TRANSMUTE. metals, 51, vi, 329. Ray. TRANSMUTATION. [of metals], 63, v, 402. Bacon.

TREPIDATION. of the balance, 1, v, 5; dismissed her daughters with the same trepidation, 51, v, 326; of impatience, 110, vi, 250. Bacon, Milton.

TROPICK. circles and tropicks, 197, vii, 331; [206, vii, 385], omitted in revision of 1754.

TUMOUR. of insolence, 98, vi, 175; of dignity, 105, vi, 217; of phrase, 125, vi, 350; (of disease, *Debates*, xiii, 300; dropsical, xiii, 309). Wiseman, Wotton. Cf. *tumid, Letters* ii, 372; *Life* iv, 39.

VACUITY. in [life], 8, v, 46; in . . . life, 35, v, 228; of mind, 39, v, 255; of our being, 41, v, 263; of recluse and domestick leisure, 85, vi, 88; of an idle moment, 128, vi, 366; [of the mind of a wit], 141, vii, 5; of actions, 152, vii, 70; of conversation, 167, vii, 161; of life, 191, vii, 295; [of] leisure . . . for contemplations, 203, vii, 367; (*Debates*, xiii, 27). Arbuthnot, Bentley, Glanvill, Milton. Cf. EVACUATE AND EVACUATION. Cf. *vacancy*, 40, v, 258; 134, vi, 402; 146, vii, 36; 149, vii, 56; 201, vii, 356; *vacant*, 32, v, 211; 124, vi, 343; 132, vi, 391; 149, vii, 53; *vacate*, 79, vi, 53.

VALETUDINARIAN. race, 48, v, 308. Cf. *valetudinary, Letters* i, 378. Browne, Cheyne.

VARIATION. [of the magnetic needle], 19, v, 129; 199, vii, 341.

VEGETATION. powers of, 48, v, 310; principles of, 135, vi, 409. Ray, Thomson, Woodward. Cf. *vegetable* n., 5, v, 31; adj., 2, v, 11; 19, v, 125; 72, vi, 8.

VEHICLE. to disguise *the catharticks of the soul*, 87, vi, 98; of instruction, 121, vi, 325. Browne.

VELOCITY. dance . . . with . . . giddy velocity, 102, vi, 200; body driven by a blow . . . moves for a time with great velocity, 127, vi, 358–359. Bentley.

VENTILATION. [of] the mind, 101, vi, 195; of gaiety, 205, vii, 376. Cf. *ventilate, Rasselas,* xi, 16, chap. vi.

VERTIGINOUS. motion, 117, vi, 297. Bentley, Woodward.

VIBRATION. [i.e., shaking] of a stick, 195, vii, 319. Newton, South, Thomson.

VICISSITUDE. contraries produced by periodical vicissitudes, 21, v, 142; of victory, 22, v, 145; of my life, 26, v, 174; 29, v, 191; 33, v, 219; 34, v, 219; of anxiety, 34, v, 223; 41, v, 268; of external circumstance, 150, vii, 57; (commotion and, *Debates*, xii, 128; of empire, xii, 378). Milton, Newton, Woodward.

VOLATILE. incidents, 60, v, 386; gratifications, 78, vi, 43; spirit of wit, 188, vii, 279; [persons], 189, vii, 283. Milton, Newton, Watts. VOLATILITY. [of] a secret, 13, v, 82. Arbuthnot, Bacon, Hale, Newton. VOLATILISE. the spirits of youth . . . volatilised by passion, 69, v, 438. Arbuthnot, Newton.

VOLUBILITY. [of lines of verse], 92, vi, 136 and 94, vi, 149; [of speech], 144, vii, 24; of tongue, 121, vi, 323. Shakespeare, Watts.

VULNERABLE. by the gentlest touch, 112, vi, 259. Browne, Shakespeare. VULNERARY. herbs, 47, v, 302. Browne.

A few philosophic words found not in the *Rambler* but in later works and in Johnson's conversation (*condense, congelation, corrode, diffusive, dissoluble, distillation, empiric, flaccidity, flux, inebriate, interstice, intertexture, laceration, putrefy, reanimate, tinct, torpescence, tumid, ventilate*) have been included in the preceding index under cognates. The following list contains some further words found in later literary and political works: *Adventurer* (A), *Idler* (I), *Rasselas* (R), *Preface to Shakespeare* (PS), *Falkland's Islands* (FI), and *Journey to the Western Islands* (WI). *Amputation,* FI, x, 59; *appendant,* WI, x, 400; *antiscorbutick,* FI, x, 42; *aquatick,* WI, x, 411; *aqueous,* I 3, viii, 10; *arable,* WI, x, 400; *armadillo,* I 81, viii, 326; *atrophy,* I 22, viii, 84; *bituminous,* WI, x, 441; *calenture,* FI, x, 63; PS, ix, 259; *coalesce,* WI, x, 435; *comet,* I 11, viii, 43; *combustible,* FI, x, 68; WI, x, 441; *concreted,* WI, x, 486; *concussion,* I 41, viii, 163; R, xi, 88; *conglobate,* WI, x, 500; *consanguinity,* WI, x, 420; *density,* R, xi, 17; *dromedary,* I 40, viii, 161; *ecliptick,* R, xi, 120; *elixir,* I 40, viii, 161; *elongation,* WI, x, 479; *emersion,* R, xi, 116; WI, x, 385; *empyreumatick,* WI, x, 381; *equinoctial,* R, xi, 116; *equinox,* WI, x, 409–410; *esculent,* WI, x, 413; *evolution,* I 70, viii, 282; *excision,* I 17, viii, 65; *feculent,* WI, x, 498–499; *focus,* WI, x, 479; *fumigation,* I 35, viii, 140; *gangrene,* I 22, viii, 84; FI, x, 59; *indiscerptible,* R, xi, 141; *inject,* I 17, viii, 65; *lacteal,* I 17, viii, 66; *loco-motive,* A 39, Chalmers xxiii, 253; *malleable,* A 99, ix, 86; *microcosm,* A 39, Chalmers xxiii, 253; *musculous,* WI, x, 466; *nautilus,* I 64, viii, 257; *ocular,* WI, x, 473; *orrery,* A 99, ix, 88; *pendent,* R, xi, 18; *perflation,* WI, x, 413; *phthiriasis,* FI, x, 78; *phthisic,* A 74, Chalmers xxiii, 204; *potable,* A 99, ix, 86; *primogenial,* A 95, ix, 82; *protuberance,* PS, ix, 252 (cf. *prominence, Rambler* 112, vi, 260); *pungent,* WI, x, 381; *refrigerate,* PS, ix, 300; *reverberation,* WI, x, 403; *saturate,* WI, x, 374, 490; *solstitial,* R, xi, 4; *spherical,* PS, ix, 252; *subterranean,* I 51, viii, 204; R, xi, 24; *subterraneous,* R, xi, 138; WI, 403, 413; *succedaneous,* WI, x, 478; *tenuity,* R, xi, 18; *torrid,* R, xi, 1, 21; *transfuse,* I 69, viii, 277; *transmarine,* WI, x, 434; *turbinated,* I 56, viii, 235; *viscous,* WI, x, 382; *zenith,* A 41, ix, 8.

Appendix B

Some Philosophic Sources of Johnson's Dictionary

THE *Rambler* words listed alphabetically in Appendix A are rearranged in the following pages according to the philosophic sources from which they are illustrated in Johnson's Dictionary. This Appendix, in conjunction with Appendix A, is thus a chart to relations between the Dictionary philosophic sources and the *Rambler* philosophic vocabulary and constitutes a documentation of the general statement made in Chapter IV (*ante* pp. 85–87).

More specifically: the 380 *Rambler* words of Appendix A are illustrated in the Dictionary, under definitions broadly relevant to Johnson's *Rambler* usage, by about 1,090 quotations. (A degree of arbitrariness in drawing the line of relevance was inevitable, but if a number of non-philosophic examples have been thus left out of consideration, so also have some of the more technically philosophic.) Of these quotations about 570, distributed among 31 philosophic authors, and about 95 distributed among five philosophic poets, Blackmore, Garth, Milton, Philips, and Thomson, are identified in this Appendix. Of the approximately 425 remaining quotations, distributed among about 60 poets and miscellaneous prose writers, the following are identified: 60 quotations from Shakespeare—because Shakespeare is the third most often quoted authority for the 380 *Rambler* words in question, coming after only Bacon and Arbuthnot, and because the aid of a concordance made the labor not extravagant; 24 quotations from Robert South—because South is a religious writer who shows typical instances of the new philosophic diction and imagery, because Johnson is known to have admired his work, and because a copy of his *Sermons* at Lichfield is one of the few surviving books which Johnson marked for the Dictionary; 8 quotations from Wotton—because the philosophic tendency of his prose invited the research. The most important sources not included in this Appendix are Dryden (50 quotations), Pope (34), Prior (13), Addison (30), Hooker (21), and Swift (24).

The title first given for each entry is that of the edition used in this study. A few standard editions of later date than Johnson's Dictionary have been used; for the rest, editions closer to the Dictionary have been preferred, when convenient, to the earliest. Neither the extent of the evidence available nor the implications of this study has demanded a meticulous concern for the editions used by Johnson himself. But see Bacon, Hale, South (Johnson's Dictionary copies); Bentley, Boerhaave, Browne, Locke, Thomson (evidence from Dictionary quotations); Arbuthnot, Chambers, Grew, Locke, Thomson (entries in the *Catalogue of the Library of Samuel Johnson*). Arbuthnot's *Tables*, 1727, Glanvill's *Scepsis*, 1665, Grew's *Musaeum*, 1681, and *Cosmologia*, 1701, Hill's *Method of Fossils*, 1748, and *Materia Medica*, 1751, and Woodward's *Fossils*, 1729, may be identified as Johnson's editions through lack of alternatives.

A few scientific dictionaries from which Johnson's *Rambler* philosophic words are not illustrated but which are important to the discussion of the Dictionary in Chapter II are listed in this Appendix. See Calmet, Hill, Miller, Musschenbroek.

JOHN ARBUTHNOT. Humble Petition of the Colliers, Cooks, Cook-Maids, Blacksmiths, Jack-Makers, Braziers, and Others [1716] (in George A. Aitken, *Life and Works of John Arbuthnot* [Oxford, 1892]. See: culinary, p. 376; rectual [i.e., radical], p. 377.

———— ———— Table of Ancient Coins, Weights and Measures. London, 1727.

> *Catalogue of the Library of Samuel Johnson*, No. 273, Arbuthnot's tables of ancient coins, 1727.

See: mensuration, p. 99.

———— ———— An Essay Concerning the Effects of Air on Human Bodies. London, 1733.
See: barometer, p. 26; emit, p. 137; repulsion, p. 25.

———— ———— An Essay Concerning the Nature of Aliments, and the Choice of Them, According to the Different Constitutions of Human Bodies. 3d ed. London, 1735.

> 1st ed. 1731. Cf. Lane Cooper, "Dr. Johnson on Oats," *PMLA*, lii (September, 1937), 789.

> See: accelerate, p. 214; accretion, p. 205; acrimony, p. a^v; aerial, p. 221; chymistry, p. 66; circulation, p. 31; cordial, p. 142; ebullition, p. a2^v; effervescence, p. a2; elastick, p. 151; emollient, p. 136; essential, p. 53; evanescent, p. 43; excoriation, p. 189; flatulency, p. 73; generate, p. 134; influx, p. 156; ingredient, p. 79; inoculation, p. 420; intermediate, p. 75; longevity, p. 203; mechanism, p. 34; medicate, p. 125; morbid, p. 152; mortification, p. 82; palpitation, p. 158; peccant, p. 14; perpetual, p. 40; phlegmatick, p. 4; putrefaction, p. 10; ramification, p. 28; relaxation, p. 157; resolvable, p. 104; restorative, p. 237; subsidiary, p. 235; tenuity, p. 37; vacuity, p. 305; volatility, p. a3^v; volatilize, p. 100.

———— ———— Practical Rules of Diet in the Various Constitutions and Diseases of Human Bodies. London, 1736. (Paged after *Essay Concerning . . . Aliments*, London, 1735.) 1st ed. 1732.
See: anodyne, p. 287; apoplexy, p. 368; balsamick, p. 307; circumvolution, p. 357; delirium, p. 318; evacuate, p. 382; exacerbation, p. 327; flaccid, p. 308; inflation, p. 300; inoculation, p. 420; irritation, p. 377; lethargick, p. 373; lethargy, p. 373; mercury, p. 413; palliative, p. 388; paroxysm, p. 330; stimulate, p. 267; suffocation, p. 264.

———— ———— Memoirs of Martinus Scriblerus (in *Works of Pope*, London, 1822, vol. vi).
See: fluid, chap. viii, p. 119; longitude, chap. xv, p. 176.

FRANCIS BACON. Works, London, 1740. 4 vols. Vol. iii.

Vol. iii contains English works. The copy in the Yale Library is that marked by Johnson in compiling the Dictionary. Cf. Gordon S. Haight, "Johnson's Copy of Bacon's Works," *Yale University Library Gazette,* vi (1932), 67–73.

(1) [Sylva Sylvarum: or a] Natural History, Nos. 1–1000. See: accelerate, No. 307; accretion, No. 602; acrimony, No. 639; adjacent, No. 771; adulteration, No. 798; adumbration, No. 187; adventitious, No. 62; animation, No. 400; assimilate, No. 680 (twice); attraction, No. 906; comminution, No. 799; compression, Nos. 9, 11, 715; concomitant, No. 126; contagion, No. 901; contiguous, Nos. 31, 865; corrosion, No. 36; coruscation, No. 115; diffusion, No. 268; dissipation, No. 98; dissolution, No. 789; ductile, No. 845; efflorescence, No. 388; emission, No. 766; exacerbation, No. 61; flaccid, No. 493; flexible, No. 796; generate, No. 124; hypochondriacal, No. 709; infection, No. 904; infectious, No. 297; ingredient, No. 998; irritate, Nos. 315, 375, 709; liquefaction, No. 294; luminous, No. 683; lunar, No. 493; magnetical, No. 75; maturation, No. 311; medium, No. 220; metalline, No. 84; momentaneous, No. 31; mortification, No. 333; operation, No. 903; percussion, No. 178; physiognomy, No. 801; preservative, No. 970; projection, No. 326; putrefaction, No. 328; radiation, No. 125; radical, Nos. 345, 601; reciprocation, No. 99; relaxation, No. 710; repercussion, No. 124; resilience, No. 245; resistance, No. 688; retardation, No. 851; rotation, No. 907; sediment, No. 881; sensory, No. 128; superinduce, No. 910; temperature, No. 816; tenuity, No. 533; transmutation, Nos. 525, 838; trepidation, Nos. 137, 793; volatility, No. 294.

(2) Physiological Remains. See: ebullition, p. 216; mortification, p. 221; mortify, p. 221; volatility, pp. 214, 219.

(3) New Atlantis. See: composition, p. 255; radiation, p. 255; register, p. 243; resuscitate, p. 254.

(4) Apophthegms. See: flexible, p. 291, No. 30.

(5) Essays. See: astronomer, No. 51; composition, No. 42; distemper, No. 19; exhaust, No. 8; percussion, No. 9; progressive, No. 36; suffocation, No. 27.

The numbers cited are those of the 1625 *Essays* rather than of the 1740 text, which includes the intrusive No. 140, *Of a King.*

(6) Colours of Good and Evil. See: anatomy, p. 387, No. 5.

(7) History of Henry VII. See: accelerate, p. 414; epidemick, p. 402; intermixture, p. 430.

Johnson quotes the *History of Henry VII* frequently in the Dictionary, but apparently used a separate edition, the text in the Yale copy being unmarked.

(8) An Advertisement Touching an Holy War. See: indissoluble, p. 547.

(9) An Account of . . . the Office of Compositions for Alienations. See: transmutation, p. 558.

(10) Advice to Sir George Villiers. See: confluence, p. 564; dissolve, p. 572; essential, p. 568.

An example under *remission* is attributed to Bacon but remains unidentified.

RICHARD BENTLEY. Sermons Preached at Boyle's Lecture (in *Works,* ed. Alexander Dyce, London, 1836–38, vol. iii).

> 1st ed. 1692–93, *The Folly and Unreasonableness of Atheism.* Johnson's quotation under the word *operation* (Sermon II, p. 39) shows that he used an edition earlier than the 4th, revised, of 1699 (Preface, p. vi).

See: aggregate, p. 35; ambient, p. 167; coalition, p. 156; coeval, p. 135; collision, p. 421; commensurate, p. 42; condensation, p. 87; confluence, p. 82; dissolution (unidentified); elastical, p. 80; essential, p. 163; expansion, p. 190; fecundity, p. 138; laxity, p. 168; levity, p. 82; luminary, p. 65; luminous, p. 178; maturation, p. 188; mechanism, p. 71; microscope, p. 58; operation, p. 39; opiate, p. 14; periodical, p. 73; physiology, p. 6; preponderate, p. 171; radical, p. 59; receiver, p. 191; rotundity, p. 197; salutary, p. 123; satellite, p. 180; tenuity, p. 152; vacuity, p. 142; velocity, p. 179; vertiginous, p. 182.

> See Johnson's tribute to Bentley in *Proposals for Printing Bibliotheca Harleiana* (*Life* i, 153, n. 7).

RICHARD BLACKMORE. Creation, A Philosophical Poem in Seven Books, London, 1712.

> See: astronomer, ii, 414; contexture, i, 647; disruption, ii, 646; effulgence, ii, 27; elastick, iv, 114; expansion, iv, 352; instrument, iii, 612; magnetick, i, 295; metallick, iii, 421; particle, iv, 468; repercussion, iv, 201; tension, ii, 632; tincture, ii, 249.

> Blackmore's *Creation,* says Johnson in his *Life of Blackmore,* "has been by my recommendation inserted in the late collection." "This poem, if he had written nothing else, would have transmitted him to posterity among the first favorites of the English Muse" (*Lives* ii, 242, 244; cf. *Life* iii, 370; *Letters* ii, 275, n. 4).

HERMANN BOERHAAVE. A New Method of Chemistry . . . Written by the Very Learned H. Boerhaave . . . Translated . . . by P[eter] Shaw, M.D. and E[phraim] Chambers, London, 1727.

> Johnson's definition of *chymistry* follows this translation of the surreptitious *Institutiones et Experimenta Chemiae,* 1724, rather than the translation by Timothy Dallowe, 1735, or that by Peter Shaw, 1741, of Boerhaave's authorized *Elementa Chemiae,* 1732.

See: chemistry, p. 51.

> The story of Boerhaave's comment on a "criminal dragged to execution" in *Rambler* 114, vi, 272 is paralleled in Johnson's Life of Boerhaave for James's *Medicinal Dictionary,* Vol. i, p. 9X. Cf. *Works* iv, 356. Cf. the allusion to Boerhaave's chemical writing in *Adventurer* 85, ix, 64.

ROBERT BOYLE. Works, 6 vols., London, 1772, Vol. i.

Johnson no doubt used the collected edition in five volumes published by Millar in 1744, the first volume of which contained all the works indicated below except *The Experimental History of Colours*, which was in the second volume. As the editions of 1744 and 1772 are the only collected editions of Boyle's works in English, No. 562 of the *Catalogue of the Library of Samuel Johnson*, "Boyle's Works, 5 v. 1774," refers no doubt to the edition of 1744. No. 30 of the *Catalogue* is "7. Boyle's Works, &c."

(1) New Experiments Physico-Mechanical Touching the Spring of the Air. See: evacuate, p. 82; metalline, p. 49; transfusion, p. 158.

(2) Two Essays Concerning the Unsuccessfulness of Experiments. See: distiller, p. 320.

(3) A Physico-Chemical Essay. See: adulterate, p. 363.

(4) The History of Fluidity and Firmness. See: adhesion, p. 412; asperity, p. 391; defecate, p. 417; distemper, p. 381; distil, p. 419; mortify, p. 425; stability, p. 401.

(5) The Sceptical Chymist. See: fermentation, p. 516; fluctuation, p. 463; indissoluble, p. 508; insipid, p. 542; intermixture, p. 513; operation, p. 484; register n., p. 502.

(6) Producibleness of Chymical Principles. See: fugacity, p. 598.

(7) The Experimental History of Colours. See: adventitious, p. 773; diffusion, p. 725; optical, p. 673.

SIR THOMAS BROWNE. Pseudodoxia Epidemica (in *Works,* ed. Geoffrey Keynes, London, 1928, 6 vols., Vols. ii and iii).

Johnson's quotations from the *Pseudodoxia* under *actuate* (Bk. III, chap. xxvii [xxv in the 1st ed., xxvi in the 2d]) and *irradiation* (Bk. III, chap. ix) show that he used some edition earlier than the 5th of 1672, perhaps the commonly obtainable folio first edition of 1646. *Catalogue of the Library of Samuel Johnson*, No. 579, Browne's vulgar errors, &c.

The following references are to book and chapter and, in parentheses, to volume and page of the Keynes edition. See: abscission, VII, xii (iii, 294); actuate, III, xxvii (ii, 301); agriculture, VI, iii (iii, 179); alexipharmick, III, xxiii (ii, 276); antidotal, II, v (ii, 158); antidote, I, vii (ii, 55); approximation, VI, ii (iii, 174); ascendant, IV, xiii (iii, 81); attraction II, iii (ii, 116); celestial, IV, xiii (iii, 77); chronical, IV, xiii (iii, 86); climacterical, IV, xii (iii, 53); condensation, V, xviii (iii, 132); declination, IV, xiii (iii, 80); ebriety, II, vi (ii, 171); ebullition, II, v (ii, 152); eccentricity, IV, xii (iii, 60); emanation, II, iv (ii, 134); emission, VI, vi (iii, 205); equilibration, II, ii (ii, 100); fluctuation, VII, xvii (iii, 318); frigidity, I, ix (ii, 68); geometrician, I, vii (ii, 51); gravity, VII, xv (iii, 307); impregnate, III, xii (ii, 224); inebriation, II, v (ii, 158); interstitial, II, i (ii, 97); involution, V, xxii (ii, 149); irradiation, III, ix (ii, 208); lunary, II, vi (ii, 170); magnetism, II, iii (ii, 131); medical, To the Reader (ii, 4); meridian, II, ii (ii, 108); meteorological, VII, iv (iii, 273); migration, IV, xiii (iii, 75); mortify, III, xxv (ii, 284); narcotick, VI, vii, (iii, 280); noxious, IV, xiii (iii, 85); periodical, IV, xii (iii, 62); postulate, VI, vi (iii, 192); preservative, VI, xvii (iii, 319–320); progression, To the Reader (ii, 6); progressive, IV, vi (iii, 31); quiescent, IV, v (iii, 26); radicate, To the Reader (ii, 4); recess, VI, ii (iii, 173); reciprocation, VII, xiii (iii, 297); scintillation, II, i (ii, 92); suffocate, III, xxi (ii, 260); supervenient, V, xiv (iii, 125); temperate, I, v (ii, 40); tortuosity, V, v (iii, 98); valetudinary, IV, xiii (iii, 86); vehicle, IV, viii (iii, 37); vulnerable, V, xxii (iii, 146); vulnerary, II, iii (ii, 131).

See the quotations from Browne in *Adventurers* 50, ix, 21; 39, Chalmers xxiii, 255.

THOMAS BURNET. The Theory of the Earth. 3d ed. London, 1697. The Two First Books. The Two Last Books (separately paged).

1st English ed. 1684–90. *Catalogue of the Library of Samuel Johnson*, No. 453, Burneti theoria sacra.

See: absorb, I, vi, p. 48; circulation (unidentified); congeal, I, iv, p. 34; exhalation, I, ix, p. 82; liquefaction, III, Preface, p. A4ʳ; rarefaction, I, vi, p. 50; relaxation, I, ii, p. 10.

AUGUSTIN CALMET. Dictionnaire Historique . . . de la Bible. 2d ed. Geneva, 1730. 4 vols. (University of Chicago.)

An English translation of Calmet had appeared at London in 1732, *An Historical . . . Dictionary of the Holy Bible*, by Samuel D'Oyly and John Colson, 3 vols. (Harvard University Library). An objection to accepting it as Johnson's source exists, however, in the absence from it of the article *swan* and in the inferiority of its prose. A comparison of Johnson's article *swan*, attributed to Calmet, with the French text of Geneva, 1730, and of Johnson's article *stork* with both French and English texts of Calmet suggests that Johnson translated for himself from one of the French editions of Calmet antedating his Dictionary—if not that of Geneva, 1730, perhaps that of Paris, 1730, or the first edition, of Paris, 1722. See Johnson's Dictionary, s.v. *chameleon, dromedary, elephant, ossifrage, ostrich, stork, swan.*

EPHRAIM CHAMBERS. Cyclopaedia: or an Universal Dictionary of Arts and Sciences. London, 1741. 2 vols.

1st ed. 1728. *Catalogue of the Library of Samuel Johnson*, No. 487, Chambers' Dictionary, 2 vols. fol. 1741.

See: balance.

GEORGE CHEYNE. Philosophical Principles of Religion, Natural and Revealed. 4th ed. London, 1734. 1st ed. Part ɪ, 1705. Part ɪɪ, 1715.
Part ɪ. See: catenarian, p. 330; cohere, p. 104; frigid, p. 258; perennial, p. 274; suffocation, p. 87; valetudinary, p. 254.

Johnson alludes to Part ɪɪ of the *Philosophical Principles*, p. Aa3ᵛ, the "infinite cone" of things, in his review of Jenyns' *Free Enquiry* (*Works* x, 227). Cf. Dictionary, s.v. *popgun*, a quotation from Cheyne, and *Letters* ii, 198, No. 702.

WILLIAM DERHAM. Physico-Theology: or a Demonstration of the Being and Attributes of God from His Works of Creation. 2d ed. London, 1714.

> The Substance of XVI Sermons Preached . . . at . . . Mr. Boyle's Lectures . . . 1711 and 1712. 1st ed. with notes, 1713.

See: barometrical, p. 17, I, ii, n. 3; equilibration, p. 298, V, ii; lacerate, p. 49, II, v, n. 2; valetudinarian, p. 72, III, iv.

> Cf. the passage on swallows conglomerating under water in *Physico-Theology*, pp. 359–360, VII, iii, n. 4, with Johnson's account in *Life* ii, 55. Johnson chose the *Physico-Theology* as Sunday theological reading at Inchkenneth October 17, 1773 (*Life* v, 323). See his recommendation of it in the Preface to Dodsley's *Preceptor*, 1748 (*Works* ix, 416).

———— ———— Astro-Theology: or a Demonstration of the Being and Attributes of God from a Survey of the Heavens. 2d ed. London, 1715. 1st ed. 1714.

See: periodical, p. 90.

SIR KENELM DIGBY. Two Treatises: in the One of Which the Nature of Bodies; in the Other the Nature of Man's Soul Is Looked into. In Way of Discovery of the Immortality of Reasonable Souls. London, 1658. 1st ed. 1644.

See: irradiation, p. 51; philosophy, p. A3.

> See the quotations from Digby in *Adventurers* 50, ix, 22; 107, ix, 98.

SIR JOHN FLOYER. The Preternatural State of Animal Humours Described by Their Sensible Qualities. London, printed . . . for Michael Johnson, 1696 (New York Academy of Medicine).

See: insipid, p. 53.

> Johnson's father was the publisher not only of his fellow townsman Floyer's *Preternatural State of Animal Humours*, but of his Φαρμακο-Βασανος: *or the Touchstone of Medicines*, 1687 (*N&Q*, 3, v, 33), and of his *Exposition of the Revelations*, 1719 (*N&Q*, 3, iv, 388).

SAMUEL GARTH. The Dispensary, a Poem in Six Cantos. 9th ed., With Several Descriptions and Episodes Never Before Printed. London, 1726.

See: cathartick, p. 64 (Canto v); coruscation, p. 48 (Canto iv).

JOSEPH GLANVILL. Scepsis Scientifica: or Confest Ignorance the Way to Science; in an Essay of the Vanity of Dogmatizing, and Confident Opinion. London, 1665.

> Johnson cites *Vanity of Dogmatizing*, the title of the first edition, 1661, in the Dictionary, s.v. *advenient*.

See: aberration, p. 58; adulterate, p. 93; adumbration, p. 50; aggregate, p. 75; coalition, p. 143; commensurate, p. 144; congruity, p. 89; constellate, p. 2; defecate, p. 17 and p. 75; equipoise, p. 82; frigidity, p. 82; involution, p. 143; magnetism, p. 98; physiology, p. aᵛ; preponderate, p. 102; quiescence, p. 58; quiescent, p. 59;

scintillation, p. 138; seminal, p. 155; sublime, p. 92; subtilize, p. 123; tenuity, p. 162; vacuity, p. 14.

——— ——— Scir$\frac{e}{i}$ Tuum Nihil Est: or the Author's Defence of the Vanity of Dogmatizing. London, 1665.
See: flatulency, p. 6; radicate, p. 35.

JOHN GRAUNT. Natural and Political Observations . . . Made upon the Bills of Mortality. 3d ed. London, 1665. 1st ed. 1662.
See: epidemic, p. 29; medicate, p. 137; theorem, p. 153.

NEHEMIAH GREW. Musaeum Regalis Societatis; or a Catalogue and Description of the Rarities Belonging to the Royal Society, and Preserved at Gresham College. London, 1681.
See: approximation, Preface, p. A4^v; effervescence, p. 354.

——— ——— Cosmologia Sacra: or a Discourse of the Universe as it is the Creature and Kingdom of God. London, 1701.

Catalogue of the Library of Samuel Johnson, No. 358, Grew's Cosmologia Sacra, 1701, &c.

See: expansion, p. 28; quiescent, p. 55; rotundity, p. 14; subtilized, p. 32.

SIR MATTHEW HALE. The Primitive Origination of Mankind, London, 1677.

The copy marked by Johnson in compiling the Dictionary is now the property of the London Philological Society. See C. T. Onions, *An Exhibition of Books Illustrating the History of English Dictionaries Held by the Bodleian Library at Oxford to Celebrate the Completion of the Oxford English Dictionary* (Oxford, 1928), p. 19.

See: adumbration, p. 46; approximation, p. 174; assimilate, p. 197; balsamick, p. 30; chronological, p. 134; coeval, pp. 167 and 169; concentre, p. 223; dissipation, p. 143; efficient, p. 5; evacuation, p. 238; influx, p. 14; irradiation, p. 2; ramification, p. 176; rotation, p. 150; volatility, p. 19.

——— ——— The History of the Common Law of England. London, 1713.
See: coalition, p. 61.

The anecdotes of Hale in *Ramblers* 14, v, 92 and 60, v, 386 are taken from Gilbert Burnet's *Life and Death of Sir Matthew Hale* (London, 1682, pp. 85, 35), a book later recommended by Johnson to Mr. Astle (*Life* iv, 311).

JOHN HARRIS. Lexicon Technicum: or an Universal English Dictionary of Arts and Sciences. 5th ed. London, 1736. 2 vols. 1st ed. 1704–10.
See: barometer, catenarian, eccentricity, fermentation.

GIDEON HARVEY. Morbus Anglicus: or the Anatomy of Consumptions. 2d ed. London, 1672. 1st ed. 1666.
See: absorb, p. 10; acrimonious, p. 60; concomitant, p. 58; defecate,

p. 16; obtund, p. 60; palpitation, p. 20; paroxysm, p. 40; perennial, p. 81; phlegmatic, p. 35.

—— —— A Discourse of the Plague. 2d ed. London, 1673. (Paged with *Morbus Anglicus,* 1672.) 1st ed. 1665.
See: preservative, p. 140.

JOHN HILL. A History of the Materia Medica. London, 1751 (The New York Academy of Medicine).

Catalogue of the Library of Samuel Johnson, No. 272, Hill's materia medica.

See: mercury, p. 58.

Johnson's longer Dictionary quotation from Hill under *quicksilver* (quoted *ante* p. 29) is an abridgment, with some rearrangement and substitution, of the account in the *Materia Medica,* pp. 53–55, 58–59.

—— —— A General Natural History, Vol. i, A History of Fossils. London, 1748.

WILLIAM HOLDER. Elements of Speech: an Essay of Inquiry into the Natural Production of Letters. London, 1669.
See: flaccid, p. 51; lax, p. 129; medium, p. 2; quiescent, p. 2; tension, p. 74.

Cf. Mrs. Piozzi's *Anecdotes* (*Miscellanies* i, 329), Johnson's hearing in a coach, and Holder's *Elements of Speech,* p. 167; cf. Derham, *Physico-Theology,* Bk. IV, chap. iii, note (u).

—— —— A Discourse concerning Time . . . for the Better Understanding of the Julian Year and Calendar. 2d ed. London, 1701 (Princeton University Library). 1st ed. 1694.
See: chronology, p. 48; excentricity, p. 51; incommensurate, pp. 13, 23.

JOHN LOCKE. An Essay Concerning Human Understanding, ed. A. C. Fraser, Oxford, 1894. 2 vols.

Johnson's Dictionary quotations under the words *impression* and *operate* show that he did not use an edition earlier than the fourth of 1700. See II, i, 23 (Fraser, i, 141); II, viii, 11 (Fraser, i, 171). See below, note on Locke's collected *Works.*

See: adhesion, II, iii, 1; anatomical, II, xv, 4; apoplexy, III, vi, 4; ether, II, xxiii, 23; expansion, II, vii, 10 and II, xv, 1; extraneous, II, xxv, 8 and II, xxxii, 4; magnet, III, vi, 5; operate, II, viii, 11 and 18; operation, II, viii, 18; philosopher, IV, iii, 16; preponderate, IV, xvi, 3; regulate, III, vi, 15; remission, II, xix, 4; resistance, II, iv, 1; superinduce, I, i, 27, II, xxv, 4 and II, xxi, 8.

—— —— Works. 7th ed. London, 1768. 4 vols.

Johnson's quotations from the *Elements of Natural Philosophy,* first added to Locke's collected works in the three-volume fourth edition of 1740, and the presence in the *Catalogue of the Library of Samuel Johnson* of No. 601, "Locke's Works, 3 v.," suggest that he used either the fourth edition or the three-volume fifth, of 1751. Cf. H. O. Christophersen, *A Bibliographical Introduction to . . . John Locke* (Oslo, 1930), pp. 78, 88.

Vol. ii, Some Considerations of the Consequences of the Lowering of Interest and Raising the Value of Money. See: preponderate, p. 9.

Vol. iv, Some Thoughts Concerning Education. See: ascendant, p. 103; astronomer, p. 113; flexible, p. 112; physiognomy, p. 59; progression, p. 125.

Vol. iv, Of the Conduct of the Understanding. See: exhaust, p. 168; progression, p. 165; physick, p. 182.

Vol. iv, Elements of Natural Philosophy. See: aerial, p. 592; eclipse, p. 584; equiponderant, p. 586; satellite, p. 583.

PHILIP MILLER. The Gardeners Dictionary . . . wherein all the Articles contained in the former Editions of this Work, in Two Volumes, are disposed in One Alphabet. 6th ed. London, 1752.

> I rely upon the description by Lane Cooper, "Dr. Johnson on Oats and Other Grains," *PMLA*, lii (September, 1937), 788–796. Professor Cooper's parallel of passages under nine cereals, including the notorious *oats* or *avena*, shows that this edition is representative of the earlier one which Johnson must have used. It was not the first, of 1724, nor the second, of 1733. I am unable to say which of the intervening editions first showed the extensive revisions which characterize Johnson's source.

JOHN MILTON.

Comus. See: aerial, 1. 3.

Paradise Lost. See: aerial, X, 667; ambient, VII, 89; assimilate, V, 412; collision, X, 1072; constellation, VII, 562; contagion, X, 544; contiguous, VII, 273; dissipation, VI, 598; dissolution, X, 1049 and XII, 459; eclipse, X, 413; effulgence, IV, 388; effuse, XI, 447; exhalation, I, 711; generate, VII, 393 and X, 894; infect, I, 453; infuse, V, 694 and IX, 836; ingredient, XI, 417; instil, XI, 416; intermix, IX, 218 and XI, 115; lax, VII, 162; luminary, III, 576; luminous, III, 420 and VIII, 140; magnetick, III, 583; meteorous, XII, 629; operation, VIII, 323 and IX, 1012; perpetual, VII, 306; philosopher, III, 601; progressive, VIII, 127; register v., XII, 335; revolution, II, 597 and VIII, 31 and X, 814; subduct, VIII, 536; sublime, V, 483; sulphur, I, 674; temperate, V, 5; texture, VI, 348; trepidation, III, 483; vacuity, II, 932; vicissitude, VI, 8; volatile, III, 603.

Paradise Regained. See: conflux, IV, 62; dissolve, II, 436; philosophical, IV, 300.

Samson Agonistes. See: dissolve, 1. 1149; humour, 1. 600; levity, 1. 880; medicinal, 1. 627; mortification, 1. 622.

HENRY MORE. An Antidote against Atheism. London, 1712. 1st ed. 1653.

See: Naturalist, p. 79, II, xii, 1.

———— ———— Divine Dialogues. 2d ed. London, 1713. 1st ed. 1668.
  See: incommensurate, p. 44; theorem, p. 4.

JOHN MORTIMER. The Whole Art of Husbandry. 5th ed. London,
1721. 2 vols. 1st ed. 1707.
  See: instrument, ii, 60; restorative, i, 223.

PIETER VAN MUSSCHENBROEK. The Elements of Natural Philosophy . . . by Peter van Musschenbroek, M.D., Professor of Mathematicks and Philosophy in the University of Leyden, Translated from
the Latin by John Colson. London, 1744. 2 vols.

> Catalogue of the Library of Samuel Johnson, No. 145, Musschenbroek, elementa
> physicae.

See: *ante* pp. 30, 55.

SIR ISAAC NEWTON. Opticks or a Treatise of the Reflections, Re-
fractions, Inflections and Colours of Light . . . Reprinted from the
Fourth Edition [1730], ed. E. T. Whittaker. New York, 1931.

> 1st ed. 1704. *Catalogue of the Library of Samuel Johnson,* No. 58, Newtoni
> optice.

  See: accelerate, p. 348; accretion, p. 256; adjacent, p. 248; aerial,
  p. 200; ambient, p. 221; assimilate, p. 387; attraction, p. 376; colorifick, p. 138; compression, p. 267; contiguous, p. 49; coruscation,
  p. 379; culinary, p. 345; ebullition, p. 377; elastick, p. 394; ether,
  p. 352; flexibility, p. 339; gravity, p. 351; inclination, p. 32; ingredient, p. 404; intermediate, p. 346; luminous, p. 97; magnetick,
  p. 267 (twice); mechanical, p. 369; medium, pp. 254, 365; particle, p. 261; percussion, p. 348; progression, p. 214; quiescent,
  p. 362; resistance, p. 365; rotation, p. 341; sensory (sensorium),
  pp. 125, 370; texture, p. 400; vibration, p. 345; vicissitude, p. 281;
  volatile, pp. 383–384; volatility, p. 359; volatilize, p. 275.

JOHN PHILIPS. Poems, ed. M. G. Lloyd Thomas. Oxford, 1927.
  Blenheim. See: absorpt, l. 242, p. 18.
  Cyder. See: concomitant, i, 220, p. 50; contexture, i, 191, p. 50;
  defecate, ii, 322, p. 78; ductile, i, 617, p. 62; exhaust, i, 124, p. 48.

> Philip Miller, "the great gardener and botanist," told Johnson that in Philips'
> *Cyder* "all the precepts were just, and indeed better than in books written
> for the purpose of instructing" (*Lives* i, 319; *Life* v, 78).

JOHN QUINCY. Lexicon Physico-Medicum or a New Medicinal Dictionary. 7th ed. London, 1757.

> 1st ed. 1719. The passage quoted in the Dictionary s.v. *laxity* shows that
> Johnson used some edition later than the second, of 1722. The fourth, 1730,
> the fifth, 1731, and the sixth, 1747, all have the qualifying passage (Army
> Medical Library, Cleveland Branch).

  See: antidote, apoplexy, athanor, atom, cathartick, chronic, corrosion, ebullition, efflorescence, electricity (s.v. *electric*), emollient,

evaporation, frigorifick, gravity, hydrophobia, infection, inoculation, lax (s.v. *laxative*), laxity, medicinal, narcotick, papilionaceous, putrefaction.

The word *papilionaceous* (*Rambler* 82, vi, 67) occurs *passim* in Miller's
Gardeners Dictionary. Cf. James, *Medicinal Dictionary,* s.v. *botany,* "Expli-
cation of the Botanical Terms," "Flos Papilionaceous."

JOHN RAY. The Wisdom of God Manifested in the Works of the Creation. 5th ed. London, 1709.

   1st ed. 1691. Successively enlarged in editions of 1692, 1701, and 1704. Cf.
   Charles E. Raven, *John Ray* (Cambridge, 1942) pp. 452, 469, 474.

   See: armature, p. 158; atom, p. 34; biennial, p. 117; comminution,
   p. 309; contemper, p. 120; disruption, p. 332; dissipate, p. 269;
   equiponderant, p. 27; fecundity, p. 346; flexure, p. 259; gregarious, p. 161; humour, p. 396; influx, p. 52; longevity, p. 231; progressive, p. 302; reciprocation, pp. 52 and 97; salutary, p. 251;
   submarine, p. 98; subtilize, p. 29; torpid, p. 79; transmute, p. 68;
   vegetation, p. 53.

   The short biography of Ray in Dr. James's *Medicinal Dictionary,* s.v. *botany,*
   Vol. i, p. 10D^v is presumably the work of Johnson (*ante* p. 35, n. 21).
   Cf. his allusion to Ray on British insects (*Life* ii, 248).

WILLIAM SHAKESPEARE.

   Johnson used *The Works of Shakespeare . . . with a Comment and Notes
   . . . By Mr. Pope and Mr. Warburton,* London, 1747, 8 vols., and later
   entered in the same volumes certain annotations which appear in his edition
   of Shakespeare. The set is preserved in the Library of University College of
   Wales, Aberystwyth (A. Cuming, "A Copy of Shakespeare's Works Which
   Formerly Belonged to Dr. Johnson," *RES,* iii [April, 1927], 208–212).

   See: anatomy, K.J. iii, 4, 40; antidote, T.A. iv, 3, 435; apoplexy,
   Cor. iv, 5, 239; balance, 2H. IV iv, i, 67; celestial, L.L.L. v, 2,
   807; confluence, T.A. i, 1, 42; contagion, C.E. ii, 2, 146; J.C. ii,
   1, 265; contagious, 2H. VI iv, 1, 7; dissolution, M.W.W. iii, 5,
   118; dissolve, M.W.W. v, 5, 237; Lear v, 3, 203; distemper n.,
   H.V ii, 2, 54; W. T. i, 2, 385; distemper v., K.J. iv, 3, 21; R. & J.
   ii, 3, 33; Othello i, 1, 99; distil v.t., Macbeth iii, 5, 26; eclipse n.,
   Macbeth iv, 1, 28; eclipse v., 1H. VI iv, 5, 53; exhalation, K.J. iii,
   4, 153; exhale, R. III i, 2, 58; R. & J. iii, 5, 13; flexible, T. & C.
   i, 3, 50; flexure, T. & C. ii, 3, 115; inclination, A. & C. ii, 5, 113;
   infect, R. III i, 2, 150; M. Ado ii, i, 257; Macbeth iv, 1, 138 and
   v, 1, 80; A. & C. i, 2, 99; Cor. v, 6, 72; H. VIII i, 2, 133; infectious,
   R. & J. v, 2, 10; A. & C. ii, 5, 61; infuse, M.V. iv, 1, 132; lethargy,
   Othello iv, i, 59; levity A. & C. ii, 7, 128; medicinal, W.T. ii, 3,
   37; medicine, Lear iv, 7, 27; Macbeth iv, 3, 214; mortify, M.V.
   i, 1, 82; H.V i, 1, 26; Macbeth v, 2, 5; nutriment, T.A. iii, 1, 61;
   operation, Lear i, 1, 113; percussion, Cor. i, 4, 59; philosophical,
   A.W. ii, 3, 2; philosophy, R. & J. iii, 3, 57; phlegmatic, T.S. iv, 2, 19

(Folio 2, 3, 4); prescription, 3H. VI iii, 3, 94; progression, L.L.L. iv, 2, 144; register n., M.W.W. ii, 2, 194; restorative, R. & J. v, 3, 166; rotundity, Lear iii, 2, 7; suffocate, H.V iii, 6, 45; T. & C. i, 3, 25; temperate, K.J. iii, 4, 12; T.S. ii, 1, 296; volubility, T.S. ii, 1, 176; vulnerable, Macbeth v, 8, 11.

SAMUEL SHARP. A Treatise on the Operations of Surgery. London, 1758. 1st ed. 1739.

See: stimulate, p. 79.

ROBERT SOUTH. Sermons Preached upon Several Occasions. Oxford, 1842. 5 vols.

The twenty-one sermons (I–XXI) in Vol. i and the first three (XXII–XXIV) in Vol. ii of this edition correspond to the two series of South's sermons published as *Twelve Sermons Preached upon Several Occasions,* London, 1692, and *Twelve Sermons Preached upon Several Occasions* . . . the Second Volume, London, 1694 (Union Theological Seminary). The copy of the 1694 volume used by Johnson for the Dictionary is now in the Lichfield Cathedral Library. For the provenance of this volume, apparently given by Johnson to Frank Barber, and some analysis of Johnson's use of it, see John E. W. Wallis, *Dr. Johnson and His English Dictionary,* Presidential Address to the Lichfield Johnson Society, 1945, pp. 13–18. That Johnson drew heavily also upon the first series of twelve sermons is indicated by the examples which follow. This volume may well have been the "old edition of South's Sermons" given to Philip Metcalfe by Johnson forty-eight hours before his death and in 1885 still in possession of Metcalfe's great-grandnephew (*N&Q,* 6, xi, 64).

See: acrimony, 23, ii, 24; ascendant adj., 6, i, 115; cohabit, 7, i, 141; concatenation, 8, i, 161; concomitant, 11, i, 235; counteract, 22, ii, 4; dissolution, 2, i, 40 and 8, i, 175 and 22, ii, 17; distemper, 4, i, 80; emanation, 2, i, 26; emission, 2, i, 36; epidemical, 7, i, 135; hypothesis, 7, i, 127; inclination, 10, i, 207; indissoluble (unidentified); lenitive, 14, i, 298; nutriment, 11, i, 231; philosopher, 2, i, 31; property, 17, i, 366; resolvable, 11, i, 234; restorative, 22, ii, 16; sediment, 2, i, 35; superinduce, 17, i, 374; vibration, 2, i, 37.

For some parallels between Johnson's ideas and the sermons of South, see *Life* iv, 530; *Letters* ii, 183, 439; *Miscellanies* i, 185.

JAMES THOMSON. The Seasons, text of 1746 (in *Poetical Works,* ed. J. L. Robertson, Oxford, 1908).

Johnson's line references for *accelerate* (*Summer,* l. 1690) and *adhesive* (*Autumn,* l. 440) are the closest marginal numbers of the 1746 edition of *The Seasons,* incorrect at these points by fifteen and four lines respectively.

See: accelerate, S.1707; adhesive, A.437; agglomerate, A.766; botanist, Sp.224; congeal, W.226; delirious, Sp.1048; dissipate, A.323; evanescent, S.303; fermentation, Sp.570; indissoluble, Sp.845; irritate, S.1114; palpitation, Sp.969; putrefaction, S.1029; rotation, Sp.629; suffocate, Sp.130; sulphur, S.1108; torpid, Sp.568; vegetation, Sp.81; vibration, S.1735.

Thomson was apparently one of four or five poets included in the *English Poets* of 1779–81 at Johnson's suggestion (*Life* iii, 109, 370). Cf. Blackmore.

ISAAC WATTS. Logick: or the Right Use of Reason in the Enquiry after Truth. 8th ed. London, 1745.

> 1st ed. 1725. *Catalogue of the Library of Samuel Johnson,* No. 262, Watts's Logic.

> See: anatomical, p. 111; concomitant, p. 216; ductility, p. 18; intermediate, p. 34; meridian, p. 40; operate, p. 233; preponderate, p. 211; preponderation, p. 259; property, p. 18; telescope, p. 111; volubility, p. 18.

———— ———— The Improvement of the Mind; or a Supplement to the Art of Logick. London, 1741.

> See: accelerate, p. xii; geometrician, p. 242; periodical, p. 230; postulate, p. 203; quadrature, p. 201; revolution, p. 221; stimulation, p. 87; temperature, p. 255; tincture, p. 239; volatile, p. 260.

> For Johnson's esteem of Watts's logical works, see *ante* pp. 72, 96.

JOHN WILKINS. Mathematical Magick; or the Wonders That May Be Performed by Mechanical Geometry. 4th ed. London, 1691. 1st ed. 1648.

> See: circumvolution, p. 279; perpetual, p. 59; radical, p. 251; submarine, p. 182.

> See the passage about a submarine reproduced by a descendant of Bishop Wilkins, the explorer Sir Hubert Wilkins, in his *Under the North Pole* (1931), p. 283.

RICHARD WISEMAN. Eight Chirurgical Treatises. 5th ed. London, 1719. 2 vols.

> 1st ed. *Several Chirurgical Treatises,* 1676.

> See: abscission, ii, 30; exhausted, ii, 395; laxity, ii, 3; regulate, i, 136; temperate, ii, 98; tumour, i, 1; vulnerary, i, 39.

JOHN WOODWARD. An Essay toward a Natural History of the Earth and Terrestrial Bodies, Especially Minerals: As Also of the Sea, Rivers, and Springs. With an Account of the Universal Deluge and of the Effects That It Had upon the Earth. London, 1695.

> See: adventitious, p. 176; agriculture, p. 105; attrition, p. 131; corrosion, p. 133; declination, p. 53; disruption, p. 80; dissipate, p. 268; dissipation, p. 204; dissolve, p. ii; effervescence, p. iii; emit, p. 145; evaporation, p. 125; fecundity, p. 102; flexibility, p. 230; fluctuation, p. 138; heterogeneous, p. 11; migration, p. 45; remission, p. 210; sediment, p. 75; temperature, p. 270; terraqueous, p. 47; vegetation, p. 84; vertiginous, p. 206; vicissitude, p. 270.

———— ———— An Attempt towards a Natural History of the Fossils of England in a Catalogue of the English Fossils in the Collection of J. Woodward, M.D. London, 1729. Vol. i.

Catalogue of the Library of Samuel Johnson, No. 23, Woodward's History of Fossils.

See: botanist, p. 118; cohere, p. 127; efflorescence, p. 154; extraneous, p. 186; petrified, p. 97; sulphur, p. 171.

Cf. *Idler* 17, viii, 66: "*Mead* has invidiously remarked of Woodward, that he gathered shells and stones, and would pass for a philosopher."

SIR HENRY WOTTON. Reliquiae Wottonianae. 3d ed. London, 1672. 1st ed. 1651.

(1) Elements of Architecture. See: concentre, p. 28; metallick, p. 20; rarefaction, p. 38.

(2) Characters of Some Kings of England. See: contexture, p. 105.

(3) Of Robert Devereux . . . and George Villiers. See: tumour, p. 174.

(4) Life and Death of George Villiers, Duke of Buckingham. See: concomitant, p. 212; eccentricity, p. 223; luminary, p. 209.

INDEX

This is chiefly an index to authors quoted, cited, or discussed in text and notes. Books are entered analytically under authors. Eighteenth-century periodicals are entered in the main alphabet. A few rhetorical and linguistic terms are included. Editors, modern translators, and persons appearing in connections other than literary or philosophical are for the most part omitted. *Johnsonian Miscellanies* and the *Catalogue of the Library of Samuel Johnson* are omitted. Boswell's works are included only where the name of Boswell or a quotation appears. Pages i–xv and Appendix A are not indexed. Appendix B is not indexed, except for entries not mentioned in Chapters I–V and for items appearing incidentally in the notes.